Merchants of Labor

Mechanics of Labor

Merchants of Labor

Recruiters and International
Labor Migration

Philip Martin

OXFORD
UNIVERSITY PRESS

OXFORD
UNIVERSITY PRESS

Great Clarendon Street, Oxford, OX2 6DP,
United Kingdom

Oxford University Press is a department of the University of Oxford.
It furthers the University's objective of excellence in research, scholarship,
and education by publishing worldwide. Oxford is a registered trade mark of
Oxford University Press in the UK and in certain other countries

First Edition published in 2017
Impression: 1

Published in the United States of America by Oxford University Press
198 Madison Avenue, New York, NY 10016, United States of America

British Library Cataloguing in Publication Data
Data available

Library of Congress Control Number: 2017935048

ISBN 978–0–19–880802–2

Printed in Great Britain by
Clays Ltd, St Ives plc

Foreword

Merchants of Labor provides valuable insights for understanding and improving the behavior of labor recruiters, the intermediaries between workers in one country and jobs in another. Labor recruiters have a long and checkered history, often associated with trickery or coercion to fill undesirable jobs, from finding soldiers in ancient Rome and sailors in the eighteenth and nineteenth centuries to moving low-skilled workers over borders today. International labor recruiters operate in settings where workers usually face serious disadvantages, relying on recruiters to deal with foreign employers and government bureaucracies at home and abroad.

Governments have struggled to regulate recruiters effectively, especially those who recruit and place low-skilled workers. Almost all governments follow a three-pronged regulatory strategy, that is, they require recruiters to identify themselves by securing licenses, set maximum fees recruiters can charge workers, and deal with complaints from workers.

Despite comprehensive laws in many countries, educational campaigns that warn workers not to overpay, and providing inspectors and supporting nongovernmental organizations (NGOs) to expose abusive recruiters, many migrant workers incur high costs to find foreign jobs; there are regular reports of migrants being trafficked into debt bondage and slavery abroad. These exposés highlight the need for better laws and improved enforcement but also justify alternative strategies to protect migrant workers from abusive recruiters.

This book explores incentives to induce better recruiter behavior. After reviewing global migration patterns, it summarizes the four phases of international labor migration, from employers testing labor markets to ensure that local workers are unavailable to the recruitment of migrant workers, their employment abroad, and their return and reintegration into their home countries. The three core functions of labor markets, recruitment, remuneration, and retention, are reviewed, as well as the complications introduced when employers in one country recruit workers in another. The various types of labor recruiters are examined, from matchers who step aside after workers are matched with jobs to temp or staffing agencies, which are the employers of the workers they send from one worksite to another.

Recruiters who move low-skilled workers across national borders are generally much better educated than the workers they recruit, and most have no experience performing the work for which they recruit workers. Most employers see low-skilled workers as interchangeable, a vision reinforced by recruiter guarantees, as when a domestic worker who is unsatisfactory is replaced by the recruiter at no additional charge. Finally, sending-country governments face trade-offs between numbers and rights: should they insist on high standards for their citizens during recruitment and employment abroad even if the result is higher costs and fewer opportunities for their residents to work abroad?

Many recruiters are short-term agents between employers and workers, aiming to maximize the fees they collect from each. By contrast, some recruiters are long-term partners interested in ensuring a series of good worker–job matches. Can governments develop a policy framework that fosters a race to the top among recruiters who aim to satisfy both employers and workers and improve equity and efficiency in international labor recruitment?

Making the transition from agent to partner recruiters requires a new business model. Recruiters must learn more about employer job requirements to ensure that the workers they recruit have the requisite skills, recouping these investments over time with multiple worker–job matches. Since migration helps individuals achieve upward mobility and can speed economic growth in poorer countries of origin, the best recruiters can be considered partners for development and treated as such, subsidized rather than taxed by migrant-sending governments.

International labor migration is the fastest and surest route to upward mobility for many of the world's low-skilled workers. Migration provides the higher earnings most migrants seek as well as remittances for their families, but too much of the wage gap that motivates workers to migrate goes into the pockets of intermediaries rather than bolstering the incomes of migrants. Providing incentives for good recruiter behavior may do more to help migrants than focusing solely on the enforcement of laws that regulate recruiters, especially when some violations are "victimless crimes," as when migrants pay recruiters too much but get what they want—foreign jobs that pay higher wages.

Government incentives to improve recruitment can be micro or macro, aimed at individual recruiters or designed to change the structure and culture of the recruiting industry. Micro-incentives could give A-rated recruiters faster processing and lower fees to speed worker departures, helping them to win business from employers and workers. A-rated recruiters could pay lower or no taxes and accompany political leaders to be introduced to "good employers" abroad.

Macro-incentives could restructure the recruitment industry, fostering fewer and larger recruiters who can achieve economies of scale and develop reputations to protect. Foreign employers could be allowed to recruit workers directly using experienced nationals of source countries who understand what is required to perform jobs abroad and are able to evaluate the credentials of local workers. Macro-incentives can favor stable employer–recruiter partnerships that invest in efficient and protective job matching over time.

Micro- and macro-incentives are not a substitute for enforcement of protective labor laws. In far too many countries, employers and recruiters conspire to charge migrants high fees, alter contracts, and take advantage of migrants who are vulnerable and unsure of their rights. However, there are unlikely to be enough inspectors to ensure that penalties alone effectuate fundamental changes in labor recruitment systems, justifying experimentation with incentives to encourage recruiters to comply with protective labor laws.

Ray Marshall
Professor Emeritus at the LBJ School
of Public Policy at UT-Austin

Austin, TX
March 2017

Acknowledgments

This book had its genesis in an April 2013 workshop convened by the MacArthur and Open Society Foundations to review the problems encountered by migrant workers as they interacted with the recruiters who had contracts to fill jobs abroad. There were many reports of workers paying high fees before departure, so that they arrived abroad in debt and vulnerable to abuse. There was discussion of the need to strengthen enforcement regimes and perhaps replace for-profit recruiters with bilateral labor agreements requiring employers and workers to use government agencies, but little discussion of the fact that for-profit recruiters are likely here to stay, and that by understanding how they operated governments could add the carrot of incentives to the stick of enforcement to improve protections for workers.

Elizabeth Frantz, with the support of Maria Teresa Rojas and later Catherine Vaillancourt-Laflamme, encouraged an exploration of recruiter incentives. As the analysis of recruiter business models proceeded, data from the International Labor Organization (ILO), the Global Knowledge Partnership on Migration and Development (KNOMAD), and International Organization for Migration (IOM) surveys of what workers paid for jobs abroad became available. Manolo Abella and I analyzed these data with the support of Nilim Baruh and Michelle Leighton of the ILO, Dilip Ratha and Soonhwa Yi of the World Bank, and Frank Laczko of IOM. Leaders of the teams that collected the data are acknowledged in each section where the data are presented.

I am grateful to the workers who provided data, to the recruiters, employers, government staff, and non-governmental organizations (NGOs) that provided insights into the often murky business of moving low-skilled workers from one country to another, and to participants in conferences where recruiter incentives were discussed. My greatest debt is to Manolo Abella, ex-director of the ILO's Migrant Branch, who has shared the goal of improving the international labor migration system over many decades.

Contents

List of Figures

List of Tables

List of Abbreviations

3-D	dangerous, difficult, and dirty
AP	*Associated Press*
BC	British Columbia
BLA	bilateral labor agreement
BP3TKI	Agency for Placement and Protection of Migrant Workers
CBA	collective bargaining agreement
CBSA	Canadian Border Services Agency
CIC	Citizenship and Immigration Canada
CIETT	International Confederation of Private Employment Agencies
CIR	Commission on Immigration Reform
CoD	countries of destination
CoO	countries of origin
DOL	Department of Labor
DOLAB	Department of Overseas Labor
DOLE	Department of Labor and Employment [Philippines]
DOS	Department of State [US]
EPS	Employment Permit System
FARMS/FERME	Foreign Agricultural Resource Management Service
FDI	foreign direct investment
FHI	Fair Hiring Initiative
FIFA	Fédération Internationale de Football Association
FRI	Fair Recruitment Initiative
GATS	General Agreement on Trade in Services
GCC	Gulf Coooperation Council
GCIM	Global Commission on International Migration
GDP	gross domestic product
GEP	Global Economic Prospects [WB]
GFMD	Global Forum for Migration and Development

List of Abbreviations

GHG	greenhouse gases
GLA	Gangmasters Licensing Authority
GLMM	Gulf Labour Markets and Migration
GNI	gross national income
HCMC	Ho Chi Minh City [Vietnam]
HLD	High Level Dialogue [UN]
HRD	human resource development
IDP	internally displaced person
IHRB	Institute for Human Rights and Business
ILC	International Labor Conference
ILO	International Labour Organization
IMF	International Monetary Fund
IOM	International Organization for Migration
IRIS	International Recruitment Integrity System
IRPP	Institute for Research on Public Policy
ITUC	International Trade Union Confederation
KNOMAD	Global Knowledge Partnership on Migration and Development
MDG	Millennium Development Goal [UN]
MOLISA	Ministry of Labor, Invalids, and Social Affairs [Vietnam]
MOU	memoranda/um of understanding
MSPA	Migrant and Seasonal Agricultural Workers Protection Act
NAFTA	North American Free Trade Agreement
NAICS	North American Industry Classification System
NAWS	National Agricultural Worker Survey
NGO	non-governmental organization
ODA	overseas development aid
OFW	overseas Filipino worker
OLEC	Organization of Labor Exporting Countries
OPEC	Organization of the Petroleum Exporting Countries
PAM	prevention, adaptation, and migration
PEA	private employment agencies
PICs	Pacific Island Countries
POEA	Philippine Overseas Employment Administration
PPP	purchasing power parity
PRB	Population Reference Bureau
PSWPS	Pacific Seasonal Worker Pilot Scheme

RM	[Malaysian currency]
RSE	Recognized Seasonal Employers [NZ]
SA	Saudi Arabia
SAWP	Seasonal Agricultural Workers Program
SDG	Sustainable Development Goal [UN]
SME	small and medium-size enterprises
SOE	state-owned enterprise
SSI	Supplementary Security Income
SWP	Seasonal Worker Program [Australia]
TFWP	Temporary Foreign Worker Program
TPP	Trans-Pacific Partnership
UAE	United Arab Emirates
UFCW	United Food and Commercial Workers
UI	unemployment insurance
UN DESA	United Nations Department of Economic and Social Affairs
UNDP	UN Development Program
UNEP	UN Environment Program
UNHCR	UN High Commissioner for Refugees
UNODC	UN Office on Drugs and Crime
VAMAS	Vietnam Association of Manpower Supply
VAT	value-added tax
VND	[Vietnamese currency]
WHD	Wage and Hour Division [US Dept of Labor]
WHO	World Health Organization
WMO	World Migration Organization
WTO(s)	World Trade Organization(s)
WWI	World War I
WWII	World War II

Prologue

Mohammed, a 30-year-old Pakistani farmer with a primary school education, paid $4,000 to get a construction job in Saudi Arabia that paid $400 a month. Mohammed did not have the $4,000 to buy a work visa and pay agent fees and transportation costs, so he mortgaged his land, hoping to repay the loan with some of the $9,600 he expected to earn in Saudi Arabia over two years. With uncertain Pakistani earnings of $100 a month and a wife and four children to support, working abroad seemed the fastest way to achieve upward mobility at home, even if half of the expected extra income from working abroad went to recruiters and other components of the migration infrastructure.

Rahul, a 30-year-old Indian construction worker with a secondary school education, paid $1,200 to get a construction job in Qatar that paid $600 a month. Rahul offered no collateral to borrow from friends and family to pay his migration costs, and expected to repay his loan from two months of foreign earnings. Rahul earned $150 a month in India, but since his employer paid for housing and food in Qatar, Rahul could achieve his goal of saving $5,000 far more quickly by working abroad.

Why did Mohammed and Rahul pay very different amounts to get similar jobs abroad? Most migrants use fee-charging and profit-seeking recruiters to get foreign jobs. In many cases, worker payments to recruiters are more like bribes to get contracts rather than payments for recruitment services that give workers the best job abroad or assure foreign employers that the recruiter has found the best worker to fill a particular job.

Migrants move in corridors between countries, such as from Pakistan to Saudi Arabia and from India to Qatar. The migration cost surveys summarized in Part II found that the corridor is the most important determinant of what low-skilled workers pay to get jobs abroad. Pakistanis paid more than Indians to get similar jobs abroad, suggesting that structural factors and government policies and engagement are more important than individual characteristics such as education and experience in determining how much workers pay to get foreign jobs. Reducing worker-paid migration costs is also likely to require corridor specific actions.

Second, the surveys found that workers who use recruiters to get jobs abroad have higher costs but not higher foreign earnings. Many workers turn to recruiters because they must; recruiters often control access to foreign jobs. A typical scenario involves an employer giving job offers to a local recruiter, who auctions them to recruiters in countries with workers. When there are more workers than jobs, workers pay recruiters for the "privilege" of earning higher wages abroad, and worker willingness to pay determines who goes abroad and who stays home.

Third, the worker surveys found that education, experience, and gender affect worker-paid costs within corridors. Workers with more education or previous experience working abroad and women pay less than first-time male migrants who are not linked to migration networks. However, women with lower migration costs often earn less abroad. Migrant domestic workers have lower costs than construction workers, but they earn $200 to $400 a month while migrant construction workers earn $300 to $600 a month. The cost differences between individuals within a migration corridor are generally less than cost differences between corridors.

Recruiters move most workers over national borders. Unlike smugglers who move asylum seekers to safe countries, the recruiters who move migrant workers over borders are usually licensed and operate legally. Some recruiters send workers into debt bondage abroad and some conspire with foreign employers to exploit workers abroad; but most are small businesses with government licenses that allow them to control access to a valuable "good," the opportunity to work abroad for higher wages. The focus of this book is on workers who are free to choose whether to work abroad or to stay at home, so we ignore those who enslave persons and move them over borders to work.[1]

In summer 2016, tens of thousands of South Asian workers were stranded in Saudi Arabia without wages or food, adding a new dimension to the risks of working abroad. The price of oil fell to half its level of summer 2014, and some Gulf governments did not pay construction firms promptly, encouraging some to stop paying their workers. Low-skilled construction workers were trapped, reluctant to leave Saudi Arabia without the wages they were owed and the bonuses they were promised for fear that once at home they would be unable to collect. The Saudi government stopped issuing new construction

---

[1] Slavery developed with social stratification in ancient civilizations, and was known in most cultures and religions. Perhaps the best known slave system was the Atlantic slave trade that moved Africans to the Caribbean and South and North America to produce sugar, cotton, and tobacco that was exported to Europe, after which slave ships returned to West Africa for more slaves, the so-called triangle trade. About 10 million slaves were involved, including 5 million taken to Brazil, 4 million to the West Indies, and up to a million to the United States.

contracts, so even if the laid-off workers were allowed to leave without the permission of their sponsor or kafala, many wanted to remain to obtain payments due them. What are the responsibilities of governments, employers, recruiters, and workers in such situations?

International labor migration is increasing. In 2015, there were 244 million international migrants who were outside their country of birth a year or more, up more than 50 percent from 155 million in 1990 and representing more than 3 percent of the world's people (UN DESA, 2015). The major motivation to cross national borders is economic, the quest for higher wages and more opportunities in a globalizing world. At least half of the world's international migrants are in the labor force of the receiving country, making international migrants an average of 10 percent of industrial country labor forces and very important to particular sectors of migrant-receiving economies, from agriculture and construction to health services and IT.

Moving workers over borders is big business. Up to 10 million workers a year leave one country to work in another, where they earn four or five times more than they would earn at home. Most are low-skilled and legal, but many arrive abroad in debt because of the high costs they incur to obtain contracts for jobs abroad. If migrants pay an average $1,000 to recruiters, moving workers over borders is a $10 billion a year business; if worker-paid costs average $2,000, labor migration is a $20 billion a year business.

Low skilled does not mean no skills. Maxwell (2006) emphasized that US employers hiring low-skilled workers expect them to be able to follow instructions, to solve problems, and to work in teams. Employers of low-skilled workers almost always report problems finding enough reliable local workers to pick crops, build homes, and staff meatpacking disassembly lines. These employers are often among the first to request permission to hire foreign workers.

Employer attitudes toward migrant workers vary. Many consider migrants vital to the success of their businesses, and express surprise when they learn that their employees incurred costs in their countries of origin to get jobs. Others know that there are more workers than jobs in migrant countries of origin, and charge workers for jobs or allow others to charge their employees. Some employers believe that a worker who has paid something for the job has made an investment and is more likely to be a reliable worker.

High migration costs and pre-migration debts make migrant workers reliable as well as vulnerable to exploitation. They also reduce remittances to families and encourage some migrants to overstay abroad in order to achieve savings targets. The UN Secretary General's eight-point agenda for action presented to the High-Level Dialogue on Migration and Development in 2013 emphasized the "enormous gains to be made by lowering costs related to migration, such as . . . fees paid to recruiters, especially by low-skilled migrants"[2] (UN Secretary General, 2013: para 113). Migrants who pay less to go abroad are more likely to be satisfied and empowered workers.

Governments in migrant-sending countries have tried to reduce worker-paid migration costs by requiring recruiters to get licenses, setting maximum worker-paid fees, and educating workers about what they should pay. However, this three-pronged licensing, regulation, and education system has not prevented some workers from paying high fees, prompting the quest for new regulations, more vigorous enforcement, and other efforts to reduce worker-paid migration costs. Many of these efforts are doomed to fail because these governments do not understand how labor markets function.

Labor Migration and Labor Markets

The first two chapters in Part I explain international migration patterns and job matching. There are four major migration corridors: south to north, or from developing to industrial countries, south to south, north to north, and north to south. The largest migration corridor involves south to south migration, as from Guatemala to Mexico or Burma to Thailand, but south to north migration as from Mexico to the US is almost as large. If south to north and north to north migration as from Canada to the US is combined, almost 60 percent of the world's migrants are in the industrial countries that have a sixth of the world's people.

International migration is likely to increase because of demographic and economic inequalities in a globalizing world marked by revolutions in communications, transportation, and rights that make it easier to learn about jobs abroad, travel to them, and stay abroad. When confronted with "too many migrants," destination governments usually react by restricting the rights of migrants, as illustrated by European efforts in 2016 to pay Turkey to prevent the exit of migrants to Greece and north through the Balkans to Austria, Germany, and Sweden. Adjusting the rights of migrants to manage migration brings governments into conflict with UN agencies that have a rights-based approach to migration based on treating migrants the same as local residents.

Labor markets have three fundamental functions: recruitment to find the best workers to fill particular jobs, remuneration or pay to motivate workers to perform, and retention to keep experienced and productive workers. Recruitment is hard because of asymmetric information. Employers know more about the requirements of the jobs they offer, and workers know more about their abilities. Within countries, employers screen applicants to find the best

---

[2] The report also called for enhancing the portability of social security and other work-related benefits and improving the mutual recognition of skills and work-related licenses.

workers, such as requiring applicants to have a high school diploma or pass a drug test, and candidates signal their abilities to employers by earning degrees and passing tests.

National borders complicate recruitment. Employers may not speak the language or understand the education and training system of workers in other countries. For this reason, employers often turn to recruiters to find workers for them. These recruiters may specialize in finding particular types of workers, such as nurses and other healthcare professionals, or in finding low-skilled construction and service workers.

There are four phases in the international recruitment process, and most worker-paid costs arise in phases two and three. First, employers receive permission from their governments to hire foreign workers, and often pay to have their need for migrant workers certified. Some employers may pass certification costs on to migrant workers, especially if governments charge monthly or annual levies for the privilege of hiring migrants. For example, Malaysia charges employers a levy for each foreign worker hired and has a minimum wage that covers migrant workers, but allows employers to deduct the cost of the levy from migrant worker wages.

Second, foreign workers must obtain contracts to fill a particular job abroad. Neither employers nor workers visit the rural areas from which most low-skilled workers come. Instead, friends and relatives of potential migrants, or a shadowy world of agents and subagents, tell workers about particular foreign jobs and arrange meetings with licensed recruiters who select a particular worker to fill a specific job. If the recruiter knows the skills of workers and the requirements of foreign jobs, recruitment may add value to the transaction and justify the fees that recruiters charge to employers and workers. However, if recruiters simply allocate jobs according to willingness to pay, both employers and workers may suffer.

The third phase involves employment abroad. Most employers of low-wage migrant workers provide them with housing and food, and some offer benefits in addition to wages, such as end-of-contract bonuses. While abroad, workers may be paying for their recruitment in several ways, including deductions from their wages to pay recruiters or in charges for housing and food, via lower-than-standard wages, or in the denial of bonuses and other benefits. In other words, just because workers do not pay for recruitment up front does not mean they did not pay for foreign jobs.

The fourth phase is return and reintegration at home. Working abroad is a trade-off that involves being away from family and friends in exchange for higher wages. Work abroad is normally an economic success, as workers return with the savings they expected and often new skills. However, some migrants do not achieve their savings targets, some are injured abroad, and many make plans to work abroad again given limited opportunities at home. Returning workers may pay for employment abroad in the form of low or reduced bonuses or other benefits that would be expected for satisfactory performance, or in injuries that prevent them from working again.

What do Workers Pay?

Governments often set maximum worker-paid recruitment fees, but they do not know what migrant workers actually pay for foreign jobs. Survey teams supported by the Global Knowledge Partnership on Migration and Development (KNOMAD) and the International Labor Organization (ILO) asked workers who were employed abroad what they paid to get their jobs, and asked returning workers what they paid to get jobs several years earlier when they left the country.[3]

Worker-paid migration costs fall into three broad categories. First is the cost of getting the contract to fill a job abroad, which involves the worker finding a recruiter who has a contract for a foreign job. Second is going through procedures mandated by governments, including undergoing health, criminal, and other checks before departure. Third are transportation costs, including travel from worker homes to government offices and travel abroad to the job.

In 2014, workers were interviewed in Korea, Kuwait, and Spain, and in 2015 as they returned to Ethiopia, India, Nepal, Pakistan, and the Philippines from jobs in Qatar, Saudi Arabia, and the United Arab Emirates (UAE). Workers interviewed in Korea, Kuwait, and Spain generally paid less than a month's foreign earnings in migration costs, there was more variance in worker-paid costs in Kuwait than in Korea and Spain, and many workers in each corridor reported different costs for standard items such as passports and medical checks.

Asian workers who arrived in Korea under the Employment Permit System (EPS) paid $1,525, or one to 1.5 months of typical earnings for 36-month contracts. If migrants earned $36,000 at $1,000 a month in Korea, or $54,000 at $1,500 a month, migration costs of $1,525 are less than 4 percent of Korean earnings. Korea is considered a very desirable destination for migrants, explaining why so many Nepalese want to work in Korea. In 2015, it was easier for undergraduates to get into Harvard than for Nepalese to be selected to work in Korea.[4]

---

[3] The KNOMAD portal for low-skilled migration is at: http://www.knomad.org/thematic-working-groups/low-skilled-labor-migration.

[4] Harvard admitted about 2,000 of 40,000 applicants in 2015, while over 60,000 Nepalis applied for 3,000 slots in the EPS.

Migrants in Kuwait had the highest migration costs ($1,900), the lowest earnings, and the most variance in migration costs. Monthly earnings in Kuwait averaged $465, making migration costs equivalent to four months earnings. Most workers had two-year contracts, earning $11,160 and paying a sixth of their earnings in migration costs. Bangladeshis and Egyptians paid an average of $3,000, versus $1,250 for Indians. Sri Lankan women paid less, about $300, but also earned less, $300 a month, as domestic workers in Kuwait.

Migrant workers interviewed in Spain had migration costs of $530 or half of their monthly earnings of $1,000. The migrants were seasonal farmworkers who stayed in Spain four to nine months, so that worker-paid migration costs were equivalent to 6 percent to 12 percent of expected earnings. Many of the migrants in Spain were from rural areas of Eastern Europe and Morocco, and working in Spain provided higher earnings than did moving from rural to urban areas at home.

Workers returning from Qatar, Saudi Arabia, and the UAE in 2015 reported widely varying migration costs. Ethiopian women returning from Saudi Arabia reported spending $900, over half in payments to recruitment agents, to get jobs paying $250 a month in private Saudi homes where they worked 90 hours a week. Filipinos returning from Qatar paid $500 to get jobs that paid $450 a month. Filipinos worked fewer than 60 hours a week in private homes, on construction sites, and in service and sales jobs.

The Indians returning from Qatar were male construction workers who paid $1,200 for their jobs, earned $600 a month in Qatar, and worked an average 60 hours a week. Many of the Indians were employed in construction at home, earning one-fourth of their Qatari wage, and reported that they could save more abroad because their employers paid for housing and food. By contrast, Nepalese returning from Qatar paid $1,100 for 70-hour-a-week construction jobs that paid $325 a month, that is, the Nepalese paid about as much as the Indians for jobs in Qatar, but earned half as much and worked more hours. Most of the Nepalese were laborers, while most of the Indians were carpenters, masons, or plumbers; many of the Nepalese did not have wage-earning jobs at home.

Pakistanis returning from Saudi Arabia and the UAE had the highest worker-paid migration costs, an average $3,000. They earned an average $400 a month abroad while working 70-hour weeks, and two-thirds borrowed money to pay for visas and other migration costs.

Most of the Indians, Nepalese, and Pakistanis were employed in construction, but they paid very different amounts for similar jobs, that is, the variance in worker-paid migration costs was much greater than the variance in worker earnings. The fact that migration costs vary by corridor suggests that policy options to reduce worker-paid costs are also likely to vary by corridor.

Rethinking Recruitment

What can be done to reduce worker-paid migration costs? The focus of this book is on recruiters, the merchants of labor who are the glue of the international labor market.

Recruiting is an economic business in which profits are revenues minus costs. The current regulatory model aims to achieve compliance by adding to the costs of recruiters who violate protective laws via penalties. Abella (2004) echoes most studies of government regulatory efforts, concluding that there is "little evidence to indicate that public authorities" who make efforts to protect workers against such [abusive recruiter] practices have been effective "because there are too few complaints and too little enforcement to make the threat of penalties an effective stick to induce compliance."

An alternative to the stick of enforcement is the carrot of government incentives that increase the revenue of good recruiters. Incentive systems that reward compliant recruiters can help to transform the recruitment industry, changing an industry now comprised of small and family-owned agents who engage in many one-time transactions into larger and more stable partners of foreign employers that develop standard contracts which reduce variance between workers, achieve economies of scale that reduce costs, and have reputations worth protecting as they place more workers abroad over time.

Three economic incentives could induce better recruiter behavior: lower processing costs; tax exemptions or subsidies; and awards and introductions. Governments could exempt A-rated recruiters from having their workers complete costly and time-consuming exit formalities aimed at educating and protecting migrants. Some governments have protective bureaucracies financed by recruiter-paid fees that are passed on to migrants, so that the lower costs of policing A-rated recruiters could justify charging them low or no processing fees.

Second, governments could exempt A-rated recruiters from some taxes, such as VAT on their revenues. If A-rated recruiters are truly partners for development, as when sending workers abroad generates public benefits in the form of remittances that have multiplier economic effects which create jobs for non-migrants, and spillover effects such as new skills embodied in returning migrants, there is a strong economic justification to exempt them from some or all corporate taxes, just as some foreign investors are granted tax holidays. Governments could go further and subsidize recruiters who open or enlarge markets for workers abroad.

Third, governments can introduce A-rated recruiters to foreign employers and give them awards that help them to expand. Just as business leaders often accompany political leaders abroad to be introduced to potential customers, A-rated recruiters could be invited to accompany political leaders to be introduced to employers seeking migrant workers. Government seals of approval for the best recruiters could help to foster a race to the top among recruiters for additional revenue rather than the current race to the bottom as recruiters and their agents try to extract payments and fees.

Moving Forward

Worker-paid migration costs are the new frontier for making the international labor migration system more efficient and protective of migrant workers. Sustainable Development Goal (SDG) Target 10.7 calls on governments to "facilitate orderly, safe, regular, and responsible migration and mobility of people, including through the implementation of planned and well-managed migration policies." Progress toward this goal is to be measured by Indicator 10.7.1, which requests data on "recruitment cost borne by an employee as a proportion of yearly income earned in the country of destination."[5]

Migration is an investment, and the best measure of worker-paid costs is their share of annual foreign earnings. A reasonable goal is to reduce worker-paid migration costs to less than 5 percent of foreign earnings, which means less than 1.2 months' earnings for a worker with a two-year contract. The best way to measure what migrant workers paid for their jobs is via labor force surveys in receiving countries, where governments ask which workers are foreign born, who is employed on a temporary work permit, and what they paid to get their jobs.[6]

Matching workers with jobs across national borders has costs that must be paid by someone. The easiest way to deal with worker-paid migration costs would be to endorse and implement ILO Conventions that call for employers to pay all recruitment costs for the migrant workers they employ. Employers do pay all or most recruitment costs for the skilled and professional migrant workers they recruit because there are more jobs than workers willing to move. However, supply often exceeds demand for low-skilled workers, allowing recruiters and in some cases employers to charge workers for jobs.

At first blush, the fact that employers pay recruitment costs for high-skilled workers while low-skilled workers pay for foreign jobs is an example of regressivity, as when the poor pay more. However, high-skilled workers typically

---

[5] SDG Target 10c calls on governments to reduce remittance costs to three percent of the amount transferred by 2030. Target 8.8 calls on governments to "protect labor rights...for all workers, including migrant workers, in particular women migrants."

[6] Collecting reliable data from migrant workers in labor force surveys may be difficult unless workers are assured that their answers will remain confidential. It may also be hard to develop questionnaires that quickly obtain data from migrant workers on the major cost items in their countries of origin.

invest in education to acquire skills, and the payoff for their investment is higher wages as well as employer willingness to pay their migration costs. There may be more low-skilled workers than jobs precisely because little investment is required to join the low-skilled labor pool.

How can migration costs be reduced when the supply of low-skilled workers in countries of origin (CoOs) often exceeds the demand for them in countries of destination (CoDs)? The current system is a hodgepodge of regulations and markets that push many worker payments into the shadows, so the first priority is to obtain better data on what workers pay. International labor migration is a normal market transaction, and moving workers over borders is as mutually beneficial as other forms of international exchange. Getting better data provides a benchmark against which to measure progress to reduce worker-paid costs.

The second priority is to better understand the recruitment business. Recruiters are usually small businesses that rely on ties to foreign employers for job offers and links to local workers to fill them. Even though CoO governments often require recruiters to be citizens in order to protect migrants during recruitment and deployment, most recruiters consider the foreign employer offering jobs a much more valuable asset than the low-skilled local workers they send abroad. Since the threat of penalties for violations of protective regulations is often hollow, can governments offer incentives to induce recruiters to be more protective of migrants?

Third, with migration costs varying so widely by corridor, policies to reduce worker-paid costs are likely to be corridor specific. The universal policy that can reduce worker costs and exploitation abroad is decent jobs at home that give workers faced with high fees for jobs abroad the power to say no. Until faster development narrows the wage differences that encourage international migration, understanding why worker-paid costs vary by corridor, and what can be done in each corridor to reduce costs, offers the best way forward.

Moving low-skilled workers over national borders is a complex process fraught with challenges. Most of those involved in regulating the movement of low-skilled workers over borders earn far more than the migrants they place and protect. The fact that the migrants are low skilled can lead to misunderstandings and complicate regulation, since it can be frustrating to obtain credible evidence of oral promises and payments for which there are no receipts. The regulatory apparatus and recruitment industry employ relatively few returned migrants, making it hard to inject migrant experiences into the industry and its regulation.

The book has eight chapters. The first reviews international labor migration, explaining that demographic and economic differences in an age of globalization promise ever more international labor migration. Chapter 2 explains the job-matching process, the four stages of matching workers with jobs over borders to highlight where worker-paid costs can arise. Chapter 3 defines the monetary and opportunity costs in the recruitment process and presents data on what migrant workers in receiving countries paid for their jobs, while Chapter 4 examines what workers returning from Gulf oil exporters paid. The fifth chapter reviews the recruitment business generally and in selected countries, while the sixth examines efforts to regulate recruiters. Chapter 7 discusses ways to encourage better recruiter behavior, and how to eliminate recruiters with bilateral labor agreements. To conclude, Chapter 8 lays out a roadmap for a new incentive-based approach to the recruitment industry.

Part I
Labor Migration and Labor Markets

Introduction

The two chapters in Part 1 explore the dimensions of international migration and the role of recruitment in labor markets. Most migration is economically motivated and most international migrants move from lower to higher-wage countries. Migration is the exception rather than the rule; but international labor migration is likely to increase because of persisting demographic and economic inequalities at a time when revolutions in communications, transportation, and rights make it ever easier to learn about opportunities abroad, move to them, and stay abroad. When faced with migration crises, the default management tool of governments involves adjusting the rights of migrants, prompting clashes with UN agencies and non-governmental organizations (NGOs) that urge equal rights for migrants.

Labor markets have the three R functions of recruiting workers, remunerating them to encourage them to perform their jobs satisfactorily, and retaining experienced and productive workers. Employers in one country and jobs in another complicate these three Rs, especially recruitment, which is why both employers and workers often turn to private recruiters to act as intermediaries between jobs and workers. Recruiters are most deeply involved in the second phase of the four-phase labor migration process, matching workers with jobs.

1

International Labor Migration

Almost half of the world's residents are economically active, meaning there were 3.5 billion workers in 2015, including more than 4 percent who were working outside the country in which they were born (ILO, 2015a).[1] Most workers never leave the country in which they were born, but 150 million were employed in another country, usually one that offers higher wages than can be earned at home.

If the world is divided into the thirty richer industrial countries with about 600 million workers and the 170 poorer countries with 2.9 billion workers, the 60 million migrant workers in richer countries are an average 10 percent of industrial country workers. The migrant worker share ranges from less than 5 percent in Korea and Japan to more than 25 percent in Australia and Switzerland. The share of migrants among all workers in poorer countries is less than 2 percent, but the range is wide, from less than 1 percent in China and India to more than 90 percent in some Gulf oil exporting states.

International migration for work is the exception, not the rule. However, international labor migration is increasing, making the recruiters who move low-skilled workers over borders ever more important. A low-skilled migrant with less than a secondary school education rarely strikes out on his/her own for a job in another country because he/she does not know how to navigate the process of obtaining a contract with a foreign employer, securing a passport and visa, and departing for the job.

Recruiters, or merchants of labor, are the key intermediaries that connect workers in one country with jobs in another; they are the glue of the international labor market. Migration involves two countries, so recruiters must know government regulations in both migrant sending and receiving countries, as well as the needs of employers seeking workers and of workers seeking jobs. In many countries, recruiters are more familiar with government regulations

---

[1] The International Labour Organization (ILO) estimated world employment at 3.3 billion in 2015, plus 200 million unemployed.

than with employer and worker needs, and some use this knowledge of government processes to extract money from employers, workers, or both.

International Migration Patterns

Before looking at how labor markets work with and without recruiters, it is useful to review the dimensions of international labor migration and the reasons why there is likely to be more. The UN defines international migrants as persons outside their country of birth for a year or more, regardless of the reason for being abroad, legal status, or plans to settle or return (UN DESA, 2015). This inclusive definition encompasses naturalized citizens, immigrants joining family members settled in the destination country, temporary students and workers, and unauthorized foreigners, refugees and asylum seekers, and anyone else abroad for at least 1 year.

The UN estimated 244 million international migrants in 2015, or 3.3 percent of the world's 7.3 billion people. The World Bank (2015), which uses a slightly different methodology, reported 249 million migrants. Both organizations distribute migrants similarly across the four major corridors: south-south, south-north, north-north, and north-south. Most migrants are in industrial[2] or northern countries—56 percent; but the largest group moved from south to south, or from one developing country to another—38 percent. Almost a quarter of international migrants moved north to north or from one industrial country to another, and 6 percent moved from north to south or from an industrial to a developing country.

Each international migrant is unique, and each migration corridor has unique features. The largest stock of migrants, 95 million or 38 percent in 2015, moved from one developing country to another, as from Indonesia to Malaysia or Nicaragua to Costa Rica (Table 1.1). The second-largest stock, 84 million or 34 percent, moved from a developing to an industrial country, as from Morocco to Spain, Mexico to the US, or the Philippines to South Korea; that is, a third of international migration involves south-north movement. Some 56 million people or 22 percent of international migrants were north to north migrants who moved from one industrial country to another, as from Canada to the US. Finally, more than 14 million people or 6 percent of migrants were north to south migrants who moved from industrial to developing countries, as with Japanese who work or retire in Thailand.

---

[2] The World Bank considers thirty-two of OECD countries to be high income (not Mexico and Turkey), plus forty-seven non-OECD countries and places, from Hong Kong and Macao to the Gulf oil exporters to Argentina, Russia, Singapore, and Venezuela.

Table 1.1 International migrants in 2015

Origin	Destination Industrial	Destination Developing	Total
Industrial	56	14	70
Developing	84	95	179
Total	140	109	249
Industrial	22%	6%	28%
Developing	34%	38%	72%
Total	56%	44%	100%

Source: World Bank Migration and Development Brief 24 2015: 28.

Some 140 million migrants are in industrial countries, making migrants more than 10 percent of the 1.2 billion residents of industrial countries. There are 109 million migrants in developing countries, where they are less than 2 percent of developing country residents and workers, and may be barely noticeable in population giants such as China and India.

Most of the world's countries participate in the international migration system as countries of origin, transit, or destination, and often all three. This is a change from the past, when most countries were either sources of or destinations for migrants. Today, Mexico sends migrants to the US, receives migrants from Guatemala, and is a transit country for Central Americans moving to the US.

Europe is *the* continent of international migration, with a tenth of the world's people and a third of the world's international migrants, some 76 million. Asia is second to Europe, with 75 million international migrants. Both Asia and Europe have a quarter of the world's 200 countries, but Asia has 60 percent of the world's people and large-scale internal migration in population giants such as China and India. Europe, by contrast, has international migration in a region with many national borders and fewer people. More than half of European countries are members of the EU, which promotes freedom of movement of EU citizens, allowing EU citizens to move to another EU country and live and work on an equal basis with citizens of that country.

North America had 54 million international migrants in 2015, almost a quarter of the world's total, including 47 million in the US and 7 million in Canada. Africa had 21 million migrants, including more than 3 million in South Africa and 2 million in Ivory Coast. Latin America and the Caribbean have more than 9 million migrants, led by 2 million in Argentina and more than a million each in Venezuela and Mexico. Oceania had 8 million migrants, including almost 7 million in Australia and a million in New Zealand.

Two-thirds of international migrants live in twenty countries. The US had 47 million or almost 20 percent of the world's migrants in 2015, followed by 12 million each in Germany and Russia; 10 million in Saudi Arabia; 9 million in the UK; and 8 million each in the United Arab Emirates (UAE), Canada, and France. The major sources of migrants were India, with 16 million born-in-India persons abroad; Mexico 12 million; Russia 11 million; China 10 million; Bangladesh 7 million; and Pakistan and Ukraine, 6 million each. The Philippines, Syria, UK, and Afghanistan each have at least 5 million persons abroad.

Migrants from some countries are concentrated in one foreign country, while others are scattered widely. Almost all Mexican migrants are in the US, while only 20 percent of Indians are in the UAE, the country hosting the most Indians. Similarly, the Filipino diaspora is widely dispersed, with a third of Filipinos abroad in the US, followed by almost a quarter in the Gulf oil exporters.

Workers and Refugees

Most migrants are young and of working age. The ILO estimated that 150 million or 65 percent of international migrants were in the labor forces of the countries to which they moved in 2013. Some 73 percent of migrants 15 years of age and older were employed or seeking jobs, compared with 64 percent of non-migrants (ILO, 2015a). Both male and female migrants have higher labor force participation rates than non-migrants; 78 percent for migrant men compared to 77 percent for native men; and 67 percent for migrant women compared to 51 percent for native women.

A third of migrant workers were in Europe, a quarter in North America, and most of the rest in Asia; three-fourths of all migrant workers were in what the ILO considers to be high-income countries (ILO, 2015a: xii). Two-thirds of all migrant workers were employed in services, 18 percent in industry (construction and manufacturing), and 11 percent in agriculture. The highest shares of migrants among all workers are in the Gulf oil exporting countries, where 90 percent or more of private sector workers are migrants.

Some migrant workers raise special concerns. The ILO estimated there were 12 million migrant domestic workers, three-fourths of them women, that is, workers who crossed national borders to work in private homes. Many work long hours in situations where they are isolated and not covered by basic labor laws, leaving them vulnerable to abuse. Migration for higher wages abroad poses difficult trade-offs for mothers, who often go abroad to take care of children while entrusting their own children to relatives (Parreñas, 2015). The demand for migrant domestic workers acting as caregivers is expected to increase in aging industrial countries.

ILO conventions and laws in many countries call for migrants to be treated equally, which means they should receive the same wages and benefits as local workers. Equal treatment is defended as the "right thing to do" as well as the best way to protect local workers from "unfair" competition from migrants, who may be willing to work for lower wages than locals. Truly equal treatment is rare, in part because migrant workers are normally required to stay with the employer with whom they have a contract, while local workers can change employers. Many of those who study guest worker programs urge governments to allow migrant workers to change employers so that they can escape from abusive employers (Marshall, 2011).

There are two other reasons why equal treatment is difficult to achieve. First, only half of the world's jobs are wage-paying jobs, and only a quarter offer work-related benefits (ILO, 2015b). In many countries, including the US, migrant workers are exempt from contributing to some benefit programs, which reduces their cost to employers who do not have to pay social security or other payroll taxes on migrant wages.[3] Second, only half of the world's countries have national minimum wages, and minimum wage laws that exist may not apply in the sectors that employ most migrants, including agriculture and domestic work.[4]

The 1951 Refugee Convention commits almost 150 countries not to practice refoulement in returning a person who is outside his/her country of citizenship and unwilling to return because of "a well-founded fear of being persecuted for reasons of race, religion, nationality, membership of a particular social group or political opinion." The UN High Commissioner for Refugees (UNHCR) registers foreigners after they leave countries where they face persecution, and at the end of 2015 counted 16 million refugees, plus almost 41 million persons displaced inside their country and 3 million asylum seekers (UNHCR, 2015). Another 5 million Palestinians registered with another UN agency.

Syria was the source of almost 5 million refugees in 2015, Afghanistan almost 3 million, and Somalia more than 1 million. Turkey hosted 2.5 million or a sixth of the world's refugees in 2015, followed by Pakistan, 1.6 million, Lebanon, 1.1 million, and Iran, almost a million. When UNHCR speaks of 65million forcibly displaced people, it should be remembered that 41 million or two-thirds are internally displaced persons (IDPs). Most IDPs are in the same countries that produce the most refugees, including Syria and Iraq, but there are also large numbers in countries that have or had civil wars, including Colombia, Sudan, and Yemen (UNHCR, 2015: 10).

UNHCR provides services to refugees, and urges governments to accept the most vulnerable 10 percent of the refugees in its care for resettlement.

---

[3] Fox (2016: 5) notes that many developing countries have comprehensive work-related benefit programs taken from industrial countries that result in high payroll taxes but poor benefits, giving both employers and employees incentives to avoid making contributions.

[4] See: www.wageindicator.org/main/salary/minimum-wage.

About 100,000 refugees a year are resettled, including three-fourths in the US and 10 percent each in Australia and Canada. However, most registered refugees eventually return home or find a country on their own in which to begin anew, as when they move to a safe country and apply for asylum.

This is what happened in 2015, when more than a million migrants, half Syrians living in Turkey, made their way from Turkey's western coast to nearby Greek islands, went by ferry to Piraeus, traveled north through the Balkans, and then continued to Austria, Germany, and Sweden to seek asylum (Martin, 2016). Because of the legacy of World War II, when some of those fleeing the Nazis perished because other countries refused to give them asylum, Germany and most other European countries have inclusive asylum guarantees in their constitutions and comprehensive systems that offer asylum seekers housing and food while their applications and appeals are considered.

Many people are seeking safety and better opportunities abroad. When German Chancellor Angela Merkel said in September 2015, "wir schaffen das" [Germany can manage] to integrate Syrian refugees, there was a mass movement from Turkey to Germany, including the arrival of a record 12,000 asylum seekers in Munich on September 12, 2015 (Martin, 2016; Teitelbaum, 2015).[5] As the number of asylum seekers continued to rise, and after terrorist attacks in Paris in November 2015, EU leaders took steps to reduce the influx, providing aid to migrants in Turkey in exchange for Turkey blocking the smuggling of migrants to Greece. Turkey agreed to accept the return of all migrants who arrived illegally in Greece in exchange for visa-free access to the EU. By summer 2016, what had been a flood of migrants from Turkey to Greece dwindled to a trickle under the fragile EU–Turkey migration agreement.

The UN is spearheading a global effort to deal with refugees and asylum seekers, which has three key elements: increase the number of refugees who are resettled; offer more assistance to countries hosting refugees; and encourage host countries to give refugees the right to work and attend schools. UN Secretary-General Ban Ki-moon, in preparation for the global Summit on Refugees and Migrants in June 2016, said: "Let us work together to resettle more people, provide legal pathways, and better integrate refugees."[6]

Governments have found it very hard to agree on a coordinated effort to reduce the number of refugees and resettle those who cannot return. The documents from the September 2016 UN summit on migration and refugees express far more generalities than specifics: "[W]e commit to a more equitable sharing of the burden and responsibility for hosting and supporting the world's refugees, while taking account of existing contributions and the

[5] Between August and October 2015 Germany suspended the Dublin Convention, which requires foreigners seeking asylum to apply in the first safe country they reach, for Syrians.

[6] See: www.un.org/apps/news/infocus/sgspeeches/print_full.asp?statID=3083.

differing capacities and resources among states." Governments made no commitment to resettle 10 percent of the world's refugees, about 1.6 million, in the face of opposition from European nations and Russia,[7] suggesting that dealing with those who flee persecution will continue to be a challenge.

Why Migration? Inequalities and Revolutions

International migration is the exception rather than the rule. Only 3 percent of the world's people have moved from one country to another for a year or more. It seems safe to predict that the number of international migrants is likely to increase, but the migrant share of the world's population should remain below 5 percent for two reasons. The first is inertia, the reality that most people will live and die without crossing a national border because they do not want to move away from family and friends and a familiar culture. Second, governments have significant capacity to regulate the entry and the activities of foreigners, and they do, with passports, visas, and border and interior controls.

The major drivers of international migration are persisting demographic and economic inequalities between countries as globalization makes it easier to learn about opportunities abroad and cheaper to travel and take advantage of them (Martin et al., 2006). Many demand-pull factors in receiving countries and supply-push factors in sending countries motivate people to cross national borders, from recruitment by some employers to environmental changes that make traditional ways of earning a living less viable. There are also more international migrants because there are more countries and more national borders to cross. The number of generally recognized nation-states rose from forty-three in 1900 to 193 in 2000, and more national borders means more international migrants.[8]

Most of the world's international migrants move for better economic opportunities; the 16 million refugees in 2015 were 6.5 percent of the world's 244 million migrants. There are several ways to categorize the countries from which migrants come and to which they move. The World Bank, which defines high-income countries as those with a per capita income of $12,736 or more in 2013 (World Bank, 2015: 28), reported that 1.3 billion or 18 percent of the world's people were in high-income countries.[9] These high-income people had

---

[7] The papers for the summit are at: http://sd.iisd.org/events/high-level-meeting-of-unga-plenary-on-addressing-large-movements-of-refugees-and-migrants/.

[8] The number of generally recognized states doubled from 90 to 180 between the mid-1960s and the mid-1990s (Held et al., 1999).

[9] World economic output in 2013 was $76 trillion for 7.1 billion people, or an average $10,700 each. At purchasing power parity (PPP), after incomes are adjusted for the cost of living, world

two-thirds of the world's $76 trillion economic output, an average $40,000 each, while the six billion people in low- and middle-income countries had average per capita incomes of $4,200, a tenth as much. Migrating from low- and middle-income countries to high-income countries can increase an individual's income by almost tenfold, providing a powerful incentive to move.

Demographics and Economics

The demographic inequality motivating international migration is straight-forward. The world's population reached an historic milestone on October 31, 2011 when, for the first time, there were 7 billion people on earth, up from 6 billion in 1998.[10]

The world's population of 7.3 billion in 2015 is projected to continue increasing by 80 million a year to reach 9.6 billion in 2050. Almost all of the additional 2.3 billion people are expected to be born in the world's 170 poorer countries, where the total population is projected to surpass 8 billion, so that the most populous countries in 2050 are projected to be India with 1.6 billion people, China with 1.4 billion, and the US and Nigeria, each with 400 million.[11] The population of the thirty wealthier countries is expected to remain stable at 1.2 billion over the next 35 years, reflecting growth in Canada and the US and shrinking populations in many European countries and Japan.

The world's population increases by 80 million a year, adding the equivalent of a Germany a year in developing countries. This means that there is a youth bulge in many African and Asian countries while workforces in Europe and Japan are shrinking, suggesting that youthful migrants could stabilize the populations and workforces of aging societies.

Since richer countries can attract migrants because of their higher wages, the decision about whether to stabilize populations via immigration is a policy choice. There are many possibilities, from industrial countries accepting immigrants to settle and integrating them and their families, opening doors to migrant caregivers and other guest workers but encouraging them to depart after a few years, or encouraging rich-country retirees to move to lower-cost countries, shifting people from higher to lower income countries rather than moving workers from poorer to richer countries.

---

economic output was $102 trillion or $14,300 each. At PPP, per capita incomes in high-income countries average $40,800, almost five times more than the $8,400 average of lower-income countries (World Bank, 2015: 28).

[10] See: www.un.org/apps/news/story.asp?NewsID=40257&Cr=population&Cr1#.WFW7XijYI04.

[11] Nigeria had 182 million people in 2015, while the US had 321 million. The total fertility rate, or the average number of children per woman, was 5.5 in Nigeria and 1.9 in the US. Nigeria will grow despite emigration, while the US will grow with immigration; but nonetheless, in 35 years, Nigeria's population is projected to be larger than the US population (PRB, 2016).

Instead of more south-north migration from poorer to richer countries, some developing countries may get rich quickly, so that their workers are reluctant to seek foreign jobs. Several countries have made the transition from emigration country to migrant destination within a generation, including Italy and Spain. However, many others, particularly in Africa and South Asia, are likely to have more workers than jobs for the foreseeable future. If countries in Europe and Japan have more jobs than workers, while African and Asian countries have more workers than jobs, demographic inequality may set the stage for compensating migration flows from faster-growing developing countries to shrinking industrial countries.

Demographic transfers from overcrowded cities in Africa to empty apartments in Europe are likely to be complex, with many hard-to-predict consequences. However, the shifting weights of Europe and Africa in global population make the challenge clear. In 1800, Europe had 21 percent of the world's 1 billion residents and Africa had 11 percent, that is, Europe had almost twice as many people as Africa. In 2000, Africa had slightly more people than Europe. By 2050, Europe is projected to shrink to 725 million of the world's 9.7 billion residents, and Africa is projected to increase to 2.5 billion or 20 percent.

When Europe had 20 percent of the world's people, there was a massive wave of emigration to the Americas; a third of the 1800 populations of many European countries emigrated in the 1900s. Will Africans emigrate when they are 20 percent of the world's population, or will Africa develop rapidly and create stay-at-home jobs for its swelling labor forces? If Africans emigrate, will they be welcomed? Books such as *Camp of the Saints* and films such as *The March* portray Africans and Asians who are desperate for survival setting out for Europe, and European leaders uncertain how to respond.[12]

Will commitments to give asylum and refuge be maintained if migration increases and public opinion favors the use of walls and force to keep migrants out? Teitelbaum (1992–93) noted that US aid policy changed in the 1980s to ignore the role of population growth in promoting conflicts and pressures to migrate, but reversed in the 1990s to acknowledge that rapid population growth can keep countries poor. There are many unknowns about fertility and development, but the demographic inequality between richer and poorer countries clearly sets the stage for more migration.

The second inequality motivating international migration is economic. The thirty high-income countries had a fifth of the world's 7.3 billion people in

[12] Jean Raspail, 1973. *Le camp des saints*, Éditions Robert Laffont, www.jrbooksonline.com/pdfs/camp_of_the_saints.pdf. *The March* is a 1990 BBC film that involves a charismatic Muslim leader from the Sudan who leads 250,000 Africans on a 3,000-mile march towards Europe with the slogan "We are poor because you are rich."

2014 but 70 percent of the world's $78 trillion of economic output, an average $38,000 per person per year, nine times more than the $4,400 average per person in the poorer 170 countries (World Bank, 2016: 52).[13] Especially, young people are motivated to migrate from poorer to richer countries for nine times higher earnings, even if higher living costs in richer countries mean that the actual income gain is less. Globalization and diaspora make potential migrants today far more aware of opportunities in a richer country than were European migrants considering a move to the Americas in the nineteenth century.

The very poorest people in poor countries often lack the resources to move to another country. However, if economic development in poorer countries gives more people some money and increases their desire for better jobs faster than the economy delivers them, migration may rise with economic growth, the paradox of the migration hump. This is what happened in Mexico, where discussion of the economic takeoff expected with the North American Free Trade Agreement (NAFTA) in 1994 was followed quickly by a deep recession and devaluation in 1995 that contributed to an upsurge in Mexico–US migration during the late 1990s, when there was a US jobs boom (Martin, 1998–99).

There is a second dimension to economic differences between countries that encourages internal and international migration. Agriculture is the world's number one employer, engaging 30 percent of the world's 3.5 billion workers as farmers or hired workers (ILO, 2015b). In rich countries, where agriculture employs less than 5 percent of workers, farmers have higher average incomes and more wealth than urban residents, and their incomes and wealth are often raised by government subsidies (Martin, 2009). In poor countries, where agriculture employs more than half of workers, farmers are poorer than urban residents, and governments often tax them by allowing monopoly input suppliers to charge high prices for seeds and fertilizers or monopoly output buyers to offer low prices for cotton, cocoa, and other commodities.

Rural youth quickly realize that they will not get rich farming as their parents and grandparents did. For many, economic mobility requires occupational and geographic mobility, getting away from farming and moving to cities. Once in urban areas, rural youth find it easier to learn about opportunities abroad and access the recruiters, travel agents, and the rest of the migration infrastructure that can help them to cross national borders for better opportunities. In this way, movement out of agriculture in developing countries can increase both urbanization and international migration.

---

[13] The World Bank reported 1.4 billion people in high-income countries in 2014 with a combined gross national income (GNI) of $54 trillion or an average $38,000 per person (Atlas method of computing GNI). The combined population of low (622 million), lower-middle income (2.9 billion), and middle income (2.4 billion) was 5.9 billion, and their combined GNI was $26 trillion or $4,400 per person, or 8.6 times more per person. The per capita GNI of sub-Saharan Africa, $1,600 was only 6 percent of the $25,000 of Europe and Central Asia.

Communications, Transportation, and Rights

Demographic and economic inequalities are like the plus and minus poles on a battery; they provide the potential for action but await a spark or link to induce migration. Three revolutions of the past half century, in communications, transportation, and rights, make it easier for potential migrants to learn about opportunities abroad, cross borders, and stay abroad. Adjusting the rights of migrants to manage migration is often the first instinct of policymakers grappling with migration crises, engendering conflict with the UN's rights-based approach to migrant workers that emphasizes the need for governments to treat migrants equally.

The communications revolution shrinks the world and makes it easier for people in one country to learn about opportunities in another. During the age of mass migration in the nineteenth century, pioneering migrants typically wrote letters to friends and family describing opportunities abroad, a slow means of communication in an era of limited literacy and slow transport (Martin and Midgley, 2010). In the 1850s, letters from the American Midwest to Scandinavia took 4–6 weeks to reach recipients. After they arrived, a literate person had to be found to read the letter and respond, so that a year could elapse between an invitation to move and migration.[14]

Communication is much faster today via cell phones and the internet. With diasporas from countries around the world settled in most high-income countries, migrants who are abroad can quickly inform friends and relatives at home about opportunities, finance the travel of newcomers, and help them after arrival. Mobile phones and Skype were not developed to facilitate international migration, but they make it easy and cheap for people in one country to learn about opportunities in another. Similarly, movies and TV shows are made for entertainment, not to encourage youth in developing countries to dream of sharing in the riches of the other countries; but the American TV shows *Dallas* and *Dynasty* about oil barons helped to persuade many youth dreaming of opportunities abroad to believe the promises of recruiters that riches await in other countries (Martin, S., 2014).

The second revolution involves transportation. Many Europeans migrating to the North American colonies in the eighteenth century could not pay for one-way transportation, so they indentured themselves for 5 years to whoever met the ship in New York or Philadelphia and paid the transportation costs. Most of the poorer British and Germans who indentured themselves worked for farmers after arrival, learning how to farm in the New World while living with the farm family for whom they were obliged to work.

---

[14] In 1870, an estimated 25 percent of the world's adults were literate. Literacy rose to 50 percent by 1950, and to 80 percent by 2000 (Kenny, 2012: Ch. 5).

Transportation today is much more accessible and cheaper, usually available in all countries and costing less than $2,500 to go anywhere in the world. Even Chinese migrants who pay smugglers $20,000 to $30,000 to reach the US typically repay their migration costs from higher earnings within 2 years, far less time than indentured servants labored to repay their transportation costs. Rapid repayment helps to explain why some Chinese in Fujian and other relatively prosperous Chinese coastal provinces continue to pay high fees to smugglers to move to industrial countries, although legal student migration has largely replaced the unauthorized smuggling of Chinese laborers (Kwong, 1998; Xiang and Shen, 2009).

The third revolution involves the rights of individuals vis-à-vis governments. Dictatorships and world wars early in the twentieth century led to the creation of the United Nations in 1945 and an emphasis on protecting the human rights of individuals that was encapsulated in the Universal Declaration of Human Rights (www.un.org/en/universal-declaration-human-rights). Many national constitutions written after World War II in postwar Europe, and in newly independent former colonies in Africa and Asia, include extensive human rights guarantees.

Governments granted individuals rights and promised them benefits to cover unemployment, old age, and ill health. There was relatively little international migration when European governments developed social welfare systems in the 1950s, and as many former colonies became independent in the 1960s, they often granted benefits to all qualifying residents and workers rather than drawing distinctions between citizens and noncitizens. One reason for universal social welfare systems was to eliminate between peoples distinctions that in the past had led to conflict.

Human and social rights guarantees make it difficult for governments to remove foreigners who want to stay. Once inside a richer country, migrants can use administrative proceedings and courts to argue that they should be allowed to remain because they have developed roots in the country or would face persecution at home. Governments have found it very difficult to draw a sharp distinction between refugees and economic migrants, even though many migrants have mixed motives for migration, that is, both economic and noneconomic motives for moving. In such cases, governments must determine whether a particular person is a refugee entitled to protection and who should be allowed to stay, or an economic migrant seeking better opportunities and who should be returned.[15]

---

[15] UNHCR recognizes the reality of mixed migration flows, and developed a 10-point plan in 2006 to provide advice to governments: http://www.unhcr.org/en-us/mixed-migration.html.

Climate Change

A potential new element has entered the demographic and economic motivations for migration: climate changes that make it impossible or less viable to continue living in a particular place. Migration linked to environmental change is not new, and most of the 19 million people displaced by natural disasters in 2015 remain within the borders of their country of citizenship (Internal Displacement Monitoring Centre).

Climate experts expect global warming to bring heavier rainstorms, bigger snowstorms, more intense droughts, and more heat waves. The world is warming: 2014, 2015, and 2016 each set records as the warmest years since accurate temperature records have been kept beginning in 1880. Global temperatures in 2016 were expected to average 1.3 degrees Celsius or 2.3 degrees Fahrenheit more than in 1880, which is close to the 1.5 degrees Celsius limit specified in the Paris climate change agreement of December 2015 between 195 countries.

The Paris Agreement went into effect on November 11, 2016, after 94 countries representing two-thirds of global emissions signed it; China, the US, and India are the three leading emitters. The goal of the Paris Agreement is to limit the increase in global temperatures over preindustrial levels to 2 degrees Celsius by having countries develop voluntary plans to reduce carbon emissions. Developing countries are reluctant to slow economic growth now to benefit future generations who are likely to be richer and to have more technologies at their disposal to cope with climate change, prompting industrial countries to offer $100 billion after 2020 to help developing countries to reduce their emissions.[16]

Climate change can be identified through significant changes in temperature or precipitation that persists for several decades. Climate change can raise temperatures because of natural factors such as changes in the sun's intensity, natural processes such as changes in ocean currents, and human activities, such as emitting gases by burning fossil fuels or deforestation that changes the composition of the atmosphere.[17]

---

[16] Many developing countries, saying that they were not responsible for the buildup of carbon in the atmosphere, argue that they should be allowed to burn carbon to reduce poverty. India, which plans to double its burning of coal by 2019 to bring electricity to 300 million more people, says it needs "carbon space" to reduce poverty.

[17] Most of the climate change focus has been on reducing emissions of carbon dioxide, which can stay in the atmosphere for decades. However, a February 2011 study by the UN's Environment Program (UNEP) suggested that it might be easier to reduce global warming by reducing emissions of two short-lived pollutants, black carbon (a component of soot that hastens the melting of snow) and ground-level ozone. The UNEP suggested that banning the burning of crop residues and introducing clean-burning biomass cook stoves for cooking and heating in developing countries could reduce black soot, while upgrading wastewater treatment and controlling methane emissions from livestock could reduce ozone.

Global warming is an increase in the average temperature of the atmosphere near the earth's surface. The earth's climate has changed many times due to natural factors, but the advent of the industrial revolution about two centuries ago increased the significance of human activities in altering the composition of the atmosphere and thus the climate. A combination of burning fossil fuels and deforestation appears to have increased concentrations of heat-trapping "greenhouse gases" (GHG) in the atmosphere, raising average global temperatures (NASA, 2009), and temperatures are likely to continue increasing because of the GHG that have accumulated in the atmosphere. Rising temperatures are likely to alter rainfall patterns, the extent of snow and ice cover, and sea levels.

The three major responses to global warming are prevention, adaptation, and migration, or PAM. Prevention aims to stop or reduce GHG emissions to slow the pace of global warming through the use of such policies as carbon taxes and cap-and-trade policies.[18] Adaptation involves countering the effects of climate change, such as changing fishing practices by switching to aquaculture and altering cropping patterns by constructing more defenses against severe storms and seawater surges that can inundate farmland. Migration, which is sometimes considered a failure of adaptation, involves moving from places made less viable by climate change to places that are more livable and offer more opportunity.

Farmers and other rural residents of the least developed countries are considered most vulnerable to global warming, and they may be most likely to migrate over national borders because getting out of agriculture requires them to change both their occupation and the place where they live (Martin, 2012). In this sense, low-skilled migration could increase as farmers are displaced or find agriculture less viable, adding to migration pressures if social networks or recruiters help them to move over borders. Most farmers will move within their own countries or to nearby countries, as from Bangladesh to India, but some may migrate longer distances.

It is very difficult to predict climate changes and their impacts on migration patterns. Even if most climate migrants are internal migrants, there is likely to be disruption that could increase international migration. In 2009, the UN Development Program (UNDP) estimated that there were 740 million

---

[18] The major issue in prevention is how much to reduce consumption now to slow global warming. The Stern Review on the Economics of Climate Change, released in October 2006, used a 0.1 discount rate to argue that 1 percent of global GDP should be invested to reduce global warming and thus avoid losses of 5 to 20 percent of GDP in the future. William Nordhaus, on the other hand, uses a 3 percent interest rate that suggests doing little to reduce carbon emissions now and instead investing to increase the physical and human capital of people so that they can better cope with climate change in the future.

internal and 200 million international migrants, including 150 million internal migrants in China. Some internal migrants later become international migrants, as with Mexicans who migrated to northern Mexico to fill jobs in export-oriented agriculture and then continued to the US. The bottom line is clear: as with development generally, climate change brings disruption to places with poor people looking for a better life, encouraging at least some to move over borders.

Managing Migration

The communications and transportation revolutions are integral components of globalization that governments do not want and may not be able to reverse. Instead, many governments respond to migrant crises by adjusting the rights of migrants. For example, during the breakup of Yugoslavia in the early 1990s, European countries generally and Germany in particular received large numbers of asylum seekers. With more than 1,000 foreigners a day applying for asylum in Germany, and asylum seekers distributed around the country to states and cities that were required to use local taxes to house and feed them, there was a backlash against migrants that included attacks on foreigners (Schuster, 2003).

European policymakers faced a dilemma between protection and protest. On the one hand, they wanted to preserve generous asylum systems enshrined in their constitutions to protect refugees in need of protection. On the other hand, governments were mindful that there was strong opposition to what many citizens saw as foreigners taking advantage of the asylum system to migrate from poorer to richer places in search of economic opportunity. Most applicants for asylum were found not to be refugees, but some remained in Europe for several years as they appealed decisions that found them to be economic migrants. As they formed and united families in Germany and other European countries, it became ever harder to remove them even after fighting in the Balkans had ceased (Martin, 2014b).

German politicians engaged in a fierce debate in 1992–93 that resulted in a compromise that preserved a generous asylum system, but made it harder for migrants to access it, an example of adjusting the rights of migrants to manage migration (Martin, 2014b). Under the compromise, foreigners who reached Germany could continue to apply for asylum and receive housing and food from the cities and towns to which they were sent while waiting for a first decision and the results of an appeal. However, the government made it harder for foreigners to get to Germany. Nationals of countries generating large numbers of asylum seekers were required to obtain visas, which prevented them from arriving as tourists and applying for asylum, and transport firms that brought foreigners into the country without proper documents were subject to fines.

Even more important were safe country lists and the EU's so-called Dublin Regulation of 1990. Citizens of countries considered to be safe could apply for asylum, but generally could not remain in Germany while their applications were pending, since they were believed not to face persecution at home. Migrants from countries in which there was persecution but who passed through safe third countries en route to Germany could be sent back to these transit countries to apply for asylum there. If a Serb had relatives in Germany, but traveled via Austria to Germany, he/she could be returned to Austria to apply for asylum there, a bid to end so-called asylum shopping. Preserving a generous right to asylum but making it harder to access the asylum system is an example of managing migration by adjusting migrant rights.[19]

The US faced a similar dilemma during the 1992 presidential campaign after Bill Clinton promised to "end welfare as we know it." President Reagan in the 1980s set the stage for welfare reform with stories of Cadillac-driving welfare queens who collected benefits in expensive cars under multiple names and addresses. Fuel was added to the fire by media reports in the 1990s of successful Asian immigrants who became naturalized US citizens, sponsored their parents for visas and promised to support them, but instead signed them up for payments from federal programs such as Supplemental Security Income (SSI) whose purpose was to help poor US citizens, not the parents of successful immigrants who brought their poor parents to the US.[20]

There were several options to deal with immigrants and the welfare system, including following the recommendation of the Commission on Immigration Reform (CIR) that needy immigrants should remain eligible for welfare benefits on the same basis as US citizens because most were intending US citizens. However, the CIR also urged the admission of fewer needy immigrants, and a change to make the commitments of US sponsors to support their relatives

[19] Asylum applications rose in Europe in 2015 due to the civil war in Syria. Some 626,000 foreigners applied for asylum in the EU in 2014, up from 435,000 in 2013, including 202,000 in Germany and 81,000 in Sweden. The largest single source country was Syria, 123,000 applications, followed by 41,000 Afghans and 38,000 Kosovars. About half of the asylum cases decided in 2014 resulted in the foreigner being allowed to stay in the EU.

[20] On February 6, 1996, the Senate Immigration Subcommittee held a hearing on the Supplemental Security Income (SSI) program and immigrants, which was then providing an average $325 a month to six million poor persons who are disabled or elderly, including a million immigrants. Immigrants must prove that they will not become "public charges" in the US in order to obtain immigrant visas, but US courts ruled that US sponsors who pledge to support those they sponsor are not binding, so the US sponsor did not break any laws by encouraging relatives to seek welfare (Congress Moves on Immigration Reform, 1996. *Migration News* 3(3) March). http://migration.ucdavis.edu/mn/more.php?id=893.

binding, so that the government could recoup welfare payments made to poor immigrants from their US sponsors.[21]

Congress rejected the CIR's advice, making no changes to the immigrant admissions system and instead denying federal welfare benefits to almost all immigrants who arrived after August 22, 1996 until they became US citizens or worked in the United States for at least a decade; another case of adjusting migrant rights to deal with a perceived migration crisis. At a time when immigrants were about 11 percent of the US population, 45 percent of the expected $54 billion in federal savings from welfare reform over its first 6 years was projected to come from denying benefits to immigrants.[22] During the economic boom of the late 1990s, some of these immigrant exclusions from federal welfare benefits were reversed, especially for poor immigrant children and the elderly.

There are many other examples of governments adjusting the rights of migrants to deal with short-term crises. For example, in the 1990s when Haitians in small boats bound for the US were intercepted at sea, they were allowed to apply for asylum on Coast Guard vessels to determine if they had a "credible fear" of persecution in Haiti. Migrant advocates complained that credible fear interviews on Coast Guard vessels were too intimidating, prompting the US government to send all those intercepted at sea to the US Naval Base in Guantanamo, Cuba, where US laws do not apply. In this example of adjusting migrant rights to deal with a crisis, the outflow of Haitians slowed when they realized that they would not get to the US mainland.[23]

Australia adopted a similar "Pacific Solution" to migrants arriving illegally by boat from Indonesia. The then Prime Minister John Howard in August 2001 declared that "We decide who comes to this country and the circumstances in which they come," and began sending migrants who arrived without visas to Pacific island nations to have their asylum applications considered. Howard said that the Pacific Solution was a safety measure, since some migrants died when their boats sank, and was a bid to discourage smuggling.[24] Australia mounted information campaigns in the countries of origin of boat people, advising them not to give their money to smugglers because, even if they reached Australian shores, they would not be admitted.[25]

---

[21] For details see: https://migration.ucdavis.edu/mn/more.php?id=465.

[22] The provisions of the Personal Responsibility and Work Opportunity Reconciliation Act of 1996 are at http://migration.ucdavis.edu/mn/more.php?id=1022.

[23] Policies toward Haitians intercepted at sea are at http://migration.ucdavis.edu/mn/more.php?id=383.

[24] An assessment of the Australian Pacific Solution is at: http://gifford.ucdavis.edu/workshop/past/australias-campaigns-discourage-migrants-how-effective/.

[25] See Australia's Campaigns to Discourage Migrants: How Effective? http://gifford.ucdavis.edu/workshop/past/australias-campaigns-discourage-migrants-how-effective/.

Most European governments stopped recruiting low-skilled guest workers from southern Europe and Turkey after the oil price hikes of 1973. However, they did not force jobless guest workers to go home, and many guest workers settled in France, Germany, and other countries that recruited them because their countries of origin were also suffering from oil-related recessions. During the 1960s, almost all guest workers were foreigners who worked; a decade later, many foreigners were not working (Martin, 2014b).

Most European governments refrained from forcing unemployed guest workers who had worked a year or more to leave, but some offered return-bonus payments to encourage those who lost their jobs to leave. France and Germany in the late 1970s and early 1980s paid expected unemployment benefits in a lump sum to those who left and gave up a right to return. Spain offered similar return bonuses to jobless workers after the 2008–09 recession, but few migrants took them, fearing they could not find good jobs at home and would be unable to return to Spain.[26] The failure of incentive programs to induce departures is one reason why governments more often adjust the rights of migrants to make it harder for them to enter.[27]

Adjusting migrant rights can quickly reduce or halt migration flows but runs counter to the rights-based approach to migration management. The fundamental principle of the rights-based approach is to treat migrants equally. Equal treatment makes sense for migrant workers in the workplace, since the best way to protect local workers from "unfair" migrant worker competition is to protect migrants and avoid the race to the bottom that could occur if employers who underpay migrants are able to expand at the expense of employers who hire native workers or treat migrant workers equally.

This review of the inequalities that motivate international migration, and the revolutions that make it easier for people to cross borders and stay abroad, envisions governments in migrant-receiving countries reacting to unwanted migration by restricting the rights of migrants. Some argue that governments cannot manage migration even by adjusting the rights of migrants. Bhagwati

[26] The Spanish government offered one-way return tickets and 40 percent of accumulated unemployment insurance benefits to jobless migrants who agreed to leave and not return for 3 years; the other 60 percent of Unemployment Insurance (UI) benefits are paid by the Spanish consulate in the migrant's home country. Details at http://migration.ucdavis.edu/mn/more.php?id=3554.

[27] Just as it is difficult to predict how many migrants will accept return bonuses and leave, it is hard to predict how many migrants will arrive if citizens of one country are granted the right to work in another. Dustman et al. (2003) predicted that 5,000 to 13,000 Poles and other East Europeans a year would move to the UK if Britain did not restrict labor migration, which it could do for 7 years. The Dustman prediction proved spectacularly wrong, as more than a million Poles and East Europeans moved to the UK, prompting a backlash against too much migration that led to the defeat of the Labor government in 2010 and the vote to leave the EU in 2016.

(2003) argued that "borders are beyond control and little can be done to really cut down on immigration," including illegal immigration.

Economist Jagdish Bhagwati and others call for a World Migration Organization (WMO) analogous to the World Trade Organization (WTO) to convince governments and their citizens that more migration is inevitable, and that nation-states should cede sovereignty to a WMO to establish minimum standards for migration, including entry doors for immigrants and windows for guest workers, in the same way that governments allow the WTO to set minimum standards to ensure the freer flow of goods and services over national borders. Governments and individuals could complain to a WMO if a member country blocks the admission of particular persons or seeks to expel migrants.

During the failed Doha Development Round of negotiations that began in 2001 to free up trade and services in ways that would benefit poorer countries, developing countries pushed for freer trade in services, including the "movement of natural persons" under the General Agreement on Trade in Services (GATS). Mode 4 of the GATS regulates the movement of workers who provide services in other countries. Developing countries said that their comparative advantage was the willingness of their citizens to work for lower wages in richer countries. They asked richer countries to open windows wider to service providers by eliminating requirements that employers first search and fail to find local workers before hiring foreigners and to end regulations that foreign-service providers must be paid at least prevailing wages and contribute to pension and other payroll-tax-financed benefit programs.

The goal of India and many other developing countries was a GATS service provider visa that would make it easy for service- providing workers from developing countries to enter and work in richer countries. Many countries opened windows to GATS services providers using the term "unbound," but then immediately closed the window with the phrase "except for measures established in immigration law." Under WTO rules, immigration is solely within national sovereignty.

The US H-1B program is an example of what India and other developing countries wanted to expand. The US at the WTO committed to providing at least 65,000 H-1B visas a year to foreigners who normally have at least a bachelor's degree and who are coming to the US to fill a job that requires such a degree. The H-1B program that makes it easy for employers to hire foreign tech workers was created in 1990, and was expected to expand quickly and then shrink as the US educated more IT professionals, but the opposite occurred. India-based outsourcers emerged to take over the IT needs of US firms, station some IT workers in the firm, and send IT work back to India for processing with lower wage workers (Lowell and Martin, 2012). Most US firms may lawfully lay off US workers and replace them with H-1B workers, and some did, including Disney and AIG, prompting protests from the laid-off US workers.[28]

With Indian-based outsourcers receiving more H-1B visas than anyone else, the US doubled the cost of H-1B visas for H-1B dependent firms to $4,500 in 2015; H-1B dependent firms are those with at least fifty employees, of whom more than half are foreigners with H-1B visas.[29] India complained to the WTO, arguing that the competitive advantage of outsourcers such as Infosys, Tata, and Wipro was reduced because of the doubling of the visa fee. The case in 2016 was before WTO arbitrators, and highlights the difficulties involved in managing the migration associated with trade under the current WTO, and foreshadows the even more complex disputes likely to arise under a WMO whose purpose is to increase mobility.

Those who argue that more migration is inevitable are often "cosmopolitans" who benefit from newcomers and favor more globalization. As many commentators have noted, governing elites rarely live with low-skilled newcomers on a day-to-day basis, so they tend to dismiss anti-migrant attitudes as racism. By contrast, many of those who adjust to newcomers on a day-by-day basis in their communities, workplaces, and schools, just as many of those who lose their jobs due to freer trade, believe that governments should protect them from the adjustments required by more migration and globalization. The oft-cited gap between the admissionist elites who welcome migration, and the restrictionist masses who fear the economic and noneconomic changes effectuated by migration is one reason that Donald Trump was elected US President in 2016.[30]

There have been many attempts to decide who is "us" and who is "them," and what responsibilities people within one nation-state owe to outsiders. Miller (2016) argues for what he calls weak cosmopolitanism, a concept that considers all humans to be equal but gives priority for limited resources to fellow citizens. He advocates national self-determination, allowing nation-states to select newcomers on whatever grounds they want, provided that their reasoning for selecting some migrants and not others is fair. This justifies, according to Miller, accepting only highly skilled migrants if a country wants immigration to bolster economic growth. Miller also argues that newcomers have a duty to integrate, and that national governments can legitimately

---

[28] Disney in 2015 laid off US workers and replaced them with H-1B workers provided by Cognizant Technology Solutions and HCL America. In response, candidate Donald Trump in March 2016 promised to "end forever the use of the H-1B as a cheap labor program." Trump said he would require employers "to hire American workers first for every visa and immigration program. No exceptions." See: https://migration.ucdavis.edu/rmn/more.php?id=1994.

[29] See: www.uscis.gov/news/alerts/new-law-increases-h-1b-and-l-1-petition-fees.

[30] Peggy Noonan, 2016, How Global Elites Forsake Their Countrymen, *Wall Street Journal*, August 13. See: www.wsj.com/articles/how-global-elites-forsake-their-countrymen-1470959258.

require them to sign "integration contracts" that require newcomers to learn the local language or risk loss of welfare support or residence rights.

Finally, there are many efforts to rank countries by their migration policies. Migration policy rankings measure inputs, asking whether governments have policies, for example, to integrate newcomers, but rarely measure the effectiveness of these policies. This means that a country with a policy to support the integration of newcomers by providing language and other orientation ranks higher than a country that does not, even if a migrant winds up jobless after learning the language in one country, while in another the migrant without local language skills finds a job. Countries with more migration policies wind up being rated higher, regardless of outcomes (EIU, 2016).

Migration and Development

Migration can generate triple wins, for migrants who move as well as for sending and receiving countries. Migrants earn higher wages and new skills, and their remittances increase family incomes at home and are associated with more education and better health care for children as well as less poverty (Adams and Page, 2003). Countries that admit migrants get jobs filled, increasing economic activity and generating multiplier effects, as when the availability of migrants creates or preserves jobs for local workers and adds to employment and economic activity. Migrant-sending countries that receive remittances and the return of workers who gained skills abroad may experience faster economic growth.

Low-skilled workers gain the most from voluntary migration. The reason is simple: the gaps in wages and opportunities between countries are largest for low-skilled workers. One study found that the average wage gains for low-skilled workers moving to the US, even after adjusting for the fact that living costs are higher in the US, were four to ten times, that is, $400 a month in Mexico becomes $1,600 in the US, and $400 a month in Vietnam becomes $4,000 in the US, largely because the better equipment available to low-skilled workers in the US makes them more productive (Clemens et al., 2009). In many cases, low-skilled workers without regular jobs at home get wage-paying jobs and work-related benefits abroad.

A series of reports, beginning with the Global Commission on International Migration (GCIM, 2004) and the UNDP's Human Development Report (UNDP, 2009), highlighted the benefits of economically motivated migration to low-skilled migrants and their developing countries of origin. These reports suggested that sending low-skilled workers abroad in one period can speed development in the next, and they called on richer countries to open more doors to low-skilled workers. The triple wins would be jobs and wages for migrants, remittances for migrant families, and the return of workers with new skills and ideas that speed up development.

The World Bank's Global Economic Prospects (GEP) (World Bank, 2005) report estimated the benefits of more migration. According to its calculations, if the number of developing country migrants in industrial countries rose by 14 million, taking the total from 28 million[31] to 42 million, global GDP would rise by $356 billion or 0.6 percent, more than the estimated gains from reducing trade restrictions (World Bank, 2005). Other estimates of the gains from more low-skilled migrants moving to richer countries are even higher, with some arguing that governments who do *not* open doors wider to migrants are leaving "trillion dollar bills" on the sidewalk, that is, keeping their economies 10 to 20 percent smaller than they could be (Clemens, 2011).

The gains from more migration are based on assumptions, including the assumption that migrants integrate seamlessly, that is, there is no unemployment among migrants or displacement of local workers by migrants. These assumptions may not hold, reducing the benefits of more migration. Borjas (2016) notes that billions of people would have to move from poorer to richer countries to double world GDP via migration, and they would have to be as productive as local workers to justify their higher wages.

Migrants receive most of the gains from migration. However, if they bring with them some of the attitudes and cultures that helped to keep their poor countries of origin poor and thus lower productivity in destination countries, there could be a net decrease in global GDP instead of an increase, a reminder that mass migration may bring unanticipated changes.[32] This so-called epidemiological case for migration restrictions argues that homogenous populations have higher levels of trust and lower levels of conflict that make them more productive.

Second, developing countries may not benefit as much from remittances and returns as imagined. The benefits of diaspora are believed to flow from the bridges they establish between poorer and richer countries, allowing advanced technologies and new ideas to flow and speed up development. Rapoport (2016) also dismisses worries about the brain drain, emphasizing that even though skilled migrants with post-secondary schooling are more than 40 percent of south-north migrants, the stock of human capital in the developing south has not decreased because of the global spread of more schooling.

---

[31] The GEP estimated that there were 28 million migrant workers from developing countries in high-income countries in 2001, including 25 million unskilled and 3 million skilled workers.

[32] Collier (2013: 257) emphasizes that migration often follows social networks, so that some migration today means more tomorrow, which could slow assimilation and the migrants achieving host-country productivity. As with GHG emissions, Collier warns that it is hard to determine the "tipping point" beyond which "too many migrants" kill the golden goose of economic growth.

However, there may have been even more skilled workers in developing countries without south-north migration, prompting skepticism that what is good for industrial countries, receiving skilled workers from developing countries, is not bad for developing countries that lose such workers.

It is important to remember that most studies of migration and development are based on assumptions, and that the potential of more migration to speed development has a pendulum quality in scholarly literature. De Haas (2010) emphasizes that there was optimism about the benefits of migration for development in the 1960s, pessimism due to the brain and brawn drains in the 1970s and 1980s, and optimism again in the 1990s as scholars emphasized the benefits of diaspora externalities and remittances.

Migrant rights advocates generally join economists in welcoming more migrant workers; but they also want transparent and protective labor migration systems, so that migrants are fully informed about the foreign jobs they will fill, charged "reasonable" recruitment fees, and paid the same wages equal to those of local workers. Calls for more low-skilled labor migration raise two issues. First, does more migration speed stay-at-home development or simply encourage more migration? Second, is there a trade-off between the number of low-skilled migrants admitted to richer countries and the rights afforded them, a topic tackled in Chapter 6.

Economic development is a sustained increase in the per capita income of an area. Income is not the only measure of development, but growth in per capita income is the most widely used shorthand indicator to compare the level of development across countries. The UNDP's Human Development Index uses a variety of development indicators to compare countries, including income as well as life expectancy, infant mortality, and education levels.[33] The UN's 2030 Sustainable Development Goals (SDGs) added sustainability, defined as development that meets the needs of current residents without diminishing the ability of future residents to meet their needs, as an important consideration.[34]

Regardless of exactly how development is defined, more development should slow the large-scale migration of low-skilled workers abroad in search of economic opportunity. When economic opportunities are similar across countries, few low-skilled workers migrate, as within the EU. Given the fact that Spain sent workers abroad in the 1980s and was receiving migrant workers in the 1990s, what can currently richer countries do to speed up stay-at-home development in poorer countries?

---

[33] http://hdr.undp.org/en/content/human-development-index-hdi.
[34] https://sustainabledevelopment.un.org/post2015/transformingourworld.

One question is whether richer countries should open their borders to more goods from developing countries, or more migrants? The logic is straightforward. Trade is the production of a good or service in one country for consumption in another. Freer trade and investment promise faster economic and job growth for most people in all trading countries, with benefits in the form of lower-priced goods and more jobs. With freer trade, economies grow faster as capital and labor is reallocated to where it is most productive, there are economies of scale in production, and competition lowers prices and increases consumption.

NAFTA was the first free-trade agreement between an industrial and developing country, and its effects on migration are instructive. NAFTA increased trade and investment between Canada, Mexico, and the US, but freer trade also speeded up changes in all three countries, including the movement of farmers out of agriculture in Mexico and deindustrialization or the closure of factories in Canada and the US. Workers displaced from factory jobs in Canada and the US did not move to Mexico, but some of the rural Mexicans who found it harder to survive with more trade in farm commodities migrated to the US.

During NAFTA's first decade, there was a Mexico–US migration hump, or a surge in legal and unauthorized migration tied to changes in both Mexico and the US. In Mexico, youth in rural areas realized that, with the US state of Iowa producing twice as much corn as all of Mexico, and at half the price, they would never achieve middle-class lives by farming in the same way as their parents and grandparents. However, these rural Mexican youth were often unable to get jobs in the auto and other factories that were created in response to NAFTA, since they lacked secondary school diplomas (Martin, 1993).

With better connections between rural Mexico and the US than between rural Mexico and booming areas of Mexico, there was an upsurge in Mexico–US migration in the 1990s, so that an average of more than 3,000 Mexicans a day were apprehended just inside the US border. During the 1990s, the Mexican labor force increased by a million a year, but only 350,000 formal sector jobs were created in Mexico each year, about a thousand a day. The US, by contrast, was adding more than 10,000 jobs each work day, and many farm, construction, and service employers were eager to hire rural Mexicans with relatively little education. NAFTA contributed to the migration hump pictured in Figure 1.1, meaning that Mexico–US migration rose alongside increased trade in goods and investment.

Mexico–US migration slowed with the 2008–09 recession and longer term changes within Mexico, including slower labor force growth and better education systems in rural areas to prepare the fewer youth there for jobs in Mexico. Meanwhile, the US has made it more difficult to enter the country illegally and work, so that the number of unauthorized Mexicans in the US has

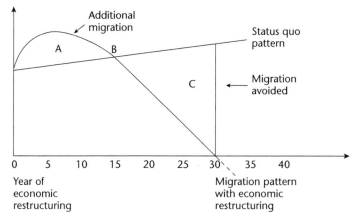

Figure 1.1 NAFTA and Mexico–US migration
Source: Author's own work.

stabilized at 6 million, making Mexicans 55 percent of the 11 million unauthorized foreigners in the US.[35]

The migration hump was anticipated by those who understood how freer trade would change the outlook in rural Mexico, where decades of recruitment of Mexican workers for US agriculture had forged strong links to US labor markets (Martin, 1993). Nonetheless, Mexican President Carlos Salinas suggested that free trade would smoothly create enough new jobs to absorb those who were displaced in rural Mexico. In advocating for NAFTA, Salinas said that the US faced a choice of "accepting Mexican tomatoes or Mexican migrants that will harvest them in the United States" (Martin, 2005).

The NAFTA experience showed that industrial countries can succeed in "attacking the root causes" of unwanted migration, but at the potential expense of a migration hump. There are many reasons for migration humps, but the simplest is that freer trade and labor displacement occur quickly as trade barriers fall, while time is required to build factories and other businesses that create jobs. If workers made worse off by freer trade have connections to jobs abroad, they may move, leading to a migration hump.

There are other reasons why trade and migration can rise together, as when countries do not share the same technologies. If tractors plow corn fields in the US and oxen pull plows in Mexico, trade theory assumes that the reason for this difference is that Mexico has more labor and lower wages, not that

[35] The estimated number of illegal Mexicans in the US was fewer than three million in 1995, reached 4.5 million in 2000, peaked at 7 million in 2007, and was 5.9 million in 2014 (Passel and Cohn, 2016).

tractors are unavailable in Mexico.[36] In reality, rural Mexicans may not have access to tractors, and may migrate to the US to earn money to buy tractors. Similarly, if the better infrastructure in the US makes Mexican workers more productive in the US than in Mexico, migration may increase alongside trade as US producers expand to supply a growing Mexican market.

Closer economic integration can raise the aspirations of potential migrants faster than economic development can fulfill them, prompting emigration. This may be happening in Africa, which experienced more than 5 percent real economic growth between 2000 and 2010 as exports to China boomed, prompting the McKinsey Global Institute to dub African economies "lions on the move." The optimism on Africa has faded since the Arab spring that began in 2011 slowed growth in northern Africa, and falling oil and commodity prices after 2014 slowed growth in other African countries.

The economic growth that occurred in Africa early in the twenty-first century raised the expectations of increasingly globalized youth much faster than local economies could create good jobs. A rural Senegalese man was profiled before leaving illegally for Europe after his brother drowned trying to get to Italy. Instead of being deterred by his brother's death in the Mediterranean, Samba Thiam concluded that he had to move 400 miles from his village to Dakar, and from there to Libya and on to Italy, in order to earn money so that his family, as well as his brother's widow and children, could buy the smart phones and televisions that have become common in migrant households.[37] Staying at home would deny Samba Thiam and other rural Senegalese the consumer items introduced by successful migrants.

Sending workers abroad is often a safety valve for countries with more workers than jobs. A safety valve allows steam to escape and protect the engine, and the safety valve of migration can create a private safety net via remittances. The major question is whether the development and migration that is occurring acts as a safety valve for countries and a safety net for individuals or drains off the energy and vitality that could lead to the reforms needed for stay-at-home development. The record is decidedly mixed.

In eastern European countries that joined the EU and whose workers got freedom of movement rights, it appears that the emigration of young and skilled workers may be slowing economic growth and development by slowing fundamental changes at home (Atoyan et al., 2016). Many young and educated Poles and Romanians leave, find jobs in Germany and the UK, and return only to visit rather than to work and invest at home. Some studies

---

[36] Trade theory assumes that differences in the labor and capital intensities of production are due solely to differences in their factor endowments.

[37] Dionne Searcey, 2016. Desperation Rising at Home, Africans Increasingly Turn to Risky Seas, *New York Times*, June 16. www.nytimes.com/2016/06/17/world/africa/african-migrants-mediterranean-sea.html.

suggest that the presence of skilled foreigners in an area such as Silicon Valley means more innovation and jobs, reflecting the benefits to concentrating skilled workers in one place (World Bank, 2009). If young and skilled people leave and concentrate in innovation hubs abroad, the countries they leave behind may wither as they become less attractive to local or outside investors.

It is not clear whether current levels of migration speed development at home or provide enough of a safety valve and net to allow governing elites to postpone difficult economic choices that could put countries on a faster road to job growth (Wickramasekara, 2015b). There are examples that prompt optimistic assessments, as with the growth of the state of Kerala in India associated with migration to Gulf oil exporters, and examples that lead to pessimism, as in Nepal or Bangladesh. Indicators of corruption, rule of law, and accountability are lower in countries such as Albania, Bulgaria, and Romania, from where skilled and educated workers are most likely to leave and not return, than in other countries (Atoyan et al., 2016: 15).

Managing international labor migration is not hopeless, but it is more difficult than many people think. People are far more complex than goods, reacting to changes in laws and regulations in ways that goods do not. This is why migration is a process to be managed on an ongoing basis rather than a problem that can be solved in a way that allows policymakers to move on to the next issue. Policies and strategies that allow migration to promote development in one country may retard migration in another, suggesting the need for careful site-specific analysis rather than sweeping generalizations (Omelaniuk, 2012).

2

Labor Markets and Migration

Work is the exchange of effort for reward. Work involves employers hiring employees, who give up control over some of their time in exchange for monetary wages and work-related benefits. Unlike many other market transactions, such as a customer buying an item in a store and never shopping there again, work is unusual because it requires a continuous relationship between employer and employee in the workplace, as supervisors assess employee performance and workers consider their satisfaction with the job. Employers may terminate unsatisfactory workers, and dissatisfied workers may quit their jobs.

There is a second important dimension of labor markets that make them unique. Goods that are purchased do not care who buys or consumes them, but workers care about their supervisors and fellow workers and the society in which they live. Workers are not clothing or tools in other ways as well. Workers are multidimensional, with lives outside the workplace that include raising families, participating in leisure activities, and voting for politicians who collect taxes and allocate resources while setting the rules of the society and economy.

Mobility is the key to labor market adjustments that ensure the "best" workers are in the "best" jobs. Employers try to recruit the best workers and develop remuneration packages to encourage them to perform their jobs well. Employers offer promotions to retain good and experienced workers to achieve higher productivity. Workers may quit one job and move to another for higher wages, better benefits, or more opportunities. The movement of workers between jobs is considered a normal component of well-functioning labor markets.

International borders and restrictions that prevent workers from changing employers while abroad complicate labor market adjustments. Instead of advertising for local workers under nondiscrimination laws, employers may specify that they will hire only male or female guest workers. Once in another country, migrant workers are usually prohibited from switching jobs unless they win the approval of both the old and new employer and a government agency. Migrant workers must generally leave the country when their contracts expire or if/when those are terminated by their employers, preventing wages and benefits rising with experience and productivity.

Labor Market Rs

Labor markets have three major functions, that is, recruitment, remuneration, and retention. Recruitment matches workers with jobs, remuneration or the wage and benefit system motivates workers to perform their jobs, and retention systems assess workers to identify and retain the best. Most workplaces have human resources departments to manage these three labor market Rs to ensure that the firm has productive and satisfied employees.

National borders complicate the three Rs. When jobs are in one country and workers in another, language differences and variance in education and training standards and certificates can make it hard to match efficiently workers in one country with jobs in another. Employers seeking workers in other countries often turn to private recruiters in their own country or abroad to find workers to fill jobs, and these intermediary recruiters can make job-matching more efficient or simply add to the cost of matching workers with jobs. Governments often regulate recruiter–worker transactions, and this regulation can improve protections for workers and reduce their migration costs or add to complications and worker-paid migration costs.

The other two R-labor market functions may also be complicated by national borders. International Labor Organization (ILO) conventions and many national laws call for equal pay for equal work, so that all workers doing the same job should receive the same wage regardless of their citizenship or work-permit status. However, it can be hard to ensure equality in the workplace. Even if migrant and local workers receive the same wages, migrants may be cheaper than local workers because employers do not have to pay work-related taxes on migrant earnings, especially if migrants will not be in the country long enough to receive benefits. For example, the US exempts employers from paying federal social security and unemployment insurance (UI) taxes on the earnings of H-2A guest workers, which can save employers up to 15 percent on payroll taxes if state laws also exempt H-2A workers from state UI taxes (Martin, 2014c).[1]

In addition to payroll tax savings, migrants may work harder than local workers because their right to be in the country depends on their satisfying the employer. The superior work performance of migrants is lauded by employers

---

[1] The H-2A program allows US farmers anticipating labor shortages to receive certification to employ guest workers, generally up to 10 months.

who emphasize that migrants are abroad in order to work and send money home to their families, making them eager to please the employer and volunteer for overtime work. Many US employers of low-skilled H-2A and H-2B guest workers cite their "reliability and loyalty," emphasizing that they are in the US to work and that they cannot easily switch employers (Martin, 2014c). British employers similarly praise the work ethic of Poles and other Eastern European workers, saying that soft skills such as being willing to work unsocial hours and reliably coming to work are more important than English language skills (Ruhs and Anderson, 2010).

Migrants are often concentrated in particular industries and occupations. Most countries welcome highly skilled migrants as immigrants, temporary workers, or as students who are allowed to stay and settle if they get job offers after graduation. Over the past two decades the global war for talent has prompted many countries to change their policies to welcome highly skilled foreigners (Fix and Kaushal, 2006).

The focus of this book is on low-skilled workers and jobs, workers who have a secondary school education or less and who fill jobs that require relatively little formal education. Rich countries have largely service economies, so that most jobs provide services rather than produce farm commodities or manufacture goods. The largest low-skilled labor market in these countries is in services, where employers stress the need for workers to have the stamina to perform repetitive tasks quickly, as with cleaning buildings (Maxwell, 2006: 7). Most migrant workers are employed in the service sector.

As some industries and occupations become dominated by migrant workers, wages in migrant-dominated sectors may not rise as fast as overall wages. If governments do not enact policies to increase wages in migrant-dominated sectors, wages can stagnate and productivity growth can slow, as occurred under the 1942–64 Mexico–US Bracero program in the commodities and areas where Braceros were the majority of workers (Martin, 2009). Instead of the labor-saving mechanization that was sweeping across most of US agriculture, commodities that relied on Bracero workers continued with labor-intensive methods, expanding employment but not raising productivity.

The final labor market function, retention, is also complicated by national borders. Most studies find that more experienced workers have higher productivity, which is why employers develop systems to identify and retain experienced workers. However, guest worker programs that require workers to depart after 2–3 years can mean the loss of experienced workers and their replacement with new hires who must be trained. Some governments allow seasonal workers to return year after year, and some permit employers to sponsor migrant workers for permanent resident status; but most guest worker programs require migrants to depart when contracts end, forcing experienced workers to leave.

Recruitment, remuneration, and retention are challenging for native employers and workers, and these three Rs are more complicated when jobs are in one country and workers in another. The fact that workers must be matched with jobs across borders adds to costs, especially during recruitment.[2]

Asymmetric Information

Labor markets are information exchanges marked by asymmetric information, meaning that one party to a transaction has more information than another. Employers with vacant jobs typically know most about the requirements of the jobs they are offering, while workers seeking jobs know more about their abilities. This asymmetry can lead to inefficiencies and exploitation: "when one party to a transaction has more information pertinent to the transaction than does the other party . . . the better informed party [may] exploit the less-informed party." For example, the seller of a car knows whether it is a "good used car," but the buyer does not.[3]

To overcome these information asymmetries, employers have developed a variety of strategies to *screen* applicants to find the best workers, including setting minimum education and experience requirements, asking current workers to refer qualified friends and relatives, and advertising or using recruiters to find qualified workers.[4] Meanwhile, workers may *signal* their abilities to employers by earning credentials and certificates and gaining experience to demonstrate that they will be good employees.

An example of screening is setting minimum requirements for applicants, such as having a high-school diploma or college degree or passing a drug or skills test; only applicants who can pass the screening test are considered for the job. An example of signaling arises when a degree suggests high ability. If high-ability persons find it easier than low-ability persons to earn an engineering degree, employers may select engineering degree holders even if the job

---

[2] Many authors attack international labor markets because many governments favor high-skilled over low-skilled migrants and often distinguish between legal and desired versus illegal and dangerous migrants (Gabriel and Pellerin, 2008).

[3] Nobel prize-winning economist George Akerlof used the example of buyers who do not know which used cars are good "cherries" and which used cars are bad "lemons" to show that buyers assume all used cars are lemons and reduce the price they will offer, which helps to ensure that only bad used cars are offered for sale (Akerlof, 1970). Independent evaluations of used cars or car sellers offering guarantees can overcome information asymmetries in the used car market. In health care, information asymmetries make it difficult for patients to evaluate the quality of healthcare providers, prompting governments to establish standards and issue licenses to healthcare professionals who satisfy them.

[4] Major trends in the recruitment of professionals include the requirement to apply online rather than via a paper resume, which allows quick screening for desirable skills and traits, and using videos, as when applicants are asked to respond to a question in a minute or two.

does not require an engineering education. Instead, earning the degree has signaled the high abilities desired by the employer. Employer screening and worker signaling have been core concerns of labor economics for several decades (Riley, 2001).

When workers and employers do not share a common language or have experience with the same education and training systems, they often rely on intermediaries to facilitate worker–job matches (Autor, 2009). Recruiters who understand the requirements of the jobs offered by employers can find and screen the best workers to fill them. When workers are low-skilled, recruiters may act as the sole port of entry into businesses that often experience high turnover. For example, some US firms offering low-skilled jobs make temporary help firms the only way for new workers to enter the workplace. New hires who have been screened by the temp firm are placed in easy-to-learn jobs and, if they prove to be satisfactory, can make the transition to regular employee of the firm.[5]

National borders add layers between workers and jobs and complicate the recruitment process. Employers may turn to recruiters in their own countries to find workers in other countries. These local recruiters may recruit foreign workers directly or transmit employer job offers to partner recruiters in countries with workers, where subagents find workers to fill jobs. National borders and different languages, cultures, and regulations combine to offer a spectrum of ways to match workers with jobs.

At one extreme, recruiters may invest and specialize to make the process of finding the best workers to fill particular jobs more efficient, as when foreign employers partner with a particular recruiter to find satisfactory employees in another country. Alternatively, recruiters can be middlemen who do not add value but increase costs to employers who need workers and low-skilled workers who cannot find foreign jobs on their own. When there are more workers than jobs, and if foreign employers see workers as interchangeable, recruiters and their agents can allocate scarce foreign jobs on the basis of worker willingness to pay.

International borders should *increase* employer investment in recruitment to ensure good worker–job matches, but in practice employers often invest little to recruit low-skilled foreign workers. Large wage gaps between origin and destination countries can create an excess supply of workers in sending countries, meaning that more workers want to work abroad than there are jobs.

---

[5] Some manufacturing firms have a branch of a temp firm such as Manpower on the premises. All new hires are Manpower employees who usually wear distinctive clothing and begin in easy-to-learn jobs. If they prove to be proficient workers, they can become "regular" employees of the factory where they work.

If there are too many workers seeking jobs abroad, employers may be able to charge for their job offers, extracting from workers some of the wage wedge that motivates migration. Selling visas may encourage some employers to hire more workers than they need, helping to explain slow productivity growth in countries where migrant workers dominate workforces. For example, average labor productivity in Gulf oil exporters where migrants dominate private-sector workforces has been falling, and the share of national income accruing to capital is among the highest in the world. Such overhiring may be in the short-term interest of employers, but not in the national interest of countries that want to raise productivity, wages, and competitiveness over time.

Recruiters and Recruitment Costs

Matching workers with jobs has costs that are usually assumed by employers seeking workers and individuals seeking jobs. Employers advertise for workers, request that current employees inform their friends and relatives about vacancies, and notify public and private employment services that they are seeking workers. Workers seeking jobs contact employers directly, ask their social networks about job openings, and turn to public and private agencies that specialize in helping workers to find jobs.

The major cost for both employers and workers in job search is opportunity cost, the cost of not having a job filled for employers and the cost of not working while engaged in job search for workers. The financial costs of advertising for workers in newspapers or paying recruiters, and worker costs to visit employers and public and private agencies, are usually small relative to these opportunity costs, which explains why most jobs are filled quickly and why most jobless workers find jobs within a few months.

International migration can slow worker–job matches. Table 2.1 shows the four major phases in the international labor migration process, and each can generate migration costs that are paid by workers. Employers set the migration process in motion by developing job descriptions, obtaining government approval to fill jobs with migrant workers (usually after seeking and failing to find local workers), and contacting workers in another country directly or via a recruiter to fill the job. If the employer utilizes a local recruiter, that recruiter may incur costs to contact workers in another country directly or via a recruiter in worker countries of origin.

Migrant workers appear in the second phase, when they learn about foreign job opportunities, obtain contracts to fill foreign jobs, apply for passports and undergo health, criminal, and other checks before receiving visas, and have their documents and contracts approved before departure. Some migrant workers receive weeks or months of language, skills, or other training before

Table 2.1 Labor migration: Worker costs in four phases

Phase	Procedure	Activity	Worker costs
Employer permission to recruit migrants	Certification vs attestation	Certification usually involves employer trying to recruit local workers under govt. supervision	Workers do not usually pay for employer costs in this phase
Worker learns about foreign job	Receive contract and permission to go abroad to work	Obtain contract, paperwork to go abroad, training, deployment	Workers make payments to agents/recruiters, govt. agencies, & others, including for transport & health checks
Employment abroad	Work for 2–3 years abroad	Earn wages and job-related benefits, receive end-of-service & other benefits	Do workers get promised wages and job-related benefits?
Reintegration or go abroad again	Return as per contract ends	Use remittance savings to open business, use skills learned abroad in job at home, go abroad again	Few worker-paid costs except to go abroad again

Source: Author's own work.

departure and, even if the training is free, there are opportunity costs during the time that migrants study rather than work. Most worker payments to recruiters and government agencies are made during this second phase of the migration cycle, and many workers take out loans to cover these costs.

The third phase involves migrant workers employed abroad, typically for 2 or 3 years. As the end of their contracts approaches, migrants may seek to have their contracts renewed and remain abroad, or return to their country of origin to rest before going abroad again. If migrants return home to stay, they can invest savings from employment abroad to start a business or to find a wage job. Some migrants are entitled to end-of-service bonuses, reimbursement of some expenses, and refunds of social security contributions upon completion of their contracts.

The fourth phase involves reintegration at home or preparation to go abroad again. The reintegration process is not well understood, so there is little reliable data on the share of migrants who return to stay versus those who cycle between work abroad, rest at home, and going abroad again. Farm employers say that workers admitted under guest worker programs that permit 8 or 10 months of employment abroad often return year after year for several decades. There are also many reports of so-called serial migrants who work 2 or 3 years abroad, return home for a year or two, and then go abroad again as their savings diminish (Parreñas, 2015).

Workers incur several types of costs in each of the four migration phases, including monetary and opportunity costs. For example, the opportunity costs of not working may be higher than the travel costs paid by rural workers who must go to capital cities to sign contracts and receive pre-departure training.

Migrants may also incur costs if they receive substandard wages and benefits abroad or if they work abroad in jobs that do not utilize their skills. In some migration corridors, maximum migration costs and their division between employers, workers, recruiters, and government agencies are specified in bilateral agreements or program rules. In others, only some or none of worker-paid migration costs are regulated.

Surveys can ask workers what they paid to learn about foreign jobs, obtain contracts, and travel to fill them. The first cost for many workers involves learning about the foreign job. What costs (if any) do workers incur to learn about foreign jobs, and can a sensible division be made between monetary, opportunity, and other worker-paid costs? Few low-skilled migrants can access databases of foreign job offers in the rural areas where they live. Instead, most migrants rely on subagents, sometimes professionals such as teachers or healthcare personnel who recruit workers as a second job, to help them learn about foreign jobs.[6]

Second, exactly how do migrants obtain contracts to fill foreign jobs? Many low-skilled migrants live in rural areas, while most foreign job offers arrive in cities where licensed recruiters are located. What payments do migrants make to recruiters and subagents? Exactly how does recruitment occur? Do recruiters and subagents rely on networks, asking current migrants to refer friends and relatives to fill jobs similar to those they are doing? Do recruiters visit villages periodically and hold job fairs in areas with workers, or do they recruit in some other way?

Third, once workers have contracts to fill foreign jobs, they must satisfy employer and government requirements before leaving their country and entering another. What are the monetary and other costs involved in obtaining passports and visas, undergoing health and criminal checks, having the contract checked, and completing any required pre-departure training and orientation? How do migrants pay these costs? Do they rely on savings or take out loans?

Fourth, after all papers are in order, migrants depart for the foreign job. Who pays transport costs: employers or migrants, or are travel costs shared? Do migrants pay first and seek reimbursement from their employers after arrival or after they have completed a certain portion of the work contract, or do employers pay transport costs and deduct them from migrant wages?

ILO conventions recommend that employers pay all costs for the migrant workers they hire. Some migrant-receiving countries have adopted this employer-pays-all-costs principle, as in the US's H-2A and H-2B guest worker

---

[6] IOM (2016) emphasizes that many subagents are trusted by workers because they are residents of their communities, and that subagents may give workers false information because they do not fully understand legal procedures and processes for working abroad.

programs, while others specify the shares of migration costs that employers and migrants must pay, as with Canada's Seasonal Agricultural Worker Programs with Caribbean countries and Mexico, and the Australia–New Zealand Pacific Island seasonal worker programs. Some migrant-sending countries, including the Philippines, set maximum worker-paid migration costs before departure at 1 month's foreign earnings or 4.2 percent of foreign earnings for a 2-year contract and 2.8 percent for a 3-year contract. It appears that no country regulates opportunity costs incurred by migrants.

Anecdotal evidence and migration cost studies suggest that many migrants pay far more than 5 percent of their expected foreign earnings in migration costs. Some South Asians moving to Gulf Cooperation Council (GCC) country destinations pay up to a third of what they expect to earn abroad, or a year's foreign earnings for a 3-year contract (Martin et al., 2006). Costs are further increased if low-skilled migrants borrow money at high interest rates, making them vulnerable abroad because they are reluctant to return with no easy way to pay mounting migration-related debts. For example, if an indebted migrant arrives abroad and learns that the wage will be lower than promised, or the job is different than was described, can he or she afford to return and face the migration-related debts that have already been incurred?

Part II
What do Workers Pay?

Introduction

Qatar is building facilities to host the 2022 World Cup with the help of South Asian migrant workers. The International Trade Union Confederation (ITUC) predicted that 4,000 of the 1.2 million migrant workers involved in the construction of World Cup facilities in Qatar would die, and called on the Fédération Internationale de Football Association (FIFA) and the Qatar government to improve working conditions for migrant workers (Booth, 2013). Subsequent stories painted a more nuanced picture, emphasizing that the problems of migrant workers often begin at home, where migrants must borrow money to pay recruiters to get jobs in Qatar. After arriving, they are expected to work hard in very hot weather to keep their jobs, which can lead to heart failure and death (Pattisson, 2013).

The Global Knowledge Partnership on Migration and Development (KNOMAD) and the International Labor Organization developed a six-part questionnaire to interview legal and low-skilled migrant workers employed abroad and as they returned home. Part 1 collected demographic and education data on the migrant, including how many family members he or she supports. Part 2 asked about the recruitment process. How did the migrant learn about the job, who was paid to get the contract, and what did migrants pay for items ranging from passports and visas to medical and police checks. Some migrants paid a lump sum to recruiters and did not know the cost of these individual items.

Many migrants did not have the $1,000 to $4,000 that was typically spent before departure, and Part 3 asked about the cost of borrowing money to pay migration costs. From whom was money borrowed, at what interest rate, and with what collateral? Part 4 asked about job-search costs. How long did it take to find the foreign job, and what were the opportunity costs in time not worked because of preparing to go abroad?

The questions in Part 5 shifted to work abroad. What do or did migrants earn abroad, what work-related benefits do or did they receive, and do or did the migrant get paid the wage that was promised before departure? Part 6 turns to work-related issues, including the cost of housing and food while abroad, hours of work and work-related injuries, and the availability of work-rights ranging from being able to form or join a union to the right to change employers.

Workers were interviewed in 2014 in Korea, Kuwait, and Spain in or near their workplaces. In 2015, workers returning from Qatar, Saudi Arabia, and the United Arab Emirates were interviewed as they returned to Ethiopia, India, Nepal, Pakistan, and the Philippines, as were Vietnamese migrants in Malaysia.

The worker-reported cost data summarized in Chapters 3 and 4 highlight three important points. First, the most important determinant of what workers pay is corridor. Bangladeshis pay more than Indians for similar jobs in Kuwait, and Pakistanis pay more than Indians for similar jobs in other Gulf oil exporters. Second, many migrants learn about foreign jobs from friends and relatives, but pay recruiters for the contracts they need to leave their countries, suggesting that migrants *must* use recruiters to get foreign jobs and raising questions about whether recruiters add value to the recruitment process or use government-granted licenses to extract some of the wage wedge that motivates migration from workers.

Third, there is variance within migration corridors in what workers pay. More skilled Indians who have been abroad before generally pay less than first-time and less-skilled Indians, but migration cost differences within corridors are much less than differences between corridors. For workers who knew the cost of individual items needed to migrate, there was a surprising variance in the cost of standard items, such as passports and health exams that should have the same cost for all workers.

3

Migration Costs in Destinations

Relatively little is known about worker-paid migration costs. Unlike the cost of remitting small sums over national borders, where it is possible to call a bank or money transfer firm and quickly learn that the cost of sending $200 averaged about 8 percent or $16 in 2015 (https://remittanceprices.worldbank. org), there is no database of migration costs by corridor.

Researchers in 2014 interviewed several hundred legal, low-skilled, and recently arrived migrant workers where they were employed, in Korea, Kuwait, and Spain. The goal of these worker surveys was to contribute to a database of what low-skilled migrants paid to work abroad.

There were three major findings. First, worker-paid migration costs were generally less than 1 month's foreign earnings except in Kuwait, where migrants paid an average 4 months' Kuwaiti wages in migration costs. Second, there is significant variation in worker-paid migration costs between migration corridors, as Bangladeshis paid more than Indians to migrate to Kuwait. Third, there was surprisingly large variation in the cost of many standard items such as passports, medical tests, and other prepare-to-depart services whose cost should be the same for all workers.

Worker-paid migration costs averaged $1,525 in Korea, or 1–1.5 months of typical earnings. Most migrant workers had 36-month contracts, so they could expect to earn $36,000 at $1,000 a month or $54,000 at $1,500 a month, depending on how much overtime they worked.[1] Migrant worker contracts can be extended for an additional 22 months at the request of migrants and their Korean employers, so average migration costs of $1,525 could be less

---

than 3 percent of expected earnings in Korea if migrants stay in Korea for the maximum of almost 5 years.

Worker-paid migration costs in Kuwait averaged $1,900, and average monthly earnings were $465, so migration costs were equivalent to 4 months' Kuwaiti earnings. With 2-year contracts, migrant workers earn $11,160, and worker-paid migration costs are a sixth of earnings. For Egyptians, many of whom were employed at home at an average wage of $165 a month, earning more than $600 a month in Kuwait was four times more than they would have earned at home.

Worker-paid migration costs to fill seasonal farm jobs in Spain averaged $530 or half a month's average earnings of $1,000. Most seasonal farm workers were employed in Spain from 4 to 9 months, making worker-paid migration costs 6 to 12 percent of Spanish earnings. Migration costs are relatively low despite only seasonal earnings because all of the workers interviewed had previous Spanish work experience and Spanish regulations require employers to pay half of worker transportation costs. When workers arrived from afar, such as from Ecuador, employers usually paid the full cost of inbound transportation and deducted transport costs from worker earnings at the rate of €90 ($100) a month. These costs are summarized in Table 3.1.

The Malaysian case was different because only Vietnamese workers employed in Malaysian factories were interviewed, and the interviews were done a year later in 2015 with a longer questionnaire. The Vietnamese interviewed in Malaysia were relatively well educated; more than half completed secondary-school. Three-fourths were employed in Vietnam before departure, but they earned almost twice as much in Malaysia, $350 a month, as they had in Vietnam, $190 a month, and remitted half of their Malaysian earnings.

Table 3.1 Worker-paid costs in Korea, Kuwait, and Spain (2014 US$)

Destination	Average worker-paid costs	Worker earnings	Costs: share of earnings
Korea	$1,525	$36,000 at $1,000 a month or $54,000 at $1,500 a month for 36 months	1 to 1.5 months of Korean earnings; could be less than 3% of Korean earnings if migrants stay max. period
Kuwait	$1,900	$465/month	4 months of Kuwaiti earnings of $11,160 over 24 months; Bangladeshis & Egyptians paid more than Indians & Sri Lankans
Spain	$530	$1,000/month	Workers employed in seasonal agri jobs for 4-9 months; all had worked in Spain previously

Source: Author's own calculations from unpublished raw data.

Most Vietnamese migrants paid recruiters a lump sum that covered 90 percent of their total migration costs of $1,375, making the costs of Vietnamese workers equivalent to 3.9 months of Malaysian earnings. Most of the Vietnamese worked in Malaysian factories for 60 hours a week and earned $1.45 an hour.

Migrants in Korea

Worker-paid costs as a share of earnings were lowest for migrants in Korea. Almost 90 percent of the migrant workers interviewed were in Korea less than 3 months.[2] Almost 80 percent were employed in manufacturing, 86 percent were men, and 61 percent were in Korea for the first time. Many of the migrants had been employed in other countries and welcomed the opportunity to work in Korea, where wages are much higher than in Malaysia or for Gulf oil exporters.

More than 95 percent of the migrants were in their twenties and thirties, 55 percent were married, and 85 percent completed secondary school or post-secondary education. Migrants supported an average of three dependents at home. Average earnings at home were $225 a month, versus $765 in Korea, for a wage gap of 3.4, although many migrants expected to earn more when they gained experience and worked overtime.

Average worker-paid costs were $1,525, but median costs were $1,300; average costs were increased by the relatively few workers who had very high costs. The average cost of the seven migration-related expenses reported by 60 percent or more of the workers was $830, including $365 for international transportation and $250 to learn Korean. The other major expenses, for passports, medical exams, security checks, welfare funds, and visas, cost $15 to $70 each.

The migrants interviewed in Korea were from Thailand, Indonesia, and Vietnam. Thais reported migration costs of $1,525, including two-thirds who reported paying recruitment fees that averaged $980. Half of the Thais borrowed money to work in Korea. Borrowers had repaid 90 percent of their loans when interviewed, but still owed significantly more, suggesting high interest rates. Median earnings in Korea were 3.3 times median earnings in Thailand, suggesting a smaller wage gain for Thais than for Indonesians and Vietnamese. More than 60 percent of the Thais completed secondary school, and an eighth had some post-secondary education, suggesting much higher levels of education than for all Thais.

---

[2] Collection of data from migrant workers in Korea was supervised by Young-bum Park.

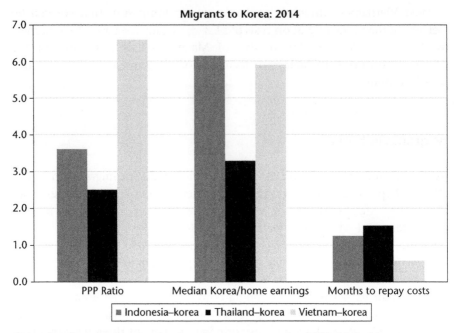

Figure 3.1 Per capita income and median earnings ratios (PPP), 2013–14
Source: Author's own work.

Indonesians had average total migration costs similar to Thais, about $1,500. More than half reported internal migration costs that averaged $420, which was more than the average $308 for international travel to Korea. Indonesians earned an average $174 a month at home, a seventh of their median earnings of $1,050 a month in Korea. More than 80 percent of the Indonesian migrants completed secondary school, but fewer than 5 percent had post-secondary education.

Vietnamese workers reported the lowest migration costs of $1,200. The median and mode costs were $630, so the average cost of $1,200 indicates very high costs for some workers. Most costs were similar to those of Thais and Indonesians, although the Vietnamese reported paying more to learn Korean and more for international travel. The Vietnamese earned a median $190 a month at home and $1,120 or six times more in Korea. More than 70 percent of the Vietnamese migrants completed secondary school, and 20 percent had post-secondary education.

The income gap between home and Korean wages is largest for Vietnamese workers, slightly more than six to one, and the ratio of median Korean-to-home earnings was also about six to one for the Vietnamese (Figure 3.1). Indonesian workers had an almost six to one median earnings gain, reflecting the fact that many were not from urban areas of Indonesia where incomes and earnings are higher. Thais also gained more than the ratio of national incomes.

The final columns show that Vietnamese could repay their migration costs with fewer months of Korean work than Indonesians and Thais, less than half a month versus more than a month.

The Korean EPS (www.eps.go.kr/ph/index.html), introduced in 2003 and since 2007 the only way for most Korean small- and medium-sized enterprises to hire non-ethnic Koreans from outside the country, functions reasonably well for most migrants, allowing them to repay their migration costs with less than 2 months of Korean earnings. Most of the high costs were incurred by relatively few workers, and these high costs were usually recruitment fees, other payments, and job searches. In the case of Southeast Asians going to Korea, reducing very high costs for the relatively few workers who incur them would reduce overall worker-paid migration costs.

Korea pays higher wages than other Asian destinations and attracts relatively well-educated migrants. In a bid to reduce corruption and high recruitment costs, the EPS involves government agencies in Korea and in migrant-sending countries. Migrants qualify to be placed on lists from which Korean employers select workers by passing Korean language tests and medical exams, and they are often interviewed via Skype by their prospective employers. High Korean wages attract well-educated Asians to learn Korean and seek to fill low-skilled jobs in Korean manufacturing, construction, and agriculture, making it easy for them to learn their Korean jobs but resulting in brain waste in the sense that many migrants do not use all of their skills while working in Korea.

The Korean EPS is an example of a bilateral guest worker program that takes advantage of wage differences between countries to help Korean employers recruit well-qualified foreign workers to fill low-skilled jobs. The pressure to seek opportunity abroad is demonstrated by the large number of applicants for each Korean job.[3]

The migration cost data suggest that the EPS works well in allowing better educated workers from Southeast Asia to earn four to six times more in Korea in exchange for migration costs that average 1–2 months of Korean earnings. The EPS is often praised as a model, and in 2011 was awarded a UN Public Service Award for Preventing and Combating Corruption in the Public Service. Nonetheless, Amnesty International (2009) condemned the EPS, titling its report, Disposable labor: Rights of migrant workers in South Korea, citing long hours of work and physical and verbal abuse of migrants by some Korean employers.

Migrants in Korea may change employers under some conditions, may join unions, and have four types of insurance to protect them from work accidents and other risks. In this sense, migrants in Korea are much better off than migrant workers in many other countries. However, migrants work in Korea

---

[3] A variety of consultants help applicants in sending countries to prepare for interviews with Korean employers.

without their families, and may stay legally in Korea only if they keep their jobs, which makes them dependent on their employers. The Korean EPS is examined in more detail along with other bilateral agreements to move workers over borders in Chapter 7.

Migrants in Kuwait

Foreigners are 70 percent of the 3.8 million residents of Kuwait, and foreign migrants are more than 90 percent of the 1.3 million workers employed in Korea's private sector. The leading countries of origin of the foreigners in Kuwait are Egypt, Sri Lanka, India, the Philippines, and Bangladesh.

More than 100 migrant workers were interviewed in Kuwait in 2014, including twenty Bangladeshis, thirty Egyptians, thirty Indians, and twenty Sri Lankans.[4] Most were men except for the Sri Lankans, three-fourths of whom were women. The median age of migrants in Kuwait was thirty-five, and most had arrived in Kuwait within the previous 5 years. Most had little education, including half who did not complete secondary school, and three-fourths were married. By country, 70 percent of Bangladeshis did not complete secondary school, compared with 50 percent of Indians and Sri Lankans. Egyptians were the best educated, with 60 percent completing secondary school and a sixth having university degrees.

Migrants in Kuwait reported an average $1,900 in migration costs and a median $1,700. Older married workers had lower migration costs than younger single workers, but some of the gap may have been due to their earlier arrival, as migration costs rose over time.

There was a wide range in costs reported by workers with similar earnings in Kuwait. Bangladeshis paid an average of more than $3,100, followed by Egyptians who paid $2,900, Indians who paid $1,250, and Sri Lankans $320. Most of the Sri Lankans were female domestic workers who paid less and earned less in Kuwait.

Many of the migrants paid a lump sum to recruiters and did not know the cost of the individual items needed for working in Kuwait. For those who reported costs, Bangladeshis paid an average $2,300 for visas and $500 for an airfare, while Egyptians paid an average $2,500 for visas and $200 for an airfare. Some of the cost differences are puzzling. For example, Egyptians reported paying an average $335 for medical tests while Bangladeshis paid $45.

Indians had lower migration costs because 80 percent did not have to pay for visas, although the Indians who had to pay for visas spent about the

---

[4] Collection of data from migrant workers in Korea was supervised by Nasra Shah.

same as Bangladeshis and Egyptians. The other major expenses for Indians were international transportation, $300, and passports, an average $45. Sri Lankans had the lowest migration costs, in part because most did not pay for visas and only half paid an airfare to Kuwait. Some of the Sri Lankan domestic workers had all of their migration costs paid or reimbursed by their employers.

Three-fourths of the migrants borrowed money to work in Kuwait. The share of migration costs that was borrowed ranged from just over 50 percent for Sri Lankans to more than 85 percent for Egyptians. Egyptians borrowed from friends and relatives, including those who were or had been migrant workers in Kuwait, while most of the Bangladeshis borrowed from pawn shops and most of the Indians borrowed from moneylenders.

The amount borrowed reflected each nationality's migration costs. Egyptians borrowed an average $3,150, while Sri Lankans borrowed an average $540. When interviewed, many migrants had repaid the amount borrowed, but owed more because of fees and interest on their loans.

Average monthly earnings in Kuwait were $465, suggesting that migrant workers who paid an average $1,900 in migration costs worked for 4 months in Kuwait to repay these costs. Average Kuwaiti wages varied by nationality, with Egyptians reporting $610 a month, Indians $500, Bangladeshis $350, and Sri Lankans $340. Egyptians earned four times more in Kuwait than at home, and Indians earned 2.5 times more in Kuwait than at home. Few of the Bangladeshis or Sri Lankans had wage-earning jobs at home.

The wage gap for Egyptians in Kuwait is illustrated in Figure 3.2. Average earnings were $165 a month or $3,960 over 24 months in Egypt, while the earnings of Egyptians in Kuwait averaged $600 a month or a total of $14,400 over 2 years. In order to get jobs in Kuwait, Egyptians paid an average $2,900, or 20 percent of what they expected to earn over 2 years.

All of the workers interviewed in Kuwait had work permits, and all were employed in the private sector, with Kuwait Visa #18 or, for domestic workers, Visa #20. Migrant workers in Kuwait must have a sponsor (*kafeel*), and at least a fifth of those interviewed were not working for their *kafeel*, although some were reluctant to acknowledge working for persons other than their sponsors, since that made them illegal. All of the Egyptians, who were the best educated and earned the highest wages in Kuwait, were employed by their sponsor, but only 60 percent of the Indians were employed by their sponsor, perhaps reflecting the well-established networks that enable Indian migrants to navigate the Kuwaiti labor market.

Many migrants were not working in the occupation for which they had been hired. For example, some domestic workers were employed as cleaners or day laborers, and some were sent to public sector enterprises such as hospitals by their private cleaning firm employers. Many of the Egyptians and Indians

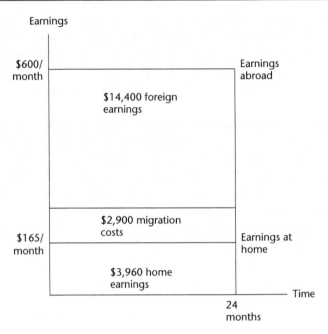

Earnings

$600/ month — Earnings abroad

$14,400 foreign earnings

$2,900 migration costs

$165/ month — Earnings at home

$3,960 home earnings

24 months — Time

Figure 3.2 Egyptian earnings at home and abroad, and migration costs, 2014
Source: Worker survey data.

worked in construction trades as carpenters, electricians, and plumbers, while most of the Bangladeshis were cleaners, helpers, or laborers.

Kuwait is a high-cost destination for low-skilled migrant workers. Migration costs averaged 4 months' Kuwaiti earnings, but there were distinct differences by nationality, with Bangladeshis and Egyptians paying far more than Indians and Sri Lankans. Migration costs vary within each corridor, with some workers paying three or more times more than their countrymen. The survey team concluded that the major reason for high and variable costs was that too many workers were seeking jobs, enabling recruiters to charge for visas as a way to allocate limited jobs among many applicants.

There is no easy way to enter Gulf Cooperation Council (GCC) countries other than with work permits that tie workers to a sponsor, so migrants pay the recruiters who control access to sponsors. If sponsors charge for visas, and then pass their right to hire migrant workers on to local recruiters who mark up the visa price before sending it to foreign recruiters who mark up the price again, the sponsorship system can create layers of intermediaries that increase worker-paid costs. There are laws against buying and selling visas, but they are not enforced against Kuwaiti citizens. When a migrant worker is found to be employed by someone other than his or her sponsor, the migrant is the only person punished, since the sponsor can report that the migrant "ran away."

Migrants in Spain

Spain was a major magnet for migrants in the first decade of the twenty-first century. The number of registered foreigners rose four-fold in a decade, from 1.5 million in 2000 to 6.5 million in 2009 (Arango, 2013). Migrants were about 20 percent of all persons employed in Spain before the 2008–09 recession, and dominated the workforces in many farming areas and especially on construction sites; a third of male migrants in Spain were employed in construction in 2005.

Spain experienced an economic crisis that began in 2008 and has not yet run its course. Employment fell 20 percent, from 20.5 million at the end of 2007 to 16.5 million at the beginning of 2013. Some migrants left the country, and Spain's population fell to 46.7 million in 2012 as more than 477,000 people left the country, almost 90 percent foreigners. Despite adverse economic conditions and an unemployment rate that has been above 20 percent for almost a decade, Spain does not have a strong anti-migrant party. Most Spaniards continue to see migrants as performing valuable if low-skilled work that natives shun, as in agriculture.[5]

Spain is a major producer of fruits and vegetables for Western Europe, exporting everything from oranges to strawberries. Most fruits and vegetables that are exported are grown along Spain's eastern and southern coasts with the help of migrant workers, as under the so-called sea of plastic around El Ejido in Almeria in southeastern Spain. Moroccans or Moros do much of the farm work in El Ejido, and there were clashes with local residents after a Moroccan killed a 26-year-old woman in 2000 that resulted in the destruction of migrant housing.[6] Most greenhouse farmers in El Ejido achieve gross revenues of over $50,000 an acre, but they do not provide housing for farmworkers, so most workers build their own housing from greenhouse materials.

Some 171 migrant workers employed in Spanish agriculture were interviewed in January–February 2014, including forty-two from Bulgaria, thirty-three from Ecuador, forty-four from Morocco, nineteen from Poland, and thirty from Romania.[7] Most had low migration costs, primarily because many did not pay for items that are common in other migration corridors, from visas to medical exams. All of the migrant workers had previous Spanish work experience, and they reported that regulations requiring employers to pay at least half of worker transportation costs were enforced. Worker-paid

---

[5] Spain is near the bottom of tables ranking negative attitudes toward migrants and refugees: www.pewglobal.org/2016/07/11/europeans-not-convinced-growing-diversity-is-a-good-thing-divided-on-what-determines-national-identity/.

[6] For details on the migrant clashes in El Ejido, see https://migration.ucdavis.edu/mn/more.php?id=2047 and https://migration.ucdavis.edu/mn/more.php?id=2119.

[7] Collection of data from migrant workers in Korea was supervised by Piotr Plewa.

migration costs were generally less than half of the typical $1,000 monthly earnings.[8]

Since the migrant farm workers who were interviewed had worked in Spain previously, and intra-EU migrants do not require visas or medical checks, fewer than half reported any costs for passports and even fewer reported costs for visas and medical checks. Travel costs were also low, less than $30 for internal travel costs in the home country and $300 for international travel costs to Spain. Moroccans had $100 in average travel costs, East Europeans $350, and Ecuadorians, who can stay 9 months in Spain, $1,100.[9]

Focusing on worker-paid costs incurred by at least forty migrants finds that transportation costs were two-thirds of the average migration costs of $530, with a wide variance reflecting the cost of getting to Spain. Three-fourths of the migrants interviewed in Spain did not take out loans to cover migration costs. The quarter that took out loans reported relatively small loans averaging $350, but debts of more than $500, suggesting high interest rates.

Most of the migrants employed to fill seasonal jobs in Spanish agriculture are from rural areas of Morocco, Eastern Europe, and Ecuador. Migrating to Spain to do farm work is an alternative to rural–urban migration within their countries of origin. Most of the migrants had less than secondary-school education.[10] For example, the Moroccan women often had less than 9 years' schooling, suggesting that migrating to Spain to do farm work was one way to remain within agriculture while working in a higher-wage country. Many of the Moroccans wanted to settle in Spain, while most of the Eastern Europeans wanted to return to their countries of origin.

Migrants harvesting fruits and vegetables in Spain were mostly unemployed or self-employed in agriculture at home, making it hard to calculate the average gain from working in Spain. Less than a seventh had wage-paying jobs before migrating to Spain. Of those who reported *any* income before migrating to Spain, from wage work or self-employment, earnings at home were $160 a month, suggesting that work in Spain increased earnings by six times.

Low-skilled migrants employed in Spanish agriculture had relatively low migration costs because many were from other EU member states and thus did not need to obtain visas or undergo medical and other checks before moving

---

[8] Earnings data were not collected from workers, but most earned the minimum wage of €39.5 or $54 for a 6.5-hour day, so they earned $270 for a 5-day week or $324 for a 6-day week and $1,080 to $1,300 a month.

[9] Spanish employers must pay half of the transportation costs of the inbound workers they recruit. Most advance the entire cost of in-bound transportation and then deduct the worker's share from earnings over the duration of their contract, typically at the rate of €90 a month. With employers advancing transportation costs, there is less need for workers to borrow money to travel to Spain.

[10] The East Europeans were best educated, but most did not complete secondary school. Many of the Moroccans had fewer than 5 years' schooling, and the Ecuadorians averaged fewer than 7 years' schooling.

to Spain. Others were recruited by Spanish employers in Ecuador and Morocco, and employers paid all or half of worker transportation expenses. Spanish farmers who want to have seasonal workers available when they are needed have been willing to invest in recruitment, unlike Kuwaiti employers who sell visas to migrants eager to work in Kuwait.

Other studies of migrants in Europe find higher costs, primarily because many migrants pay smugglers to transport them from Africa to Europe. Migrants from Egypt and Senegal interviewed in Italy in 2016 reported median migration costs of $3,200 and $1,400, respectively, to earn a median $835 and $1,000 a month, suggesting that Egyptians' migration costs were equivalent to 4 months' median Italian earnings and the Senegalese about 1.5 months. Much smaller samples of Ghanaian workers in Italy find median costs of $1,800 to earn a median $765 a month, equivalent to 2.4 months' median Italian earnings, and for Nigerians, median costs of $4,500 to earn a median $835 a month, or more than 5 months' Italian earnings.

The major difference between migrants going to Spain and migrants going to Italy in these surveys is that the migrants in Spain were reporting to the employers who hired them, and went to work upon arrival. By contrast, the migrants in Italy arrived in unauthorized or semi-authorized status and had to find jobs, which meant that their migration costs and earnings in Italy were very variable. Comparisons between migrants in Spain and Italy suggest that legal migration to a waiting job reduces costs and increases earnings.

Vietnamese in Malaysia

Malaysia is a middle-income country with a per capita GDP of $10,300 ($17,000 at purchasing power parity [PPP]) in 2012. Especially, young Malaysians are relatively well educated. In 2000, more than 90 percent of Malaysians aged twenty-five to thirty-five completed secondary school, including a third who earned college degrees. However, the labor force participation rate of educated Malaysian women in urban areas is relatively low, raising questions about whether the presence of migrants holds down wages and discourages local women from working.

About 12 percent of Malaysian GDP is from agriculture, 41 percent is from industry (construction and manufacturing), and 47 percent is from services. Malaysia runs a trade surplus, exporting electronics equipment assembled in the country as well as natural resources that range from oil and gas to farm commodities such as palm oil and rubber; the iconic Petronas Towers in Kuala Lumpur built by the national oil company are the world's tallest twin towers. About a quarter of Malaysians are ethnic Chinese, and they control more than half of the economy despite affirmative action programs for *bumiputra* or native Malays.

The number of foreign workers in Malaysia rose from fewer than 400,000 or 4 percent of the labor force in 1990 to more than 2 million or 15 percent of the labor force in 2010. By one estimate, there were 3.4 million foreign workers in Malaysia in 2012, including 2.1 million who were registered, making them 11.3 percent of the 30 million residents and 25 percent of the country's 13.8 million workers (Del Carpio et al., 2013: xiii). More than 70 percent of workers employed in Malaysian agriculture are foreigners, as well as 45 percent of workers employed in construction and 30 percent of those employed in manufacturing (Del Carpio et al., 2013: xvi–xvii).

More than two-thirds of the migrant workers in Malaysia are from neighboring Indonesia, followed by an eighth from the Philippines and 10 percent from Vietnam. Malaysia has an agreement with Bangladesh to provide workers for Malaysian plantations, but farmers appear to prefer hiring unauthorized Indonesians rather than legal Bangladeshis, so far fewer than the expected 1.5 million Bangladeshis are employed in Malaysia.[11] The number of Nepali migrants in Malaysia has been rising rapidly, leading to reports of very high migration costs paid in Nepal.[12]

The Malaysian government aims to provide employers with the workers they want to hire, even while giving local workers first priority to fill available jobs in sectors where the employment of migrant workers is allowed, that is, agriculture and plantations, construction and manufacturing, and eleven service sectors that range from domestic work to trade to restaurants. Malaysia allows employers to recruit migrant workers in fourteen Asian countries, but generally does not specify how workers are to be recruited in these countries.

The Malaysian government relies on two major mechanisms to encourage employers to favor local workers. First, employers must try and fail to find local workers to fill vacant jobs by posting their vacancies on Jobs Malaysia (http://www.jobsmalaysia.gov.my). Second, employers must pay a levy for each foreign worker they hire, an effort to make foreign workers more expensive than local workers. This levy ranged from RM410 ($124) a year for each migrant employed in agriculture or as a domestic worker to RM1,250 ($378) for each migrant in construction and manufacturing to RM1,850 ($560) in

---

[11] Malaysia banned the recruitment of Bangladeshis after thousands were stranded at the Kuala Lumpur airport after paying $3,000 or more in recruitment fees for jobs in Malaysia that did not materialize. Under a 2012 memorandum of understanding (MOU), Bangladeshis who want to work on Malaysian plantations complete an application form online and pay 40,000 taka ($520) to get jobs that pay the minimum wage of M$900 ($210) a month.

[12] http://kathmandupost.ekantipur.com/news/2016-09-19/nepali-workers-caught-in-malaysias-unfair-system.html.

2013. However, many employers pay the levy up front and deduct the levy cost from the wages of migrant workers, which makes the levy a less effective incentive to hire local workers since migrants pay the levy in the form of lower wages.

Malaysia introduced a minimum wage that required all workers (including migrants) after January 1, 2013 to be paid at least M$900 ($300) a month on the Malaysian Peninsula and M$800 in Sabah and Sarawak. The minimum wage was introduced for domestic reasons, but one hoped-for side effect was to make "migrant jobs" more attractive to local workers. The government said that it wanted to reduce the number of migrant workers by a fifth by 2020 and "ensure that, as we cut down our dependence on foreign workers over time, we will be able to find substitution in the local workforce," that is, the government wants employers to find local workers to fill jobs now filled by migrants.[13]

It has been hard to persuade Malays to fill jobs now filled by migrants because many employers who expect migrants to work long hours are dissatisfied with local workers who reject four hours of overtime every day. Since migrants generally welcome overtime hours, the cost of the levy is reduced if an employer hires migrants. For example, if migrants work 250 hours a month and local workers 160 hours, and the levy is RM100 a month, employers can pay migrants the RM900 a month minimum wage and deduct RM100 for the levy and another RM50 for housing, making the cost of migrants willing to work long hours RM750 a month, less than Malaysian workers who are paid RM900 but who do not work overtime.

Despite the minimum wage and the levy, the migrant share of the workforce in many manufacturing enterprises has been rising, the opposite of what was expected by the government, and the wage structure has been compressed as differences between higher and lower wage workers narrowed. Electronics factories have been able to keep labor costs at less than 10 percent of production costs by relying on young migrant women who have their first formal job in Malaysia at age eighteen to twenty. Most complete three two-year contracts before returning to their countries of origin.

Vietnamese migrants employed in electronics factories in Penang were interviewed in spring 2015.[14] The Vietnamese who were interviewed had been in Malaysia a median 13 months, with a range of 0–48 months. Their median age was twenty-nine, two-thirds were married, and they supported an average of three people in Vietnam. The migrants were relatively well educated; two-thirds had at least a secondary-school education.

---

[13] Quoted in https://migration.ucdavis.edu/mn/more.php?id=3776.
[14] The interviews were supervised by Lim Ai Lee of PE Research, Petaling Jaya.

Table 3.2 Migration costs of 399 Vietnamese in Malaysia (2014 US$)

	Total Cost	Share	Mean	Median	Number
Agent	496,861	90%	1,255	1,265	396
Inland trans	20,193	4%	70	44	290
Other	17,746	3%	261	195	68
Medical test	8,926	2%	28	25	320
Passport	5,269	1%	18	10	293
Total	**548,995**	**100%**	**1,632**	**1,539**	**399**

Source: Survey of Vietnamese in Malaysia, 2015 (author's calculations from unpublished raw data).

Table 3.3 Loans and repayments: Vietnamese in Malaysia (2014 US$)

	Total	Mean	Median	Number
Borrowings	380,548	1,186	1,229	321
Repaid	264,394	824	946	321
Still owed	116,154	362	0	321

Source: Survey of Vietnamese in Malaysia, 2015 (author's calculations from unpublished raw data).

For three-fourths of the Vietnamese, the job in Malaysia was their first foreign job. About 20 percent of those interviewed had worked outside Vietnam before, including one worker who had been outside Vietnam six times. Workers who had been outside Vietnam before were abroad an average of 4 years before working in Malaysia.

Two-thirds of the Vietnamese found their Malaysia jobs via recruiters and one-third via friends and relatives. Table 3.2 shows that most Vietnamese workers made lump sum payments to recruiters or agents that covered 90 percent of the total costs of working in Malaysia. This lump sum fee to the agent covered some costs that were broken out separately in other corridors. For example, no Vietnamese reported international travel costs; instead, all reported that agents paid for international travel.

Some 399 workers reported total expenses for jobs in Malaysia of $549,000 (2014 US$), an average of $1,375. The main migration costs were agent costs (average $1,255), inland travel (average $70), and other costs, usually security deposits, on average $260. The standard deviation was small, emphasizing that there were few outliers and that most migrants had similar migration costs.

More than three-fourths of the workers borrowed money to get jobs in Malaysia, and 51 percent of those who borrowed took loans from members of their household at low interest rates. Another 41 percent borrowed from banks, and 8 percent borrowed from recruiters. Those who borrowed took out loans that averaged $1,186 (Table 3.3). Workers reported borrowing a total of $380,500, repaying $264,400 by the time they were interviewed, and owing

Table 3.4 Earnings, remittances, and hours: Vietnamese in Malaysia (2014 US$)

	Total	Ratio/share	Mean	Median	Number
Earnings at home	61,696		190	179	325
Earnings abroad	142,835	2.3	354	344	404
Remittances	66,525	47%	208	191	320
Hours/week(1)	25,504		63	60	404

Note: Adjusted hours per week.

Source: Survey of Vietnamese in Malaysia, 2015 (author's calculations from unpublished raw data).

$116,154 or an average $362. A third of Vietnamese borrowers offered collateral for their loans, usually real estate or farm land.

Before departure for Malaysia, 356 or 88 percent of the Vietnamese workers were employed in Vietnam. A third were craft or construction workers and another third were employed in agriculture. About 11 percent each were employed as operators or assemblers in manufacturing, in sales and service, or in elementary occupations. The 325 Vietnamese who reported earnings at home earned an average $190 a month, ranging from $0 to $990. The total earnings of Vietnamese before departure were $61,700 a month.

The Vietnamese in Malaysia assembled electronics for an average wage of $354 a month (Table 3.4). Vietnamese workers earned a total of $142,800 a month in Malaysia, which was more than the $120,000 they were promised and more than twice the $62,000 they earned before departure. The additional earnings in Malaysia reflected overtime pay.

Migrants reported remitting (saving) $66,500 or half of their Malaysian earnings, an average $208 a month. Hours per week were a mean 63 and a median 60, and 90 percent of the Vietnamese reported one rest day a week.

All of the workers were provided with housing by their Malaysian employers, and half had some deduction from their wages to cover the cost of this housing. Only nine employers provided food to their workers in their accommodations, but all received lunch in the factories where they worked.

Some 359 workers reported being deprived of rights while in Malaysia. The most common deprivation, reported by 309 workers, was lack of access to their passports and other travel documents, followed by 178 who complained that they were unable to change employers, 160 that they could not form or join a union, 113 who complained that they did not get the same wages as natives, and 112 who complained of no social security. About 10 percent of the migrants complained of lack of job security.

Two-thirds of the Vietnamese reported sickness or work injuries in Malaysia. Common sickness was the most often reported, but flu, fever, and seasonal illness was also reported. Three-fourths of the workers reported being paid while they could not work. All of the Vietnamese entered Malaysia with work visas, and thus had a legal status.

In sum, relatively well-educated Vietnamese migrants interviewed in Malaysia paid recruiters a lump sum that covered 90 percent of their total migration costs of $1,375, the equivalent of 3.9 months Malaysian earnings. Most of the Vietnamese worked in Malaysian factories for 60 hours a week, making their earnings equivalent to about $1.45 an hour.

More than three-fourths of the Vietnamese borrowed an average 90 percent of their total migration costs, and many of the migrants were able to repay these loans, usually taken from family and friends, by the time they were interviewed. Three-fourths of the workers were employed in Vietnam before departure, earning almost twice as much in Malaysia as they had in Vietnam, and they remitted half of their Malaysian earnings. Housing was provided, but employers deducted some of the cost of housing from the wages of half of the workers. The most common worker complaint was lack of access to personal travel documents.

Malaysia employs a high share of migrants in agriculture, construction, manufacturing, and services. The government aims to reduce the employment of foreign workers, but has been unable to do so, as sectors critical to the country's economic success become ever more reliant on migrants. The World Bank concluded that migrant workers help the Malaysian economy to grow faster by keeping down labor costs, not by raising productivity, the fundamental source of long-run economic growth (Del Carpio et al., 2013). If Malaysia continues to compete on the basis of low labor costs rather than higher productivity, it may be hard to raise the earnings of Malaysian and migrant workers over time.

4

Migration Costs of Returning Workers

The six Gulf Cooperation Council (GCC) countries, Bahrain, Kuwait, Oman, Qatar, Saudi Arabia (SA), and the United Arab Emirates (UAE), offer a unique demographic and economic landscape. The current GCC population of 53 million, including over half in SA, is projected to increase by 25 percent to over 66 million by 2030, reflecting relatively high fertility rates and significant in-migration (Table 4.1).[1] The foreign share of the population in GCC countries ranges from a low of 33 percent in SA to a high of 90 percent in Qatar.

GCC countries had 10 million residents in 1975, including a quarter who were foreigners (Shah and Fargues, 2012; de-Bel Air, 2015).

The foreign share of the population was expected to decline from a third in the 1980s as the first wave of infrastructure projects after the oil price hikes of the 1970s were completed, but instead rose to reach half as foreign workers filled most of the growing number of private sector jobs and entered private homes as domestic workers.

Most of the foreigners are from South Asia. Eight countries each have more than a million citizens in GCC countries, and they collectively account for almost 90 percent of foreigners. Table 4.2 shows that the largest country of origin was India, with 7.4 million citizens in the GCC countries, including two-thirds in the UAE and SA. Bangladesh was next, with 3.3 million citizens in the GCC countries, including almost half in SA, followed by Pakistan with 3.2 million, also almost half in SA. Egypt had 2.1 million citizens in GCC countries, including almost half in SA and a quarter in Kuwait.

The Philippines and Indonesia each had almost 1.7 million citizens in GCC countries, with 40 percent of the Filipinos in SA and 30 percent in the UAE, while 90 percent of Indonesians were in SA. Nepal's 1.3 million citizens were distributed between SA, Qatar, and the UAE, while half of Sri Lanka's 1.1 million citizens were in SA and a quarter were in the UAE.

---

[1] Saudi women had a total fertility rate of 2.9 in 2015 (Population Reference Bureau [PRB]).

Table 4.1 Gulf Cooperation Council countries population, 2015 and 2030

	Pop (2015 MM)	Foreign share	Pop (2030 MM)	Increase	Shares (2015)
Bahrain	1.4	52%	1.7	21%	3%
Kuwait	3.8	69%	5	32%	7%
Oman	4.2	45%	5.5	31%	8%
Qatar	2.4	90%	2.8	17%	5%
SA	31.6	33%	39	23%	60%
UAE	9.6	88%	12.3	28%	18%
Total	53	49%	66.3	25%	100%

Note: Foreign shares of population are for 2010 (UAE) and 2014–16 (other GCC).

Source: Population data from PRB; foreign shares from Gulf Labour Markets and Migration (GLMM); PRB (Population Reference Bureau). 2016; World Population Data Sheet. www.prb.org.

Table 4.2 Foreigners in Gulf Cooperation Council countries, 2013–14

	India	Bangladesh	Pakistan	Egypt	Philippines
Bahrain	5%	3%	3%	1%	3%
Kuwait	11%	6%	4%	24%	11%
Oman	9%	19%	7%	1%	2%
Qatar	7%	5%	3%	8%	12%
SA	32%	46%	46%	47%	40%
UAE	35%	21%	37%	19%	31%
Total	7,407,592	3,272,221	3,241,112	2,144,910	1,672,888
	Indonesia	Nepal	Sri Lanka	Eight countries	
Bahrain	1%	2%	2%	687,000	
Kuwait	1%	5%	12%	2,037,436	
Oman	2%	1%	2%	1,663,852	
Qatar	2%	31%	9%	1,704,000	
SA	90%	39%	49%	9,625,000	
UAE	5%	23%	27%	6,110,530	
Total	1,671,210	1,296,000	1,121,885	21,827,818	

Source: GLMM. Most data are for 2013–14 except for Oman, which are data for 2016.

The economies of the GCC countries are based on exporting oil and gas. GCC governments use oil and gas revenues to create jobs for nationals in the public sector and jobs for foreign workers in the private sector. Government revenue from oil affects migration flows, with more foreign workers arriving when oil prices are high, enabling governments to issue contracts for major infrastructure projects. Most firms providing services to governments are private, so most foreign workers are employed in the private sector.

The price of oil, which averaged $100 a barrel between 2010 and mid-2014, has fallen to less than $50 a barrel in 2016 and is expected to remain at this level for the next few years because of new supplies—as from US shale—and pressure on OPEC suppliers including Iran and Iraq to export in order to generate revenues for governments.[2] Most projections echo the International Monetary Fund (IMF), which predicts that "oil prices will remain relatively low for some time."

Analyses of GCC demographic prospects and economic patterns conclude that the status quo is not sustainable (Forstenlecher and Rutledge, 2011; Hertog, 2013). Analysts urge GCC governments to change their policies to promote economic diversification away from oil and to persuade natives to change their norms and attitudes to accept private sector jobs that require real work.

An IMF report on the GCC noted that

> between 2000 and 2010, about 7 million jobs were created (excluding UAE), of which 5.4 million were in the private sector... nearly 88 percent of these private sector jobs were filled by foreign workers (85 percent low skilled), while nationals filled over 70 percent of public sector jobs.   (Callen et al, 2014: 12)

Another IMF report urged GCC governments to reduce "the availability and attractiveness of public sector employment... to create incentives for nationals to seek private sector jobs" (Callen et al, 2014).

The question for GCC governments is how to achieve diversification away from oil but continue to generate government revenue and nativize the private sector labor force. Dubai is often touted as a model for diversification, with construction, transportation and logistics, shopping and tourism, and finance creating a non-oil based economy that is dependent on foreign workers in the private sector. However, the Dubai model may be difficult to spread to nearby GCC countries, since there is limited demand in the region for some of the keystones of Dubai's economy, such as an airport that connects passengers traveling elsewhere.

Most studies recommend more non-oil related manufacturing and service industries such as finance to create jobs for natives and generate earnings from exports (Hvidt, 2013). Making such a transition to new industries and native workers is hard. For example, most GCC manufacturing exports are in the chemicals sector closely linked to oil, and most of the workers in the expanding chemical sector are foreigners (Callen et al., 2014: 21).

---

[2] OPEC (Organization of the Petroleum Export Countries) member states, Algeria, Angola, Ecuador, the Islamic Republic of Iran, Iraq, Kuwait, Libya, Nigeria, Qatar, SA, the UAE, and Venezuela produce about 36 million barrels of oil a day, 40 percent of the world's supply. US oil production almost doubled from 7.5 million barrels a day to 13 million barrels a day between 2010 and 2015. Shale oil has relatively low capital requirements and shorter life cycles, with most of the oil extracted from a particular formation within three years (Baffes et al. 2015).

The lack of incentives has contributed to limited economic diversification and, little labor force nativization. GCC countries have avoided Dutch disease, the rising value of the currency from oil exports that reduces non-oil exports, due to the presence of foreign workers who hold down private sector wages. Since governments distribute oil revenues via contracts to build domestic projects, private firms focus on domestic rather than export projects and use foreign workers to hold down labor costs and bolster profits (Callen et al, 2014: 23; Hertog, 2013). Native workers have incentives to seek public sector jobs that offer high wages and security rather than private sector jobs that offer lower wages and require more work.

The reservation wages of migrants are set by home country conditions. There are no national minimum wages in the GCC, and foreign workers have limited bargaining power, so reliance on migrants holds down private sector wages and allows private firms to extract rents (Hertog, 2013). As reliance on foreign workers in GCC countries increased, average labor productivity decreased, suggesting that wages for foreign workers may be lower than their marginal product, and helping to explain why the share of national income accruing to capital in GCC countries is 75 percent or more, among the highest in the world (Callen et al, 2014: 24; Hertog, 2012).

Employment in GCC countries was 24 million in 2013–14, including over half in SA. Table 4.3 shows that the share of foreigners in GCC employment averaged 75 percent, but ranged from a low of 67 percent in SA to a high of 94 percent in Qatar.

The most interesting difference in GCC employment data is the difference in the foreign share of workers between public and private sectors. A sixth of the five million public sector workers in GCC countries are foreigners, with a range of less than 10 percent in Oman and SA to almost 60 percent in Qatar (Table 4.4). However, foreigners are over 90 percent of private sector employment in GCC countries, and there is much less variance between

Table 4.3 Gulf Cooperation Council countries: Employment, 2013–15

	Employment	Foreign share	Foreigners
Bahrain	749,868	72%	539,905
Kuwait	2,328,581	82%	1,909,436
Oman	1,740,473	77%	1,340,164
Qatar	1,341,193	94%	1,260,721
SA	12,452,180	67%	8,342,961
UAE	5,147,000	88%	4,529,360
Total	23,759,295	75%	17,922,547

Note: Total and public sector labor force data for the UAE are approximate.

Source: GLMM and national statistical offices, see: http://gulfmigration.eu/percentage-of-nationals-and-non-nationals-in-employed-population-in-gcc-countries-national-statistics-latest-year-or-period-available/.

Table 4.4 Foreign shares of workers in Gulf Cooperation Council, public, and private, 2013–15

	Public	Foreign share	Foreigners	Private	Foreign share	Foreigners
Bahrain	149,868	25%	37,467	489,090	81%	396,163
Kuwait	439,204	30%	131,761	1,314,800	93%	1,222,764
Oman	378,355	7%	26,485	1,362,118	87%	1,185,043
Qatar	161,748	57%	92,196	1,039,541	99%	1,029,146
SA	3,034,201	4%	121,368	8,487,533	87%	7,384,154
UAE	1,000,000	40%	400,000	4,147,000	100%	4,147,000
Total	5,163,376	16%	809,277	16,840,082	91%	15,364,270

Note: Total and public sector labor force data for the UAE are approximate.

Source: GLMM and national statistical offices, see: http://gulfmigration.eu/percentage-of-nationals-and-non-nationals-in-employed-population-in-gcc-countries-national-statistics-latest-year-or-period-available/.

countries, from a low of 80 percent in Bahrain to almost 100 percent in Qatar and UAE.[3]

The six million GCC nationals in the labor force are a small share of persons of 15 years and older who could work. In SA, the labor force participation rate of persons fifteen plus is fewer than 40 percent, compared with a 70 percent rate in the US and 80 percent rates in Scandinavian countries.[4] The largest gap in labor force participation is for women. Fewer than 20 percent of Saudi women work, compared with over 70 percent of women in OECD countries. Even though relatively few GCC nationals work, unemployment rates are high, especially for youth aged 15 to 24 years. The International Labor Organization (ILO) reported that 22 percent of Saudi youth who wanted jobs in 1999 were unemployed, and 31 percent of Saudi youth seeking jobs in 2015 were unemployed (ILO, 2016b).

Who benefits from the current migration system, and can the migration costs paid by workers seeking jobs in GCC countries be reduced? If migrant workers each paid $2,000 for their GCC jobs, moving workers to the GCC is a $30 billion business. If migrants stay in the GCC an average 2 years, the annual revenues for the migration business are double the value of Indian cotton exports ($7.5 billion in 2015) and a quarter of Bangladeshi garment exports ($27 billion in 2015). Some of the migrant workers are skilled and have lower migration costs, while some low-skilled migrants pay more than $2,000.

The current system of dependence on foreign workers to fill private sector jobs in GCC countries is likely to continue for at least the next decade, highlighting the importance of learning what these workers paid to get jobs in GCC

---

[3] Note that some native workers are self-employed, and GCC labor force data for some countries are approximate, which explains why there are almost 24 million workers employed in the total table and only 22 million in the public and private sector table.

[4] See: https://data.oecd.org/emp/labour-force-participation-rate.htm.

countries. Workers returning from jobs in GCC countries were interviewed in 2015 to determine what they paid for the jobs they held in GCC countries. The Ethiopians, Filipinos, Indians, and Pakistanis returning from Qatar, SA, and the UAE were abroad for 2 or 3 years, and most had a legal or regular status abroad.

Ethiopians from Saudi Arabia

Some 497 Ethiopians returning from SA were interviewed in spring 2015.[5] Two-thirds were women, and the median age of all workers was 27 years, although workers' ages ranged from 17 to 52 years. Almost half of the return-ing workers were married, and almost half were single.

Returning Ethiopians had relatively little education. Over 70 percent did not complete secondary school, including 30 percent who did not complete primary school. About 30 percent completed secondary school, including 5 percent who had some post-secondary schooling. Almost 90 percent of return-ing Ethiopians were working outside Ethiopia for the first time, and they had spent a median 24 months in SA, with a wide range from 1 to 56 months.

Almost 60 percent of returning Ethiopians found jobs in SA with the help of recruiters or manpower agencies and 40 percent via friends or relatives; five workers or 1 percent found Saudi jobs with the help of government employ-ment services. However, almost 90 percent of returning Ethiopians used recruiters or manpower agencies to get the jobs from which they were return-ing. It took a median 2 months from the initial job application until departure from Ethiopia.

Returning Ethiopian workers reported paying an average $1,000 and a median $825 in total migration costs, with a range of $55 to $6,135 (2014 US$). The major worker-paid cost was for recruitment agents. Table 4.5 shows that almost 90 percent of Ethiopians reported payments to agents, a median $440 and a range from $25 to $3,780. Agent costs were half of total costs.

About 80 percent of returning Ethiopian workers incurred internal transport costs that were a median $110, but only 40 percent reported costs for inter-national travel, a median $235. Some 40 percent reported that agents paid for international travel, and 13 percent reported that employers paid for inter-national travel. Medical check costs were reported by two-thirds of workers, a median $30, and passport costs were a median $17.

Almost 30 percent of returning Ethiopian workers reported significant "other costs." When asked what these other payments were for, workers said they

---

[5] The interviews of returning Ethiopians were supervised by Adamnesh Atnafu of Addis Ababa University.

Table 4.5 Migration costs of Ethiopians returning from Saudi Arabia (2014 US$)

	Total Cost	Share	Mean	Median	Number
Agent	244,318	49%	553	441	442
Inland trans	51,494	10%	128	110	403
Int'l trans	57,138	12%	281	233	203
Medical test	12,154	2%	37	31	328
Passport	6,559	1%	19	17	341
Clearance	314	0%	1	1	284
Other	83,356	17%	604	354	138
Total	455,333	100%	998	826	497

Source: Survey of Ethiopians returning from Saudi Arabia, 2015 (author's calculations from unpublished raw data).

Table 4.6 Loans and repayments: Ethiopians returning from Saudi Arabia (2014 US$)

	Total	Mean	Median	Number
Borrowings	230,895	862	608	268
Repaid	170,832	642	497	266
Still owed	60,063	611	289	78

Source: Survey of Ethiopians returning from Saudi Arabia, 2015 (author's calculations from unpublished raw data).

were payments to brokers in Yemen who helped migrants to get into SA. At least twenty workers reported payments to police outside Ethiopia.

Most of the Ethiopians migrated through legal channels, but 40 percent did not. The migration costs of those who went to SA illegally were a median $250 more than those who went legally.

About 54 percent of the returning workers reported borrowing a median $610 to work abroad; loans ranged from $75 to $6,150 (Table 4.6). Borrowers reported repaying a median $500, which was less than they had borrowed, but the standard deviation of $710 was larger than the mean, reflecting the fact that some workers did not repay their loans, including some who owed up to $5,000. Over 90 percent of those who borrowed got loans from family and friends, usually at very low interest rates and with no collateral.

A third of returning Ethiopians reported earnings before departure for SA as a median $40 a month, but with a wide range from $4 to $375. Total earnings in Ethiopia of those with earnings were $9,900 a month (Table 4.7). Over half of the Ethiopians who reported earnings before departure had elementary occupations such as daily laborer, domestic worker, or farmer; another 10 percent reported sales or service jobs.

Ethiopians earned a median $265 a month in SA, well below the mean of $345 a month, reflecting the eighty workers who earned over $500 a month.

Table 4.7 Earnings and remittances: Ethiopians returning from Saudi Arabia (2014 US$)

	Total	Ratio/share	Mean	Median	Number
Earnings at home	9,891		63	39	157
Earnings abroad	169,082	17	343	264	493
Remittances	64,820	38%	148	122	439
Hours/week(1)	40,836		83	90	493

Note: Adjusted hours per week.

Source: Survey of Ethiopians returning from Saudi Arabia, 2015 (author's calculations from unpublished raw data).

Mode earnings were $185 a month, which is what the 40 percent of the Ethiopians who were domestic workers were paid, including those who said they provided child care and were servants. More than 120 or 25 percent reported that they were cleaners in SA, one hundred or 20 percent worked in construction or as laborers, and fifteen were shepherds. Most Ethiopians received housing and food from their Saudi employers at no cost.

Total Saudi earnings were $169,100 a month, seventeen times more than the $9,900 a month earned by those with jobs before departure; only a third of the Ethiopians had earnings at home. For many Ethiopian migrants, going abroad resulted in a wage-paying job. For the third of Ethiopians with wage-earning jobs at home, median monthly earnings were $40, while in SA they were $265, 6.6 times higher. Median migration costs of $825 were equivalent to 3.1 months of Saudi earnings and 13 percent of earnings over the median 24 months that Ethiopians were in SA.

Almost 90 percent of Ethiopians sent money home, a median $125 a month or three-fourths of median Saudi earnings. However, since not all Ethiopians remitted, total remittances of $65,000 a month were less than 40 percent of monthly Saudi earnings. One explanation is that Ethiopians were interviewed after they returned, and their monthly remittances just before returning may have been fewer because they wanted to bring money home with them.

Workers were asked if they held a skill certificate issued by a vocational testing center, and twenty or about 4 percent said they held certificates validating them as auto mechanics, cooks, or electricians. Most did not use this skill in their Saudi job. When asked if they believe that they could have found a job in SA that used their skills, a third said yes. These workers, plus another 150 workers who did not answer the question about finding a job that used their skills, estimated that if their Saudi jobs used their skills, they would have earned a median $530 a month, double their actual median $265 a month.

About 40 percent of returning Saudis worked for employers who arranged their visas and provided contracts that were signed in Ethiopia before departure, but only two-thirds of those who signed contracts before departure worked under these contracts abroad. Over half of the returning Ethiopians reported being deprived of rights while in SA, with the lack of free speech, lack of job security, and no social security were the most commonly cited deprivations. Others were unable to change Saudi employers and unable to practice their own religion; 10 percent said their travel documents were withheld by their employer.

Hours of work were a mean 82 and a median 90 a week, with many workers citing 108-hour workweeks, that is, 18-hour workdays 6 days a week. About half of the workers did not receive a rest day each week. About 20 percent of workers reported workplace injuries, and half of those who were injured were paid when they could not work. About 60 percent of the Ethiopians entered SA without a work visa, and many of those who reported their last status said it was other, which usually meant that they were illegally in SA.

Total worker-paid migration costs for the Ethiopian workers were $496,000, including $244,000, or half, in agent costs. For the 467 workers whose total migration costs were less than $2,000, there is a clear positive relationship between agent and total costs, suggesting that, for these workers, reducing agent costs would be the single most effective strategy to reduce total migration costs.

There were thirty-two high-cost workers who each reported total migration costs of more than $2,000; they had a mean $3,200 in total costs. Three observations about these high-cost migrants warrant consideration. First, the thirty-two high-cost workers were 6 percent of all workers, but accounted for over 20 percent of total migration costs reported by the entire sample. Second, after the thirty-two high-cost workers are removed, the standard deviation for the remaining 467 workers falls to less than the mean and median, suggesting that a relative handful of very high-cost workers increase dispersion measures for all workers.

Third, agent fees did not drive up total costs for the thirty-two high-cost workers. Agent fees are over half of total costs for the 94 percent of workers who paid less than $2,000, but only 37 percent of total costs for the 6 percent who paid more than $2,000. Most of the thirty-two high-cost workers reported a median $2,175 in "other costs."

Most of the Ethiopians were women who did not have earnings before departure and who worked long hours as domestic workers in SA. Many reported that they arrived and worked illegally in SA. It is hard to compare earnings at home and abroad because two-thirds of the returning migrants had no earnings in Ethiopia before departure. Overall, the earnings of the returned migrants were seventeen times higher in SA than in Ethiopia, and for those with earnings in Ethiopia, the wage wedge or gap between Saudi Arabian and Ethiopian wages was 6.6.

Filipinos from Qatar

In spring 2015, some 340 Filipino migrants returning from Qatar were interviewed in the Philippines.[6] About 55 percent were men, their average age was 39, and two-thirds were married. The Filipinos were older and better educated than migrants returning to other countries. Almost 40 percent completed secondary school, a sixth had some post-secondary education, and a quarter were college graduates.

Returning Filipinos supported an average of four people in the Philippines. Many had worked outside the Philippines before, and three-fourths of those with previous foreign work experience had been abroad at least twice before.

Over 60 percent of Filipinos reported finding their Qatari jobs via friends and relatives, followed by 30 percent who learned of the Qatari job via a manpower agency. Returning Filipinos were in Qatar a median 24 months. Table 4.8 shows that total migration costs were $177,600, an average $520 with a range from $4 to $3,300. Almost half of these total costs were for manpower agencies, although only half of the Filipinos reported paying manpower agencies for Qatari jobs.

The main components of worker-paid migration costs included agent costs, an average $490, inland travel, an average $105, medical exams, an average $67, and passports, an average $29. Workers reported that international travel, an average $915, was almost always paid by employers and agents.

Half of the Filipinos borrowed money, a total of $93,500 or an average of $530 (Table 4.9). Most borrowed from relatives and friends at low interest rates, and they had repaid $92,445 when interviewed, that is, loans were almost completely repaid before Filipinos returned.

Table 4.8 Migration costs of Filipinos returning from Qatar (2014 US$)

	Total Cost	Share	Mean	Median	Number
Agent	83,663	47%	492	443	170
Inland trans	27,794	16%	106	69	263
Medical test	14,148	8%	67	66	211
Passport	6,797	4%	29	24	232
Briefing	402	0%	4	2	111
Clearance	1,465	1%	5	4	271
Insurance	36,889	21%	40	34	93
Total	171,158	100%	522	414	340

Source: Survey of Filipinos returning from Qatar, 2015 (author's calculations from unpublished raw data).

[6] The worker interviews were supervised by Carl Daquio of the Philippine Institute of Labor Studies.

Table 4.9 Loans and repayments: Filipinos returning from Qatar (2014 US$)

	Total	Mean	Median	Number
Borrowings	93,533	528	461	177
Repaid	92,444	522	436	177
Still owed	1,089	419	274	18

Source: Survey of Filipinos returning from Qatar, 2015 (author's calculations from unpublished raw data).

Table 4.10 Earnings, remittances, and hours: Filipinos returning from Qatar (2014 US$)

	Total	Ratio/share	Mean	Median	Number
Earnings at home	55,286		229	195	241
Earnings abroad	177,364	3.2	500	435	355
Remittances	115,594	65%	337	272	343
Hours/week(1)	22,197		62	56	357

Note: Adjusted hours per week.
Source: Survey of Filipinos returning from Qatar, 2015 (author's calculations from unpublished raw data).

Two-thirds of the Filipinos reported being employed before departure, with domestic and farm work, service and sales work, and craft and related trades the most common occupations. Total earnings for workers before departure were $55,285, an average $230 a month (Table 4.10).

Qatari earnings were a total $177,365 a month or an average $500. Over 98 percent of workers reported being paid regularly in Qatar as they worked in construction or private households. Filipinos reported remitting $115,600 a month, two-thirds of their Qatari earnings, an average $335 a month.

Almost all Filipinos reported that housing and food were provided by their Qatari employers at no charge. A sixth or fifty-eight workers reported being deprived of rights in Qatar, with seventeen citing the lack of free speech rights, fifteen unequal treatment compared to natives, and fifteen having their travel documents withheld.

Workweeks averaged 62 hours, with a median 56 hours and a standard deviation of 20; almost all workers reported receiving a rest day each week. Almost a quarter of Filipino workers reported a workplace injury, often fevers, cuts, and fatigue; three-fourths said they were paid for time not worked. Almost 92 percent entered Qatar with work visas, and only one was illegal before departure.

Another 480 Filipinos returning from SA were interviewed between May and July 2016, including over half being women who had been domestic workers. The median age of the returning workers was 34, half were married, and three-fourths were working abroad for the first time. They were abroad a median 24 months.

Workers returning from SA paid a total $135,000 in migration costs, an average $285 and a median $220. The largest costs were placement fees, $46,000, and internal transportation before departure, $45,000. The third of returnees who paid placement fees had median costs of $320, that is, their placement fees were more than the median total costs of all returning workers. Internal transportation costs were paid by 80 percent of returnees, but were much lower, a median $75.

Some 280 returnees or 58 percent had earnings at home before departure, earning a total $57,000 or a median $160 a month. Earnings in SA were almost $220,000 or four times more, a median $400 a month. Remittances totaled $155,000 or 70 percent of Saudi Arabian earnings, and workers were employed a median 73 hours a week abroad. Almost half of the returnees borrowed money for migration costs, almost always from family or relatives at low or no interest rates.

The data collected from returning Filipinos demonstrate that most have relatively low migration costs, meaning they can repay their pre-departure costs with a month's foreign earnings or less. The returning Filipinos earned four times more in SA, and were able to remit over two-thirds of what they earned, so that even for those with earnings before departure, remittances of $280 a month were almost twice local earnings of $160 a month.

There were three major differences between returning Filipinos and returning Ethiopians. First, the Filipinos were older, better educated, and had lower migration costs than the Ethiopians, paying half as much and almost always having employers pay for their international travel. Second, Filipinos had higher earnings abroad, a median $435 a month versus $265 for Ethiopians. Two-thirds of Filipinos, versus one-third of Ethiopians, were employed before departure.

Third, Filipinos worked fewer hours a week than Ethiopians, a median 56 hours in Qatar and 73 in SA, versus 90 for Ethiopians, in part because a higher share of Ethiopians were domestic workers. The major conclusion is that older and better educated Filipinos paid less for foreign jobs, earned more abroad, and were better able to repay loans and remit a higher share of their earnings.

Indians from Qatar

The 400 Indian migrants returning from Qatar in spring 2015 had a median age of 31.[7] The returning Indian migrants had more education than all Indians,

---

[7] The interviews in India were supervised by Sasi Sasikumar of the V.V. Giri National Labour Institute and Prabhu Mohapatra of the University of Delhi.

which was fewer than 5 years for adults in 2013.[8] Almost 60 percent of the returning Indian migrants completed 10 years of schooling, 30 percent completed primary (6 years) but not secondary, and 12 percent had post-secondary schooling, such as technical training.

The quality of post-secondary technical training varies. The Indian government is committed to upgrading the skills of its citizens, but many of the instructors in technical training institutions are poorly paid and may not impart useful skills to students. The Ministry of Skill Development and Entrepreneurship aims to coordinate the many programs that are trying to raise the skill levels of Indian workers to international standards.

The returning Indian migrants supported an average of six people in India; the range of people supported was from zero to fourteen. For most of the returnees, the job in Qatar was their first foreign job. Most learned about jobs in Qatar from friends or relatives, 63 percent, followed by 25 percent who used recruiters or brokers, and 12 percent who used manpower agencies to find Qatari jobs; however, almost all of the Indians used agents to get contracts for the Qatari jobs. Respondents were abroad a mean 35 months and a median 38 months. None learned Arabic before departure.

Returning migrants reported total expenses for jobs in Qatar of $456,000 (2014 US$), an average of $1,140 and a range of $350 to $1,690 (Table 4.11). The main components of migration costs were agent costs, an average $550, international travel, an average $295, and other costs, an average $97. Most migrants reported similar costs, explaining why mean and median costs were similar.

Table 4.11 Migration costs of Indians returning from Qatar (2014 US$)

	Total Cost	Share	Mean	Median	Number
Agent	219,420	48%	551	559	398
Int'l trans*	118,399	26%	296	297	399
Other	35,452	8%	97	93	364
Inland trans	28,105	6%	70	71	400
Medical test	20,757	5%	52	52	399
Passport	17,649	4%	46	45	387
Briefing	8,918	2%	24	25	365
Skills test	2,920	1%	11	11	264
Insurance	2,606	1%	7	6	397
Total	454,226	100%	1,140	1,156	400

* Seventeen workers had their international transportation costs reimbursed.

Source: Survey of Indians returning from Qatar, 2015 (author's calculations from unpublished raw data).

[8] See Human Development Report: http://hdr.undp.org/en/content/mean-years-schooling-adults-years.

Table 4.12 Loans and repayments: Indians returning from Qatar (2014 US$)

	Total	Mean	Median	Number
Borrowings	120,019	628	609	191
Repaid	118,342	620	578	191
Still owed	1,677	152	175	74

Source: Survey of Indians returning from Qatar, 2015 (author's calculations from unpublished raw data).

Table 4.13 Earnings, remittances, and hours: Indians returning from Qatar (2014 US$)

	Total	Ratio/share	Mean	Median	Number
Earnings at home	58,634		147	146	398
Earnings abroad	236,376	4.0	591	599	400
Remittances	163,930	69%	411	408	300
Hours/week(1)	23,683		59	60	400

Note: Adjusted hours per week.

Source: Survey of Indians returning from Qatar, 2015 (author's calculations from unpublished raw data).

Almost half of workers borrowed money to get their jobs in Qatar, and 93 percent of those who borrowed took out loans that averaged $630 from members of their household at low or no interest rates and for which they offered no collateral. Workers reported borrowing a total of $120,000, repaying $118,000 by the time they returned to India, and owing $1,677 (Table 4.12).

Before departure, almost all of the returning workers were employed in India, usually as construction craft workers. They earned an average and median of $145 a month, and total earnings before departure were $59,000 a month.

Almost all of the returning Indians were employed in construction in Qatar, the same sector that employed most in India. Qatari employers arranged for their work visas, almost all workers signed contracts before departure, and this was the same contract under which they were employed in Qatar. The most common occupations in Qatar were carpenter, driver, electrician, fitter, mason, and plumber. None of the Indians changed jobs while in Qatar.

Qatari earnings averaged $590 a month with relatively little variation because Qatari contractors paid the reference wage for each occupation set by the Indian embassy (Table 4.13). Workers earned a total of $236,000 a month in Qatar, which was four times the $59,000 they earned in India before departure.

Migrants reported remitting (saving) $164,000 or almost 70 percent of their Qatari earnings, an average and median $410 a month. The high savings rate is explained by the fact that food and lodging was provided at no cost by Qatari employers.

Thirteen workers reported a union in their workplace, including eight that joined the union, and seventeen reported being deprived of rights while in Qatar. Hours per week were a mean and median 60, and all reported one rest day a week. Some twenty-four workers reported injuries at work; the most common injury reported was fever, and twenty-two workers reported being paid while they could not work. All of the Indians entered Qatar with work visas, and thus were legal in Qatar before they returned.

Indians returning from Qatar paid median migration costs of $1,160 to earn $600 a month, or 1.9 months of median Qatari earnings. For the median 38 months that the Indians were in Qatar, earnings were $22,800, making median migration costs 5 percent of total foreign earnings. The survey data support the hypothesis that structural and policy factors, not individual characteristics, best explain worker-paid migration costs, that is, employer and agent behavior and government policies better explain worker-paid migration costs than do individual characteristics such as age, education, experience working abroad, or rural versus urban residence in India.

Why are migration costs relatively low in the Indian–Qatari construction corridor? The Indian government scrutinizes the large Qatari contractors who are registered with and monitored by the Indian embassy in Qatar. Almost all of the Indian workers were employed in construction before departing for Qatar, where they held similar carpenter, mason, and plumber jobs but earned four times more and, because food and housing was provided, could save most of their higher earnings. Achieving savings targets quickly was the reason cited by many Indians for working in Qatar.

Nepalese from Qatar

The 350 Nepalese migrants returning from Qatar in spring 2015 had a median age of 30.[9] Most had little education: seventy-eight or 22 percent reported no schooling, 123 or 35 percent reported incomplete primary schooling, fifty-eight or 16 percent reported complete primary schooling, sixty-five or 18 percent reported some secondary schooling, and twenty-six or 7 percent reported complete secondary schooling.

Almost 80 percent of the returning Nepalese migrants were married, and they supported an average five people in Nepal; the range of people supported was two to eighteen. For three-fourths of the returnees, the job in Qatar was

[9] The Nepalese surveys were supervised by Ujwal Gurung of the Nepal National Institute of Development Studies.

their first foreign job. Most returning migrants learned about jobs in Qatar from manpower agents, about 62 percent, followed by 36 percent who learned about Qatari jobs from friends or relatives. Respondents were abroad an average 30 months.

The Nepali migrants who reported total expenses for jobs in Qatar paid $369,000 (2014 US$), an average $1,055 and a range of $70 to $2,835 (Table 4.14). The main components were agent costs, an average $875, inland travel, an average $110, and passports, an average $75. For the thirty-one workers who reported international travel expenses, the average cost was $400.

The noteworthy features of Nepalese migration costs are high costs overall, a median $1,100, and the fact that agents accounted for three-fourths of these costs. Nepalese reported fewer itemized costs than did migrants in other corridors, suggesting that they paid agents a flat fee to cover their migration costs.

Almost two-thirds of the Nepalese borrowed money to get their jobs in Qatar, including a quarter who borrowed from moneylenders and three-fourths who borrowed from family and relatives at low or no interest rates. Those who borrowed took out loans averaging $1,100 (Table 4.15). Workers reported borrowing a total of $234,100, repaying $301,800, and owing $2,600. Very few borrowers offered collateral for their loans.

Table 4.14 Migration costs of Nepalese returning from Qatar (2014 US$)

	Total Cost	Share	Mean	Median	Number
Agent	278,869	76%	874	877	319
Int'l trans	12,447	3%	402	302	31
Inland trans	31,610	9%	108	66	293
Medical test	10,190	3%	34	29	299
Passport	25,905	7%	75	60	344
Briefing	1,115	0%	9	8	135
Visa	11,160	3%	319	170	35
Insurance	5,442	1%	37	35	149
Total	376,738	100%	1,054	1,088	350

Source: Survey of Nepalese returning from Qatar, 2015 (author's calculations from unpublished raw data).

Table 4.15 Loans and repayments: Nepalese returning from Qatar (2014 US$)

	Total	Mean	Median	Number
Borrowings	234,088	1,097	1,031	227
Repaid	301,808	1,330	1,294	227
Still owed	2,579	332	330	8

Source: Survey of Nepalese returning from Qatar, 2015 (author's calculations from unpublished raw data).

Before departure, almost 40 percent of workers had earnings in Nepal; farmer and laborer were the most common pre-departure occupations. Average monthly earnings for the 139 Nepalese with pre-departure earnings were $110 a month. The total earnings of Nepalese with jobs before departure were $15,100 a month (Table 4.16).

Almost all of the returning Nepalese were employed in construction in Qatar; laborer was the most common occupation abroad. Qatari employers arranged for work visas for 95 percent of the Nepalese, and 90 percent reported that they signed contracts before departure and that the contract they signed in Nepal was the same contract under which they worked in Qatar.

Total earnings in Qatar were $119,000 a month, 7.6 times the $15,600 of Nepalese with earnings in Nepal. Median monthly earnings in Nepal were $325 or 2.2 times the median $110 a month of Nepalese with earnings in Nepal.

Migrants reported remitting (saving) $72,500 or 61 percent of their Qatari earnings, an average $205 a month. The high savings rate is explained by the fact that food and lodging was paid by employers in Qatar. All Nepalese were provided with housing at no cost, and most were provided with food at no cost; twelve workers reported deductions for food.

Almost 60 percent of Nepalese reported being deprived of rights while in Qatar. The most cited deprivations were withheld travel documents, reported by half of those who answered this question, lack of free speech reported by 40 percent, denial of the right to join a union reported by 35 percent; a quarter complained of being unable to change employers.

Hours per week were a mean sixty-eight and a median seventy, and all workers reported one rest day a week. Some thirty-four workers reported injuries at work, including fevers, heat stress, and cuts, and eighteen or almost half reported being paid while they could not work. All of the Nepalese entered Qatar with work visas, and thus were legal in Qatar before they returned.

Like the Indians, almost all Nepalese were employed in construction in Qatar. However, unlike the Indians, most Nepalese were not employed in Nepal or, if employed, were not employed in construction. The Nepalese

Table 4.16 Earnings, remittances, and hours: Nepalese returning from Qatar (2014 US$)

	Total	Ratio/share	Mean	Median	Number
Earnings at home	15,573		112	109	139
Earnings abroad	118,957	7.6	339	326	351
Remittances	72,466	61%	207	197	350
Hours/week(1)	23,752		68	70	351

Note: Adjusted hours per week.

Source: Survey of Nepalese returning from Qatar, 2015 (author's calculations from unpublished raw data).

had low levels of education and were mostly helpers and laborers in Qatar, earning a median $325 a month in Qatar versus $600 a month for Indians. Like the Indians, all of the Nepalese entered Qatar with visas and were legal when they left to return home.

Indians and Nepalese paid about the same amount to get construction jobs in Qatar, but Indians earned almost twice as much as Nepalese, helping to explain why the Indians remitted almost twice as much as the Nepalese. Nepalese reported working a median 70 hours a week, versus 60 hours a week for Indians, and more Nepalese complained of withheld documents and other deprivations of rights while in Qatar. It should be noted that almost all of the Indians held construction jobs in India before departure, while the 40 percent of Nepalese who had earnings before departure were generally not employed in construction. Going from Nepal to Qatar was, for many Nepalese, a way to get a wage-earning job and, with housing and food paid by employers, a means to achieve a savings target.

Pakistanis from Saudi Arabia and the United Arab Emirates

The 634 Pakistanis who were interviewed as they returned from SA (375) and the UAE (260) in spring 2015 were a median 27 years old.[10] Almost 60 percent were married, and they supported an average eight and a median seven people. The largest single group completed primary school, 170 or 27 percent, followed by 160 or 25 percent who completed secondary school. Some 135 or 21 percent completed primary but not secondary school, and 105 or 16 percent had no schooling or did not complete primary school. The remaining sixty-five had post-secondary schooling, including twenty college graduates.

Over 85 percent of Pakistani returnees were abroad for the first time; the average stay abroad was 23 months. The largest share of workers, 350 or 55 percent, found foreign jobs via relatives and friends, while the others found foreign jobs via recruiters or manpower agencies.

Returning Pakistanis reported a total of $2.3 million in migration costs, including $1.7 million or 77 percent for visa costs, $178,000 or 8 percent for agent costs, and $160,000 or 7 percent for international transportation; these three items were 92 percent of total costs (Table 4.17). The most costly item was visas, which cost an average $2,860, followed by an average $463 for agent costs and $411 for international travel. There was a large variation around these averages, suggesting that migrants paid very different amounts for visas, agents, and travel.

[10] The survey team was led by Nasir Iqbal of the Pakistan Institute of Development Economics.

Table 4.17 Migration costs of returning Pakistanis (2014 US$)

	Total Cost	Share	Mean	Median	Number
Visa	1,746,882	77%	2,859	2,432	611
Agent	177,800	8%	463	375	362
Int'l trans	160,691	7%	411	386	391
Inland trans	38,508	2%	73	55	526
Medical test	28,471	1%	59	55	486
Passport	28,061	1%	46	45	609
Contract	19,501	1%	74	73	265
Insurance	7,206	0%	32	30	223
Other	19,491	1%	44	30	441
Total	2,226,611	100%	3,558	3,040	634

Source: Survey of Pakistanis returning from SA and UAE, 2015 (author's calculations from unpublished raw data).

Table 4.18 Loans and repayments: Returning Pakistanis (2014 US$)

	Total	Mean	Median	Number
Borrowings	1,035,069	2,441	2,007	424
Repaid	872,306	2,057	1,654	424
Still owed	162,763	900	495	139

Source: Author's own calculations from unpublished raw data.

Two-thirds of the workers borrowed money to get foreign jobs, and 97 percent borrowed from family and relatives at low or no interest rates. Those who borrowed took out loans averaging $2,240 and a median $2,005, with a standard deviation of $1,510 (Table 4.18). Workers reported borrowing a total of $1 million, repaying $872,306, and owing $162,763, that is, workers financed 43 percent of their migration costs without borrowing. Very few borrowers offered collateral for their loans, which were mostly taken from family and friends at low or no interest.

Before departure, 81 percent of workers had earnings in Pakistan; farmer and laborer were the most common pre-departure occupations. Average earnings were $155 a month and the total earnings of the Pakistanis who had jobs before departure were $80,300 a month.

Of the 500 workers who reported their occupation abroad, almost two-thirds were laborers, helpers, or craftsmen in construction. Earnings abroad totaled $283,500 a month, or 3.5 times earnings in Pakistan, and were a mean $450 and a median $395 a month (Table 4.19). Two-thirds of Pakistanis reported being paid regularly abroad.

Migrants reported remitting (saving) $140,888 or half of their foreign earnings, an average $238 a month. A quarter of workers reported changing employers while abroad, and 28 reported that their employer supplied labor to other firms.

Table 4.19 Earnings, remittances, and hours: Returning Pakistanis (2014 US$)

	Total	Ratio/share	Mean	Median	Number
Earnings at home	80,297		156	122	514
Earnings abroad	283,478	3.5	448	396	633
Remittances	140,888	50%	238	196	594
Hours/week(1)	43,035		68	72	633

Note: Adjusted hours per week.

Source: Survey of Pakistanis returning from SA and UAE, 2015 (author's calculations from unpublished raw data).

Almost 96 percent of Pakistanis reported being deprived of rights while abroad. The most cited deprivations were withheld travel documents, reported by 90 percent of those who answered this question, no job security cited by 73 percent, lack of free speech reported by 63 percent, inability to join a union reported by 62 percent, not having the right to change employers by 59 percent, and not having rights to social security by 58 percent. Except for religion, a majority of workers who responded to deprivation questions reported deprivations.

Hours per week were a mean 68 and a median 72, and 85 percent reported one rest day a week. Some 300 workers, almost half, reported injuries at work, including fevers, heat stress, and cuts, and a quarter reported being paid while they could not work. Over 99 percent of the Pakistanis were abroad with work visas, and thus were legal abroad before they returned.

Pakistanis Returning from Saudi Arabia (2014 US$)

There were two subgroups of Pakistanis: some returned from SA and some from the UAE. The 375 Pakistanis returning from SA were a median twenty-eight and mostly married, supporting an average eight people. Almost 90 percent were abroad for the first time, and they stayed in SA an average 27 months.

Half of the returnees from SA found jobs via relatives and friends; the other half found jobs via recruiters or manpower agencies. They reported a total of $1.6 million in migration costs, including $1.3 million or 79 percent for visa costs, $127,000 or 8 percent for agent costs, and $94,000 or 7 percent for international transportation; these three items were 93 percent of total costs (Table 4.20). Visa costs were an average $3,500, agent costs were an average $575, and international travel was an average $450.

Almost three-fourths of the workers borrowed money to get jobs in SA, and almost all took loans from family and relatives at low or no interest rates and offered no collateral. Those who borrowed took out loans averaging $2,900, for a total of $781,129 or about half of their migration costs (Table 4.21). They

Table 4.20 Migration costs of Pakistanis returning from Saudi Arabia (2014 US$)

| | Costs reported by Pakistani workers returning from SA (2014 US$) | | | | |
	Total Cost	Share	Mean	Median	Number
Visa	1,296,209	79%	3,494	3,198	371
Agent	127,237	8%	576	502	221
Int'l trans	93,816	6%	449	441	209
Inland trans	27,416	2%	81	61	337
Medical test	22,047	1%	60	55	369
Passport	16,895	1%	46	46	366
Contract	10,307	1%	71	66	146
Insurance	4,259	0%	32	30	133
Other	12,245	1%	46	28	266
Total	1,610,431	100%	4367	3970	375

Source: Survey of Pakistanis returning from Saudi Arabia, 2015 (author's calculations from unpublished raw data).

Table 4.21 Loans and repayments: Pakistanis returning from Saudi Arabia (2014 US$)

	Total	Mean	Median	Number
Borrowings	781,129	2,904	2,473	269
Repaid	681,608	2,534	2,206	269
Still owed	99,521	1,050	551	77

Source: Survey of Pakistanis returning from Saudi Arabia, 2015 (author's calculations from unpublished raw data).

had repaid $681,600 before they returned, that is, they had repaid less than they borrowed.

Before departure, 83 percent of workers had earnings in Pakistan, usually in construction, with average monthly earnings of $165 a month. Total Pakistani earnings before departure were $51,282 a month.

Of the 375 workers who reported their occupation abroad, almost two-thirds were laborers, helpers, or craftsmen in construction; almost 20 percent were drivers. Earnings abroad totaled $180,000 a month, or 3.5 times earnings in Pakistan, and were a mean $485 a month (Table 4.22). Two-thirds of Pakistanis reported being paid regularly abroad.

Migrants reported remitting (saving) $66,229 or 37 percent of their Saudi earnings, an average $160 a month. Seemingly low remittances may reflect the fact that Pakistanis were interviewed as they returned, and that some returned with remittance savings rather than sending them ahead.

Over 96 percent of the Pakistanis returning from SA reported being deprived of rights while abroad. The most cited deprivations were withheld travel documents, reported by 93 percent of those who answered this

Table 4.22 Earnings, remittances, and hours: Pakistanis returning from Saudi Arabia (2014 US$)

	Total	Ratio/share	Mean	Median	Number
Earnings at home	51,282		164	122	312
Earnings abroad	180,014	3.5	486	433	374
Remittances	66,229	37%	160	358	594
Hours/week(1)	25,288		68	72	374

Note: Adjusted hours per week.

Source: Survey of Pakistanis returning from Saudi Arabia, 2015 (author's calculations from unpublished raw data).

question, not having the same rights as other workers, 75 percent, no job security cited by 74 percent, lack of free speech reported by 62 percent, inability to join a union reported by 60 percent, not having the right to change employers, 60 percent, and not having rights to social security, 59 percent.

Hours per week were a mean 68 and a median 72, and 85 percent reported one rest day a week. Over half of workers, 192 of 375, reported injuries at work, with most citing fever, heat, or temperature as the cause of their injury; forty-eight or a quarter of those with injuries reported being paid while they could not work. Almost all of the Pakistanis, 371 of 374, were abroad with work visas, and thus were legal abroad.

Pakistanis Returning from United Arab Emirates

The 259 Pakistanis returning from the UAE were a median twenty-seven, half were married, and they supported a median seven people in Pakistan. About 40 percent of the Pakistanis had a primary school education or less, and 40 percent had a secondary school education or more.

Over 82 percent were abroad for the first time, although the fifth who had been abroad before had worked a median twice abroad before. Among returnees from UAE, the average stay abroad was 18 months and the median stay was 16 months.

Over 60 percent of the returnees found UAE jobs via relatives and friends and 35 percent found foreign jobs via recruiters or manpower agencies. However, over 70 percent of the returning workers got contracts for jobs in the UAE from recruiters and manpower agents, followed by 25 percent who got contracts from relatives.

The returning migrants had a total of $618,370 in migration costs, including $450,700 or 73 percent for visa costs, $44,475 or 7 percent for agent costs, and $66,875 or 11 percent for international transportation; these three items were 91 percent of total costs (Table 4.23). Almost 93 percent of

Table 4.23 Migration costs of Pakistanis returning from United Arab Emirates (2014 US$)

	Total Cost	Share	Mean	Median	Number
Visa	450,673	73%	1,878	1,606	240
Agent	44,474	7%	323	197	141
Int'l trans	66,874	11%	367	331	182
Inland trans	11,091	2%	59	49	189
Medical test	6,423	1%	55	59	117
Passport	11,166	2%	46	45	243
Contract	9,193	1%	77	80	119
Insurance	2,947	0%	33	30	90
Other	7,246	1%	41	35	175
Total	610,087	100%	2,388	2, 095	259

Source: Survey of Pakistanis returning from UAE, 2015 (author's calculations from unpublished raw data).

Table 4.24 Loans and repayments: Pakistanis returning from United Arab Emirates (2014 US$)

	Total	Mean	Median	Number
Borrowings	253,940	1,638	1,456	155
Repaid	190,698	1,230	1,004	155
Still owed	63,242	713	495	62

Source: Survey of Pakistanis returning from UAE, 2015 (author's calculations from unpublished raw data).

returning Pakistanis had visa costs that averaged $1,878, 54 percent had agent costs that averaged $323, and 70 percent had international travel costs that averaged $367. Total costs were an average $2,390, and median costs were $2,095.[11]

Almost 60 percent of the workers borrowed money to get jobs in the UAE; 95 percent of the loans were from family and relatives who charged low or no interest rates and demanded no collateral. Borrowers took out loans averaging $1,638 and a total of $253,940, repaying $190,700, and owing $63,242, that is, they repaid and are expected to repay less than they borrowed (Table 4.24).

Before departure to the UAE, 79 percent of workers had earnings in Pakistan, with 60 percent in elementary occupations including domestic and farm work; about 7 percent held certificates from vocational schools in Pakistan. Average monthly earnings before departure were $144 a month, and median pre-departure earnings were $125 a month. The total earnings of Pakistanis returning from jobs in SA before departure were $29,015 a month.

---

[11] Some thirty-six Pakistanis who had been abroad before reported mean and median $2,400 costs to get previous foreign jobs.

Table 4.25 Earnings, remittances, and hours: Pakistanis returning from United Arab Emirates (2014 US$)

	Total	Ratio/share	Mean	Median	Number
Earnings at home	29,015		144	126	202
Earnings abroad	103,464	3.6	399	323	259
Remittances	50,869	49%	217	176	234
Hours/week(1)	17,747		69	72	259

Note: Adjusted hours per week.

Source: Survey of Pakistanis returning from UAE, 2015 (author's calculations from unpublished raw data).

A quarter of returning Pakistanis said that their UAE employer arranged for their work visa, 44 percent reported signing a contract before departure from Pakistan, but only two-thirds said that they worked under this contract in the UAE. The most common job in the UAE was laborer, the occupation of 44 percent of the returning Pakistanis, followed by 20 percent with construction crafts such as mason, welder, and electrician.

UAE earnings totaled $103,465 a month, or 3.6 times earnings in Pakistan, and were an average $400 a month and a median $325 a month (Table 4.25). Some 64 percent of Pakistanis in UAE reported being paid regularly.

Migrants reported remitting (saving) $50,869 or half of their UAE earnings, an average $217 a month. An eighth of workers reported changing employers while abroad, and a quarter reported that their employer supplied labor to other firms.

Over 99 percent of the Pakistanis returning from the UAE reported being deprived of rights while abroad. The most cited deprivations were withheld travel documents, reported by 84 percent of those who answered this question, not having the same rights as other workers, 81 percent, no job security cited by 72 percent, lack of free speech reported by 62 percent, inability to join a union reported by 67 percent, not having the right to change employers, 56 percent, and not having rights to social security, 54 percent. Except for religion and remittances, a majority of workers who responded to deprivation questions reported deprivations.

Hours per week were a mean 69 and a median 72, and 85 percent reported one rest day a week. Some 108 workers, 42 percent, reported injuries at work, with most citing fever, heat, or temperature as the cause of their injury; twenty-seven or a quarter reported being paid while they could not work. All of the Pakistanis returning from the UAE were abroad with work visas, and thus were legal.

Migrant Costs and the Gulf Cooperation Council

The migration cost data provided by low-skilled workers returning from GCC countries show that median migration costs were lowest in the

Table 4.26 Worker-paid migration costs and foreign earnings (2014 US$)

	Mean Costs	Median Costs	Mean Earnings	Median Earnings
Ethiopia–SA	998	826	343	264
Philippines–Qatar	522	414	500	435
India–Qatar	1,140	1,156	591	599
Nepal–Qatar	1,054	1,088	339	326
Pakistan–SA	4,367	3,970	486	433
Pakistan–UAE	2,388	2,095	399	323

Source: Surveys of returning workers in 2015 (author's calculations from unpublished raw data).

Philippines–Qatar corridor at $400 and highest in the Pakistan–SA at almost $4,000, a 10:1 gap in worker-paid costs between corridors (Table 4.26). Median earnings ranged from a low of $265 a month for Ethiopians in SA to a high of $600 for Indians in Qatar, a 2.2:1 gap. The variance in average migration costs by corridor, 10:1, was much larger than the 2:1 gap in worker earnings.

A second dimension of worker-paid migration costs is rarely noted—that of super-payers. Especially in Ethiopia, Nepal, and Pakistan, some workers had very high costs, paying between $6,000 and $9,000 to get jobs that paid $300 or $400 a month abroad. In these countries, the 10 percent of workers with the highest costs accounted for 20 to 25 percent of the total costs of all workers.

As with superusers in health care, where the most expensive 1 percent of people account for 15 to 20 percent of total health-care spending, super-payer migrants raise questions about why some workers pay so much for foreign jobs. Superusers and super-payers raise the question of whether the optimal strategy to reduce costs is to deal with their special issues or to focus on reducing costs for all workers.

Was migration economically worthwhile for the millions of workers who spent 2 or 3 years in GCC countries, mostly in construction and working in private homes? First, with the notable exception of India, most migrants did not have wage-paying jobs before moving to GCC countries, that is, going abroad gave them wage employment. Also, with the exception of India, the jobs migrants filled abroad were not the types of jobs they held at home (if they had jobs at home).

Second, most migrants who borrowed money to pay migration costs took out loans from family and relatives at very low interest rates, and most repaid their loans with foreign earnings, that is, there was relatively little borrowing from moneylenders at high interest rates, with the possible exception of some of the Ethiopians. Third, most migrants were able to repay migration costs with 1 to 9 months of foreign earnings (Table 4.27). Filipinos and Indians in Qatar were able to repay their migration costs with 2 months of foreign earnings, while Pakistanis in SA needed 9 months of foreign earnings to repay their migration costs.

Table 4.27 Months of foreign work needed
to repay migration costs (2014 US$)

	Mean	Median
Ethiopia–SA	2.9	3.1
Philippines–Qatar	1.0	1.0
India–Qatar	1.9	1.9
Nepal–Qatar	3.1	3.3
Pakistan–SA	9.0	9.2
Pakistan–UAE	6.0	6.5

Source: Surveys of returning workers in 2015 (author's
calculations from unpublished raw data).

The most remarkable finding is that, for most workers, migration costs were less than 10 percent of foreign earnings. This is remarkable because the perception is that many workers pay a third or more of their foreign earnings to get foreign jobs, arrive abroad in debt to moneylenders who charge high interest rates, and work abroad while deprived of human and labor rights.[12] None of these "stylized facts" proved to be true for most of the workers returning from jobs in GCC countries.

There are workers who are trafficked and enslaved, and one such worker is one too many. However, just as it is hard to examine the health of a nation's population by interviewing only persons in hospital emergency rooms, so it is hard to examine the health of a migration corridor by interviewing only migrants with complaints.[13] Migrant complaint centers reveal misery as well as strategic thinking, as when workers file complaints near the end of their contracts to obtain a 1 to 6 month of "free visa" to work for any employer while their complaint is resolved.

The fact that many workers with similar earnings abroad pay very different amounts in migration costs at home suggests the need to examine the factors that influence migration costs in origin countries. In some cases, reasons for high migration costs lie in destination countries, as when GCC countries reduce the number of visas available to particular nationalities, allowing GCC employers and recruiters to auction the limited visas among recruiters

---

[12] For example, *The Guardian* has a special section devoted to "modern day slavery" among migrants in Qatar (https://www.theguardian.com/global-development/series/modern-day-slavery-in-focus+world/qatar).

[13] Wickramasekara (2013) details the problems encountered by migrant workers in GCC countries: "Deception and provision of misleading information; excessive fees, non-transparency of fees, and non-issue of receipts for payments; collusion between intermediaries at origin and destination; employment contracts either not issued or, when issued, not understood by migrant workers nor enforceable at destination; substitution of inferior contracts at destination; withholding or confiscating passports or travel documents; visa trading and sending workers under irregular situations and into forced labour situations and/or into hazardous employment; and violation of migrant workers' fundamental rights as workers in countries of destination through the sponsorship (kafala) system."

in migrant-sending countries, who in turn pass high visa costs on to workers willing to pay.[14] In other cases, layers of intermediaries between licensed recruiters and workers, combined with a lack of receipts and corruption in government agencies, help to explain why migration costs are high.

Migration costs vary systematically by corridor, and policy options to reduce worker-paid costs are also likely to be different in each corridor. Some policies will always reduce worker-paid costs, including the long-term empowerment of workers that accompanies opportunities to find decent jobs at home. Shorter-term options are more likely to involve micro-incentives that induce recruiters to avoid overcharging workers, and macro-incentives that change the recruitment industry from one that profits from auctioning the limited number of foreign jobs available among workers eager to move to one that partners with foreign employers and local workers to satisfy both.

Two final notes deserve mention: prospects for fewer jobs for migrants in GCC countries and the unanticipated consequences of efforts to improve the system for training and deploying migrant workers in India and other migrant-sending countries. GCC governments, aware that the Arab Spring uprisings of 2011 began with frustrated youth who could not find jobs, are trying to encourage more native youth to accept private sector jobs, a Herculean task given decades of reliance on foreign workers willing to work for low wages. Nativization policies that require private employers to hire a certain share of natives often lead to hiring natives in-name-only, that is, natives are hired but do not show up to work, prompting some countries to make entire sectors off limits to foreign workers.

The second development is the "cleaning up" of recruitment in GCC countries, especially the enforcement of regulations that require households to pay $5,000 or more to employ domestic workers and to cover all of their migration costs. Reducing abuses in GCC countries at a time when the number of jobs for migrants is shrinking may increase competition in migrant-sending countries for ever fewer jobs, increasing corruption there. The paradox of reducing worker-paid fees in one part of the migration system only to have fees rise elsewhere suggests there should be both cautious and holistic approaches to migration policy reforms.

Juridini (2016) provides a comprehensive review of the problems involved in recruiting Asian workers for jobs in the GCC, emphasizing the layers in the migration infrastructure between employers and workers that extract payments from workers. His preferred solution is to prohibit recruiters in

---

[14] Rahman (2011) suggests that three-fourths of the average $2,750 paid by Bangladeshi migrants for jobs in GCC countries are for fees and kickbacks to intermediaries in the migration system, including employers and recruiters in GCC countries and subagents and brokers in Bangladesh.

migrant-sending countries from charging any fees under the argument that opening the door to a "reasonable" fee puts workers in the mindset that they must pay for foreign jobs and allows recruiters to collect hard-to-trace extra payments. Juridini recommends that migrant-receiving governments insist that their employers pay all of the costs of migrants in both sending and receiving countries, and that GCC governments urge migrant-sending governments to be tougher on recruiters, many of whom are linked to politicians.

What would happen if recommendations that employers pay all recruitment costs were followed? There are already more workers than jobs. Policies that eliminate worker-paid fees would make foreign jobs even more desirable, attracting more workers to seek them and making it ever harder to police corruption. Juridini (2016: 37) acknowledges that making work in the GCC more attractive by eliminating recruiter fees could lead to fewer jobs for low-skilled Asian workers and more competition to get them, but does not explore the consequences.

Part III
Regulating Recruitment

Introduction

Merchants of labor are private businesses that match workers in one country with jobs in another. There are thousands of licensed recruiters, and many more who operate as travel agents in the international migration infrastructure. Chapter 5 explains that most recruiters are agents who aim for maximum profits from each transaction rather than partners who expect repeat business with particular employers and workers. An analysis of recruiters in several Southeast Asian countries highlights the strategies that enable many to act as price discriminators, charging each worker as much as he or she is willing to pay.

Chapter 6 turns to national and international efforts to regulate recruiters. The fundamental principle of the International Labour Organization (ILO) is clear, that is, employers should pay all migration costs for the migrant workers they employ. Some countries of destination (CoD) governments including the US have incorporated this principle into national legislation, but most countries of origin (CoO) governments allow recruiters to charge workers, often setting a maximum worker-paid fee. Government efforts to enforce maximum fee laws usually fail because few workers complain if they get what they want, a foreign job offering high wages.

There have been many efforts to close regulatory gaps in ways that better protect low-skilled workers and reduce worker-paid migration costs. Codes of conduct promise compliant recruiters seals of approval that they can use to attract more employer and worker clients. Some migration corridors are governed by bilateral labor agreements that eliminate private recruiters but not necessarily worker-paid migration costs, as with Southeast Asians in Korea.

Part III
Regulating Recruitment

Introduction

5

The Recruiting Business

Recruiters are information brokers between employers in migrant-receiving countries and workers in migrant-sending countries. Recruiters who match workers with jobs are paid for their services, and governments more often aim to regulate the fees recruiters charge *workers* rather than the fees they charge *employers*. Most governments allow markets to determine employer-paid fees to recruiters.

Many governments set maximum worker-paid fees at less than what workers are willing to pay for higher-wage foreign jobs. As a result, alternative allocative mechanisms determine who goes abroad, including the willingness of workers to pay recruiters and their agents. The "unfairness" of low-wage workers paying high upfront fees for 3-D (dangerous, difficult, and dirty) jobs in richer countries, and often borrowing money at high interest rates to pay recruitment costs, often makes recruiters the villains of international labor migration. Migrant workers arrive abroad in debt and are vulnerable because they do not want to lose their jobs and return to recruitment debts at home that were incurred in anticipation of high foreign wages.

Recruiters, as with information brokers in other markets where prices are not always transparent, can charge different prices for similar services. Such differential pricing is an example of price-discriminating monopoly. If a recruiter controls access to workers that the employer wants to hire, employers "desperate" for workers will pay more to recruiters than employers who can wait to fill jobs. Price discrimination may also work in reverse. If employers "sell" jobs to recruiters, they can effectively auction their job offers to the recruiter willing to pay the most.

When an employer is the only or dominant place for nurses, professional athletes, or farm workers to get jobs, the employer may act as a monopsony, which is a monopolist in the labor market. For example, hospitals may pay more to traveling nurses who fill less-desirable jobs at night or on weekends to avoid having to raise wages for all nurses. Similarly, farmers may hire local workers to fill year-round jobs and guest workers to fill harvest jobs to avoid having to raise wages to find sufficient local workers to harvest. In both cases, even if traveling nurses or guest workers cost more, monopsony employers can save money because they do not have to raise wages for current workers.

Recruiters who place workers in jobs abroad can charge them different prices for their services if they can determine how much workers are willing to pay. The key to determining what workers will pay are agents and subagents who live in or visit villages with low-skilled workers. These agents get to know potential migrants, can determine what workers are willing to pay, and inform the recruiter, who often collects from the worker and reimburses the agent.

There are limits to recruiter power vis-à-vis foreign employers and local workers because of competition between recruiters and when workers have other job options. Indeed, many recruiters in Asian CoO would say that foreign employers are price-discriminating monopolies, pitting recruiters against each other in order to collect fees in exchange for job offers. Employer power rises when CoD governments restrict the number of workers from particular countries, so that Bangladeshi recruiters must compete with each other to obtain job offers from Malaysia or Saudi Arabia.

Some CoD governments make it hard for migrants to avoid recruiters. Workers abroad and returned workers can inform migrants about usual migration costs. However, even if workers know that the recruiter is charging "too much," he or she may have to use a particular recruiter to get a foreign job.

The first half of this chapter covers three topics: the difference between recruiters who are long-term partners of the employers to whom they provide workers versus recruiters who act as short-term agents for employers and workers; the division of the wage wedge between employers, workers, and the other parties involved; and the relative success that cooperation between governments has brought to reducing remittance costs versus the difficulties of reducing recruitment costs. The second half of the chapter reviews the activities of recruiters in Indonesia, the Philippines, and Vietnam.

Agents versus Partners

Wage gaps between countries motivate international labor migration. Most workers will not pay this entire wage gap to recruiters, since that would mean that migration away from family and friends generates the same wages as working at home. However, many workers will pay more than the typical 1 month's foreign wages or less than 5 percent of foreign earnings on a 2-year contract that some governments specify as the maximum amount that private recruiters should charge.

Dividing the wage wedge that motivates international labor migration between employers, workers, and recruiters is a major issue in migration and development, a subject discussed at a UN High-Level Dialogue (HLD) in October 2013 (www.iom.int/hld2013). In light of ILO recommendations that employers should pay all recruitment costs, the international community is seeking policies to reduce worker-paid migration costs. The HLD's concluding statement laid out five priorities, beginning with the need to integrate migration into the global development agenda and to make migration a catalyst for development by protecting the rights of migrants and lowering migration costs; subsequent UN meetings have echoed these priorities.[1]

Recruiters who match workers and jobs are paid for their services by employers, workers, or both. Employers generally pay some or all of the recruitment costs of highly skilled workers, including managers, healthcare professionals, and engineers, because there are relatively few such workers and the consequences of poor worker–job matches can be costly to the employer. Some recruiters, especially those who match college-trained workers with foreign jobs, become *partners* of employers, anticipating repeat business that makes it worthwhile to fully learn employer requirements and spread this investment in understanding the employer's needs over many placements. For example, one Indian recruiter reported spending $10,000 to recruit each nurse placed in the US, including the costs of required tests, visa costs, and travel expenses (Maybud and Wiskow, 2006: 232).

Recruiters who place low-skilled workers in foreign jobs are more often *agents* than partners. Agents often bring parties together for a one-time transaction, which gives them less incentive to learn about employer and worker needs. In low-skilled occupations such as domestic service and construction labor, where there are often more workers seeking foreign jobs than there are jobs available, agent recruiters can charge workers to move up the queue of those waiting to go abroad. Even if low-skilled workers know they are paying higher-than-government-set maximum fees for foreign jobs, they may not complain if they get what they want, a foreign job that offers a higher wage.

The distinctions between agents and partners can be clarified by examining the nature and frequency of three types of transactions, that is, real estate, recruitment, and remittances. Real estate and recruitment are similar in the sense that each transaction is unique, reflecting the needs of particular buyers

---

[1] The second HLD priority is to improve lives and work for migrants by lowering remittance costs and improving the recognition and transfer of skills over borders. Third is to develop plans to help migrants in crisis and fourth is more data on migrants moving within the various migration corridors, including migrant characteristics and migration and remittance costs. The fifth HLD priority is to develop a strategy to achieve the first four priorities, and to have the strategy endorsed by governments at the Global Forum for Migration and Development meetings in May 2014 in Sweden.

and the attributes of each house, just as worker traits and job characteristics are unique. Housing and recruitment transactions occur rarely, sometimes only once in a lifetime, and often require navigating several markets, such as both the labor market and the credit market.

Sending remittances, by contrast, involves a standard commodity and is a transaction repeated frequently. The consequences of bad decisions are also different. Home buyers and migrant workers are often "locked in" by the loans taken to buy a house and find a job abroad, while a poor remittance transaction usually results only in the loss of a portion of worker earnings.

There are other similarities between real estate and recruitment transactions. Even though many homes and condos are similar or identical, heterogeneity allows agents to charge high commissions because each buyer is unique. Agents may invest time to learn buyer needs and priorities in terms of space, neighborhood, price, and other factors, so that "finding exactly the right house" works against transparency and competition, minimizing the cost reductions expected with more transactions. Similarly, recruiters may offer similar or identical jobs abroad to low-skill workers, but justify charging differential fees by saying that they are investing to learn which foreign job is best for a particular worker. Making what appear to be homogeneous transactions to outsiders but heterogeneous to participants helps recruiters to extract money from employers and workers.

Real estate transactions in their frequent reliance on credit are similar to low-skilled workers going abroad. Many home buyers rely on credit to purchase homes, just as many migrant workers take out loans to pay recruitment fees. In both cases, people are forced to negotiate two unfamiliar markets, for housing or foreign jobs, and for credit to complete the transaction. Home buyers seeking credit can do so in a fairly transparent market because of regulation and the security of the house being purchased; but migrants seeking credit for the costs of foreign jobs must usually navigate a less transparent credit market that offers less security to lenders, since the foreign work contract may not generate the expected earnings to repay the loan.

There are other similarities between buying real estate and working abroad. Housing has both investment and consumption benefits, just as moving abroad to work generates income, may lead to new skills or settlement abroad, and can help rural youth to escape conservative rural villages. There is usually mobility in both real estate and migration transactions, as people move over local borders to new homes just as migrants move over national borders to jobs.

Important differences between real estate and recruitment involve principal–agent issues and subagents. Employers and migrants are the principals in recruitment, and both may use the services of recruiters. Recruiters should act on behalf of the principals who are paying them, but may act in their self-interest, filling a job quickly and cheaply, especially if jobs and workers are perceived to be homogeneous, that is, the jobs do not require skills and workers are low skilled. Recruiters in sending countries often rely on subagents to find low-skilled workers, introducing another opportunity to put self-interest ahead of the interest of the worker, recruiter, and foreign employer.

Other differences between real estate, recruitment, and remittance transactions arise in fee setting and agent commissions. In most housing markets, agents compete to represent sellers of homes (get listings) and to find buyers for them. Each agent may represent multiple buyers and sellers, but should represent the best interest of a buyer or seller in a particular transaction. In most home sales, there are different agents for the seller and the buyer, and local cartels often fix the commission and how it is divided between selling and buying agent.

For example, in many US housing markets, the commission is 5 or 6 percent of the sale price, with half going to the agent representing the seller and half to the buyer's agent. The buyer ultimately pays the commission in the price of the house, with the commission normally deducted from the seller's sale proceeds. The selling agent has some incentive to have the sale price be higher, and the buying agent to have the price be lower, but the major incentive of both agents is to complete the transaction so that they share the commission.

Recruiters in CoD may be able to charge employers fees that depend on the job's skills level, the employer's cost of leaving the job unfilled, and the number of recruiters competing for the employer's job offers, that is, destination country recruiter charges may not be linked explicitly to wages paid. Sending country recruiter charges to workers reflects the number of workers who want to fill foreign jobs versus the number available. The imbalance between supply and demand normally rises as skill levels fall. At the lowest wage levels, there may be five or ten workers available to fill each foreign job, allowing the recruiter to effectively auction foreign jobs.

The internet has made the real estate market more transparent, lowering the cost of bringing home buyers and sellers together. However, in most countries, the internet has not eliminated licensed agents representing most home buyers and sellers or even significantly reduced agent commissions. Similarly, despite technology and the experience gained via social networks from workers who have gone abroad and returned, worker-paid migration costs remain high in many corridors.

In some cases, both buyers and sellers believe that "discount agents" will not represent their interests as well as full-commission agents. FSI Worldwide, a recruiter that does not charge fees to the workers it places in foreign jobs, reported trouble recruiting Kenyan construction workers for foreign jobs because they believed that FSI's no-fee system of recruitment meant that the foreign jobs were not "real."[2]

There have been efforts to standardize recruitment transactions and thus reduce fees. Standard contracts, easily available information on foreign jobs and worker skills, and government regulation of employer- and worker-paid fees are efforts to move recruitment away from the real estate and toward the remittance model. However, recruitment in many sending countries defies standardization that could reduce costs, because migrants typically begin with agents of licensed recruiters rather than recruiters with job offers. These agents consider the desires of the migrants they represent as well as the fees or commissions offered by each recruiter, adding a fee-charging layer to the recruitment process.

Remittance versus Recruitment Costs

Sending money over national borders is a standardized transaction whose total cost reflects the price charged for the service, the exchange rate, and the cost of receiving money. Workers making frequent remittance transactions quickly learn these total costs. Remitters can advertise one or all three costs, and economies of scale reduce remitter costs. Competition and education has lowered the cost of sending small sums via regulated financial institutions and prompted some remitters to offer additional services, such as a phone call or text message to the recipient that the money is arriving.

International cooperation between governments helped to reduce remittance costs. After the 9/11 terrorist attacks, governments encouraged financial institutions to extend services to small remitters, issued identification to unauthorized foreigners that was acceptable to banks, and regularly distributed information on the cost of sending $200 via various remitters. These policy changes plus new technologies such as phone transfers reduced the cost of sending $200 from one country to another from 15 percent or $30 to less than 10 percent or $20 over the past decade. The World Bank's 5x5 program aimed to reduce remittance costs by another 5 percentage points over 5 years, that is, to lower average remittance costs to 5 percent by 2014. However, average remittance costs were 7.7 percent of the amount transferred in 2015 (World Bank, 2015).

---

[2] Nick Forster said that Kenyan workers weren't coming forward because FSI wasn't charging fees: "They didn't believe it [recruitment for foreign jobs] was real." Quoted in Electronics Firms Vote to Ban Charging Workers Fees for Jobs, 2015 *Wall Street Journal* April 8, see: http://blogs.wsj.com/riskandcompliance/2015/04/08/electronics-firms-vote-to-ban-charging-workers-fees-for-jobs/.

Recruitment is the new frontier to lower migration costs and increase the development payoff of labor migration. The benefits of lower recruitment costs are manifold. Low recruitment costs and good worker–job matches result in satisfied workers and employers. If migration costs are low, migrant workers capture more of the wage wedge that encourages migration, and employers have highly motivated workers.[3] Low worker-migration costs can help governments to manage migration by reducing the need for them to deal with dissatisfied, terminated, runaway, and overstaying workers.

High migration costs can have the opposite effects. High costs can prompt migrant workers to seek jobs for which they lack necessary skills in a quest for higher wages to repay migration debts, to take second jobs while abroad that make them irregular, or to overstay their visas to achieve savings targets. Employers may be dissatisfied with the performance of workers who are worried about repaying recruitment debts as well as workers sent by recruiters more interested in collecting recruitment fees than in making good worker–job matches.

Given the benefits of good rather than poor worker–job matches, why do high migration costs and poor worker–job matches persist? There are many reasons, including perverse incentives. Remittance transactions are frequent, so money-transfer firms have an incentive to offer low-cost services to win repeat business. Recruitment occurs less frequently, and employers may not care who is recruited if their major business is selling job offers that result in the issuance of work visas. Similarly, recruiters may not care who they send abroad if their major source of revenue is charging workers before departure.

Making money by being merchants of labor rather than sending workers abroad to produce useful goods and services creates perverse incentives. Consider the example of low-skilled Bangladeshis recruited as laborers in Gulf Cooperation Council (GCC) countries for $250 a month. These workers, who will earn $3,000 a year or $9,000 over 3 years, often incur $2,000 to $3,000 in migration costs, perhaps financed by selling or mortgaging the family's land. Once abroad, some of the workers may take second jobs to earn more money to achieve a savings target, but second jobs make them irregular. In this case, the fact that wages are low and migration costs are high gives migrants incentives to engage in behavior that can make them worse off, as when they are detected working illegally and deported.

---

[3] Wage differences can act as efficiency wages, as when employers pay more than the market wage to workers who are hard to monitor in order to encourage them to work without close supervision. Higher-than-market efficiency wages motivate workers because they know that loss of their job would result in lower wages.

Recruiters in Indonesia, Philippines, and Vietnam

The key characteristic of recruitment is the competitive nature of the industry. The major assets of recruiters are job offers from foreign employers and the ability to find workers to fill those jobs. There are relatively low barriers to entry, since the major cost of doing business is an office and staff. Many recruiters began as employees of recruiting firms, got to know foreign employers seeking workers, and started their own firms. Most recruiters maintain good ties with employers who provide them with job offers, and rely on networks, employees, or independent agents to recruit and screen workers to fill jobs.

At higher skill levels, both the employer offering the job and the worker filling the job are important, since mismatches can be costly. For example, foreign hospitals want to hire healthcare personnel who can obtain the required local licenses and who are competent to perform their jobs, making them willing to pay recruiters the equivalent of 3–4 months' salary to find the best workers. As skill levels decline, the value of foreign employers who offer many jobs rises in the eyes of recruiters, while the value of migrant workers who fill these jobs declines. Many employers and recruiters see low-skilled workers as interchangeable.

A 1969 study of private employment agencies in Detroit noted the "cloak of social disapproval" surrounding them (Skeels, 1969: 160). Much of the disrepute arose from the secrecy that recruiters thought was necessary for protection from competition. For example, many recruiters would not tell workers exactly where jobs were located until they paid recruitment fees or signed contracts committing them to pay fees for fear that workers might go on their own to the employer and be hired.

Many recruiters tried to prevent their staff from breaking away to start their own recruitment businesses by requiring them to sign non-compete agreements. When owners retired, recruitment businesses were more often shut down than sold because of the difficulty transferring the major asset—ties to employers seeking workers—leading to the conclusion that "competition forces even the ethical private employment agent toward questionable activity" (Skeels, 1969: 160).

Indonesia

Indonesia is a country of 255 million people with a per capita income of $3,600 in 2014, or $10,200 at purchasing power parity (PPP). Indonesia is the world's largest island country, and successive governments have tried to move Indonesians from the most populous island of Java to less densely populated islands and abroad.

There were 515 licensed recruiters in Indonesia in 2014. Recruiting licenses are normally valid for 5 years, and they allow the establishment of an unlimited number of branch offices. However, the recruiter's main office, usually in Jakarta, must be the place from which workers are deployed to foreign jobs.

Lindquist (2010) described the recruitment of Indonesian migrants, also known as TKI, on the Indonesian island of Lombok just east of Bali. Lombok men were recruited to work on palm oil plantations in Malaysia for $235 a month, while women were recruited to work in Saudi Arabia as domestic workers for $215 a month (Lindquist, 2010: 127). Most Lombok recruiters were branch offices of Jakarta-based recruitment agencies, known as PJTKI; these branches receive payment for their recruiting efforts from their PJTKI head office when the migrant travels to Jakarta and departs to the foreign employer.

Women going to Saudi Arabia do not pay recruitment fees, according to Lindquist. The local PJTKI office receives $600 of the $1,400 that the Jakarta-based office is paid by Saudi recruiters for each domestic worker (Lindquist, 2010: 127), and most of this $600 is redistributed to the agents who act as independent contractors to find women willing to work abroad. Branch office profits can be only $30 a migrant, explaining why branches are closed if they have "bad luck" with the workers they recruited, as when migrants are fired by their foreign employers or run away from the employer to whom they are assigned.

Women willing to work abroad are valuable to recruitment agencies. Many agencies house them at the agency until they are ready to depart so that they do not become pregnant or change their minds about working abroad (Lindquist, 2010: 129). Women are often trained while waiting to go abroad and once again after they arrive in Saudi Arabia.

In contrast to the women, Indonesian men pay about 2 months' wages to get a job on Malaysian palm oil plantations, with half going to the recruiting agency and half to the agent who recruits them. Men often borrow from moneylenders at 100 percent interest rates, using family homes or land as collateral, and repay their recruitment debts from their foreign earnings (Lindquist, 2010: 128).

Most Indonesian men leave illegally, while women go abroad legally. Legal exits begin with a letter from the village chief approving the departure plus a letter from a branch of a recruitment agency confirming the foreign job offer. These letters are reviewed and approved by the local government employment agency before the worker can get a medical check at a provincial hospital. The next step is to get a passport, attend a briefing at the local office of the Agency for Placement and Protection of Migrant Workers known as BP3TKI about migrant rights and responsibilities abroad, and then undergo training of at least 200 hours for workers headed to Malaysia and 300 hours for workers going to Singapore.

The legal procedure takes 3–4 months because of paperwork and training. Once abroad, migrant expenses are typically deducted over 3–5 months, so there can be a 9-month gap between when a worker decides to go abroad and when remittances begin to flow home. The alternative is to go abroad illegally, paying a smuggler the equivalent of 1–2 months' wages to get into Malaysia and relying on social networks and smugglers to find jobs.[4] Going illegally is cheaper and faster, which explains why most Indonesian men go illegally to Malaysian plantations.

The Indonesian example of legal and unauthorized exits highlights another way to look at the key asset of recruiters. Instead of recruiters acting as information brokers, their core business is "the negotiation of immigration and emigration rules" on behalf of employer and worker clients. Jones (2015: 56) noted that many recruiters want complex regulations to prevent employers and workers from contacting each other directly. In the Indonesian case, a complex regulatory system meant to protect migrants winds up creating incentives for Indonesian men to migrate illegally to save money and time.

Philippines

The Philippines is a country of 99 million people with a per capita income of $3,500, or $8,500 at PPP in 2014. There are 7,000 islands, but half of Filipinos live on the main island of Luzon, including 20 percent who live in metro Manila.

The Philippines has been sending millions of workers abroad for decades. Over 1.8 million were deployed in 2014, including 400,000 to work on the world's ships. Of the 1.4 million Filipino workers leaving to work on land, two-thirds were being rehired by foreign employers and a third were going abroad for the first time.[5] Most overseas Filipino workers, known as OFWs, work in Gulf oil exporters such as Kuwait, Qatar, Saudi Arabia, and the United Arab Emirates (UAE), while smaller numbers go to Southeast Asian destinations including Singapore, Hong Kong, Taiwan, and Malaysia.

Most Filipino workers are matched with jobs abroad by one of the 1,250 licensed recruiters. The major asset of licensed recruiters is ties to foreign employers seeking migrants to fill jobs. Licensed recruiters are required to have offices, and the major issue facing "good recruiters" is competition that encourages employers to pay little or nothing to find OFWs and encourages some recruiters to charge workers for jobs.

---

[4] Migrant workers build hopes on dry land, 2015. *Jakarta Post*, April 26, see: www.thejakartapost.com/news/2015/04/26/migrant-workers-build-hopes-dry-land.html-0.
[5] These data are from POEA OFW statistics: www.poea.gov.ph/ofwstat/ofwstat.html.

The Philippines makes it relatively hard to become a recruiter. The Philippine Overseas Employment Administration (POEA) requires applicants for recruiting licenses to be college graduates, Filipino citizens, and to have at least 3 years' experience in recruitment. Recruiters must invest at least two million pesos ($45,000) in their business and post a one million peso escrow deposit, have a bank account of at least 500,000 pesos, provide 2 years of tax returns for any shareholders of the business, and rent an office of at least 100 square meters and register this place of business with POEA.[6]

An applicant for a recruiting license must convince a foreign employer to give him or her an offer of at least 100 jobs before POEA will issue a recruiter license, a stiff requirement since employers can turn to already licensed recruiters for Filipino migrants. After satisfying these requirements, a new recruiter gets a 1-year probationary license that can be renewed for 3 years.

The fact that foreign job offers are critical to obtaining a recruiting license means that some new recruiters take over an ongoing recruitment agency, often requiring or encouraging the owner and key staff to stay. Senior staff may leave established recruiters after they have earned the trust of a foreign employer who provides them with job offers, prompting the owners of recruitment agencies to restrict competition from ex-staff with non-compete agreements and compartmentalization so that even senior staff have access to only a few foreign employers.

Most recruiters are small, staffed by the owner and ten to fifteen employees, including relatives of the owner. After deploying one hundred workers, recruiters can retain their licenses even if they send fewer workers abroad in subsequent years. Established recruiters complain that foreign employers try to reduce the fees they pay, often requesting discounts if they are recruiting one hundred or more workers. Some Filipino recruiters "cold call" foreign employers and offer discounts to get their job offers.

The major challenge facing Filipino recruiters is obtaining sufficient foreign job offers. This issue is compounded by so-called "front" recruiters, agencies nominally owned by the Filipino wife of a national of a Gulf State who knows employers in these destinations and can get job offers from them. Front recruiters are believed to charge employers less for Filipino migrants and to charge fees to workers in ways that are hard to detect, which prompts other recruiters to follow suit in order to continue receiving job offers.[7]

---

[6] Would-be recruiters must also pay a license fee of 50,000 pesos ($1,120) and provide a surety bond of 100,000 pesos ($2,280).

[7] For example, the East West Placement agency (www.eastwest.com.ph), largest in the Philippines and making more than 10,000 placements in some years, is reportedly owned by a Bangladeshi married to a Filipina. Over 60 percent of the Filipinos deployed by East West are for the Saudi oil and gas and heavy construction sectors.

There are several ways to operate recruitment businesses. The owner and senior staff may be paid $2,000 a month or more to deal with foreign employers, while lower-paid staff recruit and screen migrants. Some agencies pay recruitment-and-screening staff salaries of $400 to $500 a month and have productivity quotas, such as expecting staff to recruit twenty-five to thirty workers a month for whom employers pay fees of $500 per worker. Other agencies pay their staff piece rates, offering them a fee for each worker who is selected by a foreign employer.

Once a migrant is selected by a foreign employer, a staff person is assigned to that migrant and has almost daily contact, checking on progress to secure documents. At this point, the employer, migrant, and agency have made investments in the person going abroad, and the constant contact aims to avoid having the migrant decide to withdraw.

An ongoing issue is dealing with foreign employers who want to reduce fees they pay to Filipino recruiters. Some recruiters estimate that 80 percent of Filipino recruiters who send workers to Gulf states do not charge employers the full or normal $500 per worker fee for service workers who are paid $500 a month, instead charging workers who are eager for foreign jobs. For example, if the recruiter charges a Gulf employer $400 instead of $500 for one hundred workers, the employer saves $10,000.

Many Gulf employers say that they want migrants to pay something to recruiters so that their new employees have an investment in the foreign job (IOM, 2016). Philippine law allows recruiters to charge the workers they send abroad 1 month's foreign earnings, but some recruiters say that opening the door to *any* worker-paid fees makes it impossible to police how much workers pay. For example, if migrants going to work in Gulf hotels are charged 2 months' salary, it can be hard for regulators to detect the extra payment unless workers complain, which they are unlikely to do if they get the higher-wage jobs they want.

The Philippines is often considered a best-practice model for protecting migrant workers during recruitment and deployment. However, with more than a million new entrants to the labor force each year and a tradition of achieving upward mobility by working abroad, it is very hard for the government to prevent Filipinos from paying more than 1 month's wages for foreign jobs. Recruiters caught between foreign employers who want to reduce payments to recruiters and Filipinos eager to go abroad can make ethical recruitment very difficult, especially as other countries with English-speaking workers such as India and Sri Lanka, or countries with very low wages such as Bangladesh, Myanmar, Nepal, and Vietnam, step up efforts to send more workers abroad.

The POEA's hard-to-enter and easy-to-exit regulatory model leads to frequent suspensions and withdrawals of licenses, so that the threat of losing a license becomes a major reason for recruiters to resolve worker complaints. Many recruiters resent the POEA's tough enforcement approach, noting that relatively minor infractions can halt an agency's business, as when a complaint by one worker stops POEA from processing any applications from that recruiter. In such cases, in order to stay in business the recruiter often compensates the aggrieved worker.

Employers generally pay all recruitment fees for skilled workers earning $500 or more a month and professionals such as health-care workers who earn even more. Two major "manual" occupations generally do not charge workers for foreign jobs: domestic workers and seafarers. Fees for domestic workers are prohibited by regulations that established the "supermaid" program in 2007, when household service workers were required to have their skills certified before departure, to be paid at least $400 a month abroad, and to pay no recruitment fees.

The seafaring industry operates under both ILO and national guidelines developed in conjunction with shippers and maritime unions. The manning firms that sometimes train seafarers may charge them for training, but generally not for placement.

Filipino law makes local recruiters jointly liable with foreign employers to fulfill the terms of the contracts that Filipino migrants have as they depart, including unpaid wages and work-related benefits, an effort to increase protections for OFWs (Migrant Forum, 2014). Joint liability should make recruiters careful about the foreign employers they deal with, but recruiters complain that joint liability can cost them money for the actions of foreign employers over which they have no control. In some cases, employers say that they need to charge workers so that they can compensate workers if foreign employers do not abide by their promises.

At the behest of recruiters, the Migrant Workers Act that establishes joint liability was amended to limit compensation due to workers to 3 months per year of work abroad that was not paid as called for in a worker's contract. However, the Philippine Supreme Court in August 2014 struck down this limited compensation provision, ruling in the case of Joy Cabiles, who went to Taiwan on a 1-year contract and was terminated after a month, that Cabiles could collect the remaining 11 months of her salary of 15,060 New Taiwan dollars ($491) a month from her Filipino recruiter, the Sameer Overseas Placement Agency.[8] Many Filipino recruiters bill foreign employers for early termination wage claims, but they have little recourse if foreign employers refuse to pay.

---

[8] http://www.chanrobles.com/cralaw/2014augustdecisions.php?id=629.

Migrant advocates say that joint liability is good practice but often fails to compensate aggrieved workers fully. Returned workers who were not paid the wages or benefits due them abroad often lack the funds to await the legal process. If a recruiter defends against the worker's complaint, the legal process could stretch 3–5 years. Once a worker files a complaint and the recruiter prepares a defense, workers may settle for much less than the amount they are seeking because they cannot afford to wait for the legal process (Gordon, 2015: 31–2). In several cases where workers pursued legal action, recruiters went out of business, giving migrants hollow victories. Furthermore, foreign employers who do not abide by worker contracts may not be punished at all, and simply turn to another recruiter to get more OFWs.

Vietnam

Vietnam is a country of 91 million people with a per capita income of $1,900, or $5,400 at PPP in 2014. Vietnam is an S-shaped country, with identity in the north shaped by resisting China and absorbing Chinese culture and the south influenced by Khmer culture.

There are about 500,000 Vietnamese working abroad; almost 100,000 Vietnamese workers went abroad in 2014, to Taiwan (60,000), Japan (20,000), South Korea (7,000), Malaysia (5,000), Saudi Arabia (4,000). The Vietnamese government wants to send more workers abroad in order to accelerate development; it expects foreign employers to train rural and minority workers while abroad and hopes that remittances speed development in lagging areas.

Vietnamese workers often incur high costs to go abroad with the help of 170 licensed recruitment agencies. Most Vietnamese migrants arrive abroad in debt, prompting some to "run away" from the employers to whom they are assigned to escape deductions from their wages for migration-related costs; over a third of the Vietnamese in Korea run away from their employers in a bid to escape deductions for migration debts. Some Vietnamese overstay their contracts in order to achieve savings targets that are delayed by high recruitment costs, prompting some to say that Vietnamese are going abroad to "debt mountains."[9]

The major government response to high worker-paid migration costs is to punish workers who become illegal abroad. Departing workers must post bonds of $5,000 or more that are forfeited if the worker absconds or overstays. One reason for absconding is that migrants with debts often have repayments deducted from their wages, so that they may be able to earn more as unauthorized workers; overstayers may try to achieve savings targets that take longer

[9] Tan Lieu, 2015. Going to Debt Mountain. *The Economist*, February 14, see: www.economist. com/news/asia/21643235-working-abroad-no-bargain-going-debt-mountain.

to reach than expected because of pre-departure debts. It is not clear whether Vietnamese migrants who return properly get refunds of what they paid for bonds.

Licensed Vietnamese recruiters are not supposed to charge fees to migrant workers. However, migrants usually pay unlicensed brokers to help them through the process of learning about a foreign job, in completing required pre-departure training and documentation, and accompanying the migrant to licensed recruiters and to the departure airport.

During the 1980s, Vietnam sent workers abroad to socialist countries and the Middle East under the auspices of a government agency, a system that ended in the early 1990s. Some of the Vietnamese sent to work in the Czech Republic and East Germany settled abroad, so that there are up to 200,000 Vietnamese in these countries.

Vietnam began sending workers abroad again in November 1991, when Decree 370 established regulations that allowed enterprises to send their employees abroad. Subsequent directives and decrees called sending labor abroad an "important and long-term strategy" to generate remittances and improve the skills of Vietnamese workers. In 2006, the eight-chapter, 80-article Law on Vietnamese Workers Working Overseas under Contract was enacted, with provisions for licensing and regulating private recruiters. In October 2013, decrees were issued that required departing workers to post bonds and fine-tuned the regulation of recruiters.

The government encourages labor migration from poor and minority areas to jump-start development there. PM Decision 71 in 2009 approved a plan to send 120,000 workers abroad from sixty-one poor and minority districts in nine provinces between 2009 and 2020, and a 2014 decision makes workers leaving from these poor districts eligible for grants and loans to cover the cost of training and documentation to go abroad.

The government's use of migration as an anti-poverty strategy poses problems for recruiters, who emphasize that both Vietnamese and foreign employers prefer to hire better educated urban workers rather than rural farmers from poor districts of Vietnam. Rural workers are sometimes found unfit by foreign employers and sent home. For example, between 2009 and 2012, some 7,500 workers from poor districts of Vietnam were sent to Malaysia and the Middle East, where many were terminated by their employers or elected to return early (Ishizuka, 2013: 4).

Recruiters and others emphasize that minorities, who are half of the poor in Vietnam, often have low self-esteem and ambition, which contributes to problems during training and once abroad. Instead of down skilling, as when well-educated workers from a low-wage country work for higher wages abroad in jobs that do not use their skills, the Vietnamese government aims for up skilling via migration, or having foreign employers train Vietnamese workers.

This is a dubious strategy on many grounds, from employer acceptance to worker protection.

The Department of Overseas Labor (DOLAB) within the Vietnamese Ministry of Labor, Invalids, and Social Affairs (MOLISA) regulates recruiters and other aspects of labor outmigration. Vietnam issues recruitment licenses to firms headed by college graduates with at least 3 years' experience in recruitment. Recruiters must post bonds of at least $250,000 and make a deposit of at least $50,000. To keep their licenses, recruiting agencies must send at least one worker a year abroad.

As of June 2010, there were 167 licensed agencies, including thirty that were completely private, thirty-nine in which the state owns up to half of the stock, and ninety-eight that are mostly or completely state-owned enterprises (SOEs). Most are small; only seventeen sent more than 1,000 workers abroad in 2009, and only eighteen specialize in sending workers abroad (Ishizuka, 2013: 5).

Licensed agencies can establish up to three branches in three provinces, but these branches are not allowed to collect fees from migrants. Brokers or local governments often recruit workers and, when they have screened a sufficient number of prospective migrants, the licensed agency sends its employees to interview migrants and select those to present to foreign employers.

The Vietnam Association of Manpower Supply (VAMAS) is a voluntary association that includes 80 percent of the licensed recruiters (www.vamas. com.vn). VAMAS in 2010 developed a code of conduct that is being implemented among forty-seven of its member recruiters that send half of Vietnamese migrants abroad. The code calls on recruiters to abide by the law in posting job offers and recruiting workers, prohibits charging fees to workers but in a seeming contradiction also calls for the issuance of receipts for worker payments, and outlines complaint-and-resolution mechanisms. VAMAS is trying to get more recruitment agencies to endorse the code of conduct and have their staff undergo training.

It is not clear why Vietnamese workers have high pre-departure costs. Most observers highlight the gaps between relatively poor and rural workers with little education and licensed recruiters in Hanoi and Ho Chi Minh City (HCMC) who rely on intermediaries to do an initial screening of workers before employees of the licensed recruiter visit the area to make the final selection. Since there are more workers who want to go abroad than there are jobs available, families often pay intermediaries in a bid to have them persuade a licensed recruiter to select a particular worker.

The government recognizes that high migration costs are a problem. Korea stopped recruiting Vietnamese workers under the Employment Permit System (EPS) in August 2012 when over half of Vietnamese workers who had been admitted were illegal. The runaway–overstay rate dropped to less than 40 percent in 2013 and recruitment of Vietnamese resumed, with a quota of

2,900 Vietnamese for 2015 and a goal to reduce runaways and overstays to less than 30 percent. Vietnam is planning to post the names of Vietnamese workers who become illegal abroad and fine them when they return, a move criticized by some non-governmental organizations (NGOs) because it may "trap" migrants in bad jobs abroad.

Migrant worker complaints focus on two issues. First, some Vietnamese pay fees and pass tests but are not selected to go abroad and have difficulty getting their deposits returned. For example, a worker who deposited VND 30 million ($1,400) with a recruiter to go to Taiwan complained of trouble getting this deposit refunded after not being selected. Second, many returned migrants note that they worked very hard abroad, in part because there were few disruptions due to lack of materials, power interruptions, or labor disputes, and that "too much" work was expected in Korea and Taiwan. However, many returned migrants do not work while waiting to go abroad again rather than doing wage work in Vietnam.

6

Regulating Recruiters

This chapter has four sections. The first outlines the major International Labour Organization (ILO) and UN conventions that protect migrant workers, emphasizing that ILO Conventions 97 (1949) and 143 (1975) were enacted largely in response to European concerns about migrant workers at the time they were enacted. The 1990 UN Migrant Workers Convention, on the other hand, reflected the concerns of migrant-sending countries such as Mexico that were seeking to improve conditions for their citizens abroad (de Guchteneire et al., 2009); few migrant-receiving countries have ratified the 1990 convention (Ruhs, 2013).

The chapter then turns to remittances, the savings from migrant wages that reduce poverty in families receiving them and may fuel faster economic growth. Remittances to developing countries surpassed overseas development aid (ODA) in the mid-1990s, and are now over three times ODA and rising. Like many aspects of migration, remittances are a mixed blessing, providing more money for families at the expense of at least one parent being away, and generating scarce foreign exchange but also increasing the value of the currency in migrant-sending countries, which can lead to reduced exports and fewer factory jobs for non-migrants.

The next topic is the trade-off between migrant numbers and migrant rights introduced in Chapter 1 and reflected in tensions between UN agencies such as the ILO, which are concerned mostly about the rights of migrant workers, and those such as the World Bank that are more concerned with increasing remittances to speed development in migrant-sending countries. The ILO emphasizes the need to treat migrant workers in the labor market the same as the local workers with whom they work, while the World Bank focuses on maximizing remittances that reduce poverty in families receiving them. More labor migration and better protections for migrants are both desirable goals, but which should get higher priority if governments must choose between them?

The normal response to regulatory gaps that result in the abuse of migrants is to call on governments to ratify ILO and UN conventions and translate them into national laws and regulations that are enforced effectively. Enforcement is often a problem, as when recruiters routinely charge fees to low-skilled migrants that exceed government-set maximums. If migrant workers complain, the recruiter can usually escape enforcement by giving migrants what they want, jobs abroad at a higher wage, which usually leads to a withdrawal of the complaint and end to enforcement activity.

The chapter ends with a discussion of positive incentives to induce recruiters to protect the rights of migrants in exchange for tangible economic benefits. Such an inducement policy would represent a shift in many countries, which have more often added new requirements and penalties on recruiters in response to abuse. However, inducement policies may be more effective in maintaining desirable recruiter behavior over time.

International Standards

The International Labor Organization, the oldest UN agency and founded in 1919, has a constitutional mandate to protect the rights of all workers, including migrant workers. The ILO was founded after World War I to promote peace through social justice by assuring decent work for all workers, including those who find employment abroad. The ILO defines decent work as work that offers opportunities, is productive, and delivers a fair income, security in the workplace, and social protection for families. Decent work also offers prospects for personal development and social integration and freedom for people to express their concerns as well as the right to organize and participate in the decisions that affect workers' lives.[1]

The ILO is unique among UN agencies in having a tripartite structure, with those closest to the workplace, employers' and workers' organizations, joining governments to approve conventions that promote decent work for all; there are usually two government representatives for each representative from employers and labor. The ILO's 190 conventions create international labor standards that apply to all workers, including migrants, unless migrant workers are specifically exempted. Eight ILO conventions, including the freedom of workers to form and join unions, no forced and child labor, equal pay for all workers, and no discrimination, are considered to be fundamental conventions that protect all workers.[2]

---

[1] The ILO's Decent Work agenda is at http://www.ilo.org/global/topics/decent-work/lang–en/index.htm.
[2] ILO Conventions and Recommendations. www.ilo.org/global/standards/introduction-to-international-labour-standards/conventions-and-recommendations/lang–en/index.htm/.

The ILO has long favored no-fee public over private employment services. ILO Convention 2, approved in 1919, called for "a system of free public employment agencies under the control of a central authority," and recommended that governments "prohibit the establishment of employment agencies which charge fees or which carry out their business for profit." If private recruiters already existed, governments were advised to require them to obtain licenses and "abolish such agencies as soon as possible" (Gravel, 2006: 145). ILO Convention 34 (1933) renewed the call to abolish private employment agencies within 3 years and, when it was not widely ratified, Convention 96 (1949) gave governments a choice: eliminate private employment services or regulate them.

The gap between the ILO preference for no private recruiters and their spread in the 1980s and 1990s led to another ILO convention, 181, in 1994. Convention 181 recognized that public employment services were matching fewer workers with jobs, and that private recruiters were the norm in many labor markets, from models and actors to farm workers. Article 7 of Convention 181, the Private Employment Agencies Convention, prohibits private employment agencies from charging "directly or indirectly, in whole or in part, any fees or costs to workers."[3] However, Article 7 allows governments to "authorize exceptions ... in respect of certain categories of workers, as well as specified types of services provided by private employment agencies."[4]

Article 8 emphasizes the need to protect migrant workers, calling on host governments "to provide adequate protection for and prevent abuses of migrant workers recruited or placed in its territory by private employment agencies." However, ILO hostility to private recruiters is evident in its recommendation that governments negotiate "bilateral agreements to prevent abuses and fraudulent practices in recruitment, placement and employment." Most bilateral agreements rely on government agencies rather than private recruiters to move workers over borders.

Since most countries have both public employment services and private recruiters, Convention 181 calls for cooperation between them: "Where countries recognize the capabilities of private agencies in the recruitment and placement of migrant workers ... measures should be taken to promote cooperation between private agencies and the public employment services ... both migrant-sending and migrant-receiving countries should supervise [their] activities" (Guidelines on special protective measures for migrant workers recruited by private agents, Annex II, 1997, 2.3 and 3.1). Few governments

---

[3] C181 negated C96 (1949), which called on ILO member states to abolish fee-charging private recruitment agencies and strengthen public employment services.

[4] www.ilo.org/dyn/normlex/en/f?p=NORMLEXPUB:12100:0::NO::P12100_INSTRUMENT_ID:312326.

have ratified Convention 181, and there are very few agreements between public employment services and private recruiters (Gravel, 2006).

The unions that often drive the ILO's agenda remain opposed to private recruiters. In 1980, Swiss unions declared that they "can not accept that workers are placed in employment by intermediaries seeking profits." Malaysian unions similarly in 2005 called for "all middlemen or recruiters [in labor markets] to be eliminated" (Demaret, 2006: 160). Unions in many EU countries complain of "social dumping," as when Polish workers hired by a Polish temp agency are posted to Germany. Polish migrants must be paid the German minimum wage of at least €8.50 an hour while employed in Germany, but are covered by Polish rather than German work-related benefits, which reduce labor costs.

Two ILO conventions, 97 (approved in 1949) and 143 (1975), and their associated recommendations, apply specifically to migrant workers who cross national borders to work for wages. The bedrock principle of C97 is to treat all workers equally, so that migrant and local workers receive the same wages, have the same working conditions, and enjoy the same rights to form or join unions. The justification for this principle is straightforward: by protecting migrants, governments protect local workers from unfair competition. C97 was approved in the aftermath of World War II, after borders were redrawn in Europe and millions of people were resettled in new countries; equal treatment aimed to avoid allowing distinctions that could lead to tensions and fuel another conflict.

C97 aimed to ensure that all workers in rebuilding Europe were treated equally, regardless of where they were born or their status in the country where they worked. C97 also dealt with the recruitment of migrant workers, calling on "Each Member...to maintain...an adequate and free service to assist migrants for employment, and in particular to provide them with accurate information" (Article 2). The ILO continues to call on its member governments to operate no-fee labor exchanges or employment services and ensure equal treatment in the workplace.

After European governments stopped recruiting guest workers in southern and Eastern Europe in the early 1970s in the wake of oil-price hikes, the ILO developed C143 to urge governments to hold employers of irregular migrants accountable and to integrate migrants and their families who had settled.[5] Most "guest workers" who arrived in the 1960s departed as expected, but the

---

[5] Conventions 97 and 143 define a migrant worker as "a person who migrates from one country to another with a view to being employed otherwise than on his own account and includes any person regularly admitted as a migrant for employment." The 1990 UN Convention on the Protection of the Rights of All Migrant Workers and Members of Their Families has a broader definition, calling a migrant worker "a person who is engaged or has been engaged in a remunerated activity in a State of which he or she is not a national."

number of migrants was so large that, even if less than a quarter settled, many European countries developed significant minority populations. Public perceptions that guest workers would leave with their savings to achieve upward mobility at home were belied by host-country policies that gave most migrants the right to form or unify families after 1 year of work and to earn permanent residence status after 5 years (Miller and Martin, 1982).

C143 urged governments to crack down on employers and others who facilitated irregular migration, and to take steps to integrate migrants and their families who were unlikely to return. This call to integrate migrants and their families was controversial at a time when Germany openly declared that it was "not a country of immigration." First France and then Germany offered jobless migrants and their families return bonuses to encourage them to give up their work and residence rights and return home, but relatively few migrants accepted them.[6] During the 1960s, almost all foreigners in Germany were foreign workers. By the 1990s, there were three foreign residents for each foreign worker (Martin, 2014b).

Migrant workers are often the majority of domestic workers in private households in the countries where they work. C189 (2011), the Domestic Workers Convention, calls on governments to treat work in private households as employment and to set a minimum age for domestic workers, generally at least 18. Host governments are also urged to "ensure that domestic workers, like workers generally, enjoy fair terms of employment as well as decent working conditions and, if they reside in the household, decent living conditions that respect their privacy." C189 calls for written contracts for migrant domestic workers that spell out wages and working conditions as well as worker rights and responsibilities.

The ILO encourages its member states to ratify and implement its conventions. However, the migrant worker conventions, C97 and C143, have not been well ratified, especially by migrant-receiving states in both industrial and developing countries (Ruhs, 2013). As of April 2015, only forty-nine countries had ratified C97, which is over 60 years old, and most migrant-receiving countries excluded themselves from some of its provisions. Only twenty-three countries ratified C143, including Italy and Sweden as major hosts to migrant workers. C181 on private employment agencies was ratified by twenty-eight countries and C189 on domestic work by seventeen countries. The countries that host most of the world's migrant workers, from the US and

---

[6] The French and German governments offered lump-sum payments to jobless non-citizen workers who gave up their work and residence permits under the theory that the jobs from which they were laid off were unlikely to return after economies were restructured in the wake of 1970s oil price hikes. In both cases, relatively few migrant workers accepted the return bonuses and left, largely because economic conditions at home were also challenging and there were few prospects of being able to return.

Germany to Saudi Arabia (SA) and the United Arab Emirates (UAE), have not ratified the relevant ILO conventions.

In the twenty-first century, the ILO has taken a renewed interest in international labor migration. The Multilateral Framework on Labor Migration developed in 2006 contains principles and recommendations for a rights-based approach to improve the governance of international labor migration, that is, to have governments emphasize the rights of migrant workers. The Multilateral Framework grew out of a General Discussion on Migrant Workers at the International Labor Conference (ILC) in June 2004 that led to a "Resolution concerning a fair deal for migrant workers in the global economy," including a Plan of Action covering seven migrant-related issues (ILO, 2004).

The ILO's Multilateral Framework deals with rights, not numbers. It lays out the minimum standards and equal treatment norms that are included in international labor and human rights conventions to protect migrant workers, but does not suggest how many migrants should move over national borders.[7] The Multilateral Framework has nine elements: decent work; international cooperation; global knowledge base; effective management of labor migration; protection of migrant workers; prevention of abusive migration practices; migration process; social integration; and migration and development. Each of these elements is followed by several guidelines that can be implemented globally, regionally, and in particular countries, but there are no priorities established among the nine elements or the more numerous guidelines.

In June 2014, the ILO's annual conference discussed recruiters under the rubric of "fair migration." After acknowledging the importance of private recruiters in moving workers over borders, the ILO report noted

> substantial evidence of widespread abuse connected with the operation of these agencies. These [abuses] ranged from excessive rates and sometimes extortionate fees, to deliberate misinformation and deception concerning the nature and pay and conditions of work that is on offer. Migrants will often have little or no means of redress in the face of unscrupulous intermediaries once they get to their destinations and problems become apparent. This type of situation can give rise to extremes of exploitation, as in cases where workers acquire very high levels of debt to pay recruitment fees.   (ILO, 2014: 15–16)

To remedy recruiter abuses, the ILO called for "renewed efforts and cooperation with governments to ensure the adequate regulation of such agencies, and to offer workers who are victims of malpractices access to remedies." The Fair Recruitment Initiative commits the ILO to increase knowledge about recruitment practices, strengthen national laws that regulate recruitment and their

---

[7] The Multilateral Framework was noted by the ILO's Governing Body during its 295th session in March 2006.

enforcement, and promote fair recruitment practices via social dialogue and partnerships. The overall goal is to develop a regulatory framework that respects "the principles enshrined in international labour standards," and the concrete goals are to end the practice of recruiters charging migrant workers for foreign jobs and instead have more workers move over national borders under the terms of bilateral agreements.

The Fair Recruitment Initiative is aspirational, since there is little evidence that governments are replacing private recruiters with bilateral agreements. What may be more realistic is for the ILO to promote cooperation between governments to better police recruitment activities and engage in joint prosecution of violators.

The ILO is not the only UN agency that aims to improve migrant protections. Most ILO conventions cover legal migrant workers, not irregular workers and members of migrant worker families. The UN General Assembly on December 18, 1990, adopted the International Convention on the Protection of the Rights of All Migrant Workers and Members of Their Families to reinforce the rights of legal migrants and to extend protections to irregular workers and migrant family members. In celebration of the 1990 UN Convention, December 18 is celebrated as International Migrants Day (www.un.org/en/events/migrantsday/).[8] However, relatively few countries have ratified the 1990 UN Convention; only thirty-eight as of April 2015, almost all migrant-sending countries.

Remittances and Development

The ILO and UN General Assembly focus on protecting migrant workers and migrants, while the World Bank and other development institutions focus on the potential of remittances that migrants send to their countries of origin to speed development. If remittances are as important to development as some believe (Clemens, 2011), then more labor migration can be a shortcut to faster development.

Remittances to developing countries—monies sent by international migrants to their countries of origin—topped $1 billion a day a decade ago and were $442 billion in 2016, about the same as 2015. Remittances have risen much faster than the number of international migrants, doubling between 1990 and 2000 and tripling between 2000 and 2010.

Remittances are often the grass roots capital needed to reduce poverty in rural areas of developing countries, which can speed economic and job growth in

---

[8] The text of the 1990 convention is at www.ohchr.org/EN/ProfessionalInterest/Pages/CMW.aspx. The website for December 18 is at www.un.org/en/events/migrantsday/index.shtml.

both migrant-sending areas and elsewhere as the spending of remittances creates jobs for non-migrants. Unlike foreign direct investment (FDI) and private capital flows, remittances were stable during the 2008–09 recession, while FDI and private capital flows to developing countries fell sharply (Sirkeci et al., 2012).

Six countries received over half of remittances to developing countries in 2014. India received $70 billion, followed by China, $64 billion, the Philippines $28 billion, Mexico $25 billion, and Nigeria and Egypt, $20 billion each. Remittances are the largest share of gross domestic product (GDP) in a diverse group of countries, including ex-USSR countries whose Soviet industries collapsed, such as Tajikistan (remittances are half of GDP); island countries such as Tonga (24 percent); and Central American countries with large diasporas in the United States, including Honduras and El Salvador (16 percent).

Governments want to maximize remittances; many leaders cite the level of remittances as a shorthand indicator of the value of migration. Studies agree that the best way to maximize the volume of remittances that migrants send home voluntarily is to have an appropriate exchange rate and economic policies that promise growth (Ratha, 2005). Sound economic policies are a far better magnet for attracting remittances than special programs that target migrants to encourage them to send money home or require them to remit.

Government "forced savings" programs, under which employers withhold some wages and send them to designated banks in migrant countries of origin, have been plagued by problems and largely abandoned. For example, under the 1940s Mexico–US Bracero program, US farmers withheld 10 percent of worker wages and sent them to a Mexican bank that "lost" them. The ex-Braceros and their families sued, and in 2006 the Mexican government established a compensation fund to pay up to 250,000 former Braceros up to $3,500 each.[9]

There is more debate about comparing the remittances from workers abroad versus earnings from the export of goods. Bangladesh is the most populous of the forty-eight least-developed countries as defined by the UN,[10] and 80 percent of its exports are readymade garments sewn by four million women for wages of about $50 a month. Bangladesh's garment exports in 2015 were $25 billion, but they required the import of $13 billons' worth of cloth and other items, so that the "net earnings" of the garment sector were only $12 billion in local value added. Remittances to Bangladesh were $15 billion in 2015, prompting some to say that sending workers abroad is "more valuable" in terms of generating foreign exchange than garments.[11]

---

[9] For details see: Braceros: History, Compensation, 2006. *Rural Migration News* 12(2) at https://migration.ucdavis.edu/rmn/more.php?id=1112.

[10] www.un.org/en/development/desa/policy/cdp/ldc_info.shtml.

[11] See the reports of the Centre for Policy Dialogue: http://cpd.org.bd/index.php/cpd-working-paper-112-advancing-the-interests-of-bangladeshs-migrant-workers-issues-of-financial-inclusion-and-social-protection/.

Workers going abroad are often breadwinners for their families, so most remittances replace earnings at home and are used for consumption. The fact that migrant workers are supporting their families from abroad helps to explain why remittances can remain stable even as exchange rates and investment outlooks change.[12] For example, migrants abroad can send more money if there is a health emergency or a natural disaster at home.

By earning more abroad than would have been earned at home, families receiving remittances have more income and can also save and invest. Many studies have documented the positive effects of remittances on the families receiving them (Ratha, 2005), including reduced poverty and increased spending on education and health care for children, especially when mothers are remitting from abroad or spending remittances at home (Pritchett, 2006). Children in remittance-receiving families often get more years of schooling than non-migrants, especially girls, and fare better on health measures. However, there is also the psychological cost of parents being separated from their children.

The record on migrant investments at home is more mixed, in part because many migrants are from areas that offer few opportunities for investments that can improve livelihoods over time. Remittances may encourage farm families to buy more farm equipment or vehicles, but such purchases may not raise farm productivity if breadwinners remain abroad. In some farming areas where men go abroad, remaining family members switch from crops to livestock and leave some farm land idle for lack of labor to farm.

Remittances can improve the lives of families receiving them, but may not speed the development of migrant-sending countries. An International Monetary Fund (IMF) paper concluded that remittances

> have contributed little to economic growth in remittance-receiving economies... the most persuasive evidence in support of this finding is the lack of a single example of a remittances success story: a country in which remittances-led growth contributed significantly to its development... no nation can credibly claim that remittances have funded or catalyzed significant economic development.   (Barajas et al., 2009)

There are several reasons for this pessimism about remittances transforming economies from poor to rich. The first is simple: the dramatic increase in global remittances and remittance flows may reflect better measurement rather than more money flowing to developing countries. Second, outmigration and remittances can keep entrenched elites in power and slow overall economic growth if the migration escape valve reduces pressure on governments to make the policy changes necessary for faster growth. The vice-president of Moldova, the

---

[12] Automatic stabilizers in developed countries, such as unemployment insurance, help to stabilize the flow of remittances to developing countries that have the same economic cycles as the countries in which their migrants work.

poorest country in Eastern Europe, was quoted in 2004 as saying that if young and ambitious Moldovans could not migrate to Russia and Eastern Europe to work, they may protest at home and force a then-communist dominated government to change its policies. Talani (2014) makes a similar point about vicious circles in North Africa, where outmigration of the most able who cannot get ahead at home allows corrupt elites to remain in power and block the fundamental reforms necessary for sustainable growth.

Remittances can also be a two-edged sword in narrower economic terms. Countries such as Moldova that send workers abroad need to develop other export industries to keep workers at home in the future. However, if remittances raise the value of the currencies of migrant-sending countries, exports can fall, displacing workers in export-oriented sectors and choking off their growth.

This is an example of Dutch disease: the rising value of the Dutch guilder after natural gas was discovered in the North Sea in the 1950s shrank the manufacturing sector and eliminated factory jobs. Many migrants are from countries with small export sectors, and the remittances that benefit migrant families may simultaneously hurt other families whose jobs depend on exporting manufacturing and agricultural goods that become more expensive as remittances drive up the value of the local currency (Acosta et al., 2009; Atoyan et al., 2016: 21).

A shrinking export sector and a higher share of the young and elderly among residents who depend on government programs can mean less tax revenue and more demand for government services. Governments must finance services for the elderly and children, and if they do so by raising taxes on ever fewer workers and their employers because many prime-aged workers are abroad, the economy's ability to produce goods and services competitively is reduced.

When a developing country produces workers for richer countries, the result can be a virtuous circle in which sending workers abroad in one period leads to stay-at-home development later, or a vicious circle in which villages turn into nurseries for children and nursing homes for the elderly that depend on external lifelines. There are examples of both virtuous and vicious circles between migration and development, suggesting skepticism when confronting assertions that migration speeds or slows development.

Migrants: Numbers versus Rights

The first priority of the ILO is the protection of migrant workers, while the first priority of the World Bank is speeding economic development. There is little guidance available to governments when these desirable goals conflict. Should governments first stress sending workers abroad, as the Philippines did in the

1970s and 1980s, and later stress protections for migrant workers, as the Filipino government did in the 1990s? Should governments give migrant protections and remittances equal priority at all times, or should migrant protections be prioritized?

Many government leaders cite the volume of remittances as a shorthand indicator of the value of migration to their countries. Some, including the Filipino and Mexican presidents, symbolically welcome home several returning migrants during holidays to remind those who did not migrate of the sacrifices and hard work abroad that earn remittances. Some governments tout the number of workers deployed, and announce "record deployments," but remittances are the usual reference for governments summarizing the impacts of migration. A common goal is to maximize remittances while minimizing complaints of migrant worker abuse and exploitation.

There is little advice available to migrant-sending governments when they are forced to choose between migrant numbers and migrant rights (Martin, 2011). When there is a civil war in the destination country that may require the government to rescue its citizens, they may try to stop their citizens from departing under the theory that the government may be required to later rescue them. But when the issue is more nuanced, such as whether women may go abroad to work in private homes, there can be a conflict between the individual rights of women to decide whether to work abroad and governments that want to "protect their women." Jones (2015: 4) reviewed the monitoring of recruitment in Asia and noted the "tension between . . . a reduction in exploitation of migrants and successful labor export programs" that measure success in terms of the number of workers deployed.

Migrant-receiving countries also face numbers and rights dilemmas that arise from the fact that migrant rights can cost taxpayers money. Countries with more low-skilled migrant workers, such as Gulf oil exporters and Singapore, afford migrant workers fewer rights than countries with fewer of them. One reason is that rights for low-skilled migrant workers may have costs financed by host-country taxes. If low-earning temporary migrant workers have access to social welfare programs, taxes on residents may have to be raised to cover the cost of the benefits they receive, which could increase opposition to the admission of such workers.

On the other hand, if employers are required to pay the same wages and benefits to low-skilled migrants as they do to similar local workers, the costs of migrants rise and the demand for them falls. In the Scandinavian countries that require employers to pay migrants the same wages as local workers and to provide migrants with the same work-related benefits as local workers, there are relatively few low-skilled migrant workers.

If rights impose costs on host-country taxpayers, then restricting the rights of low-skilled migrants may increase their economic benefits and open doors wider to them. Singapore's policy is explicit: low-skilled migrant workers are admitted to hold down the cost of non-tradable goods such as the construction of housing and to lower the cost of domestic work so that more Singaporean women can work for wages outside the home. Other countries are more circumspect, but most have policies that aim to ensure that low-skilled migrants leave when their jobs and contracts end, that is, low-skilled migrant workers are to be sojourners rather than settlers (Ruhs, 2013).

For high-skilled workers, there is an opposite positive relationship between rights and numbers. The US attracts more college-educated migrants than European countries because wages are often higher in the US, many US firms offer stock options, English is the language inside and outside the workplace, and most high-skilled temporary migrants are allowed to arrive with their families and eventually become immigrants.

When admissions of low- and high-skilled migrants and migrant rights are plotted, the result is an X-shape. The right or rising part of the X shows that, for *high-skilled* migrants, numbers and rights increase together, while the left or falling part shows that for *low-skilled* workers, numbers rise as rights fall. An example of high-skilled policies is the US versus Japan, and for the low-skilled Scandinavia versus Gulf oil exporters. The US allows most high-skilled migrants to arrive with their families and to adjust to immigrant status while they are temporary workers, while Japan has a less open door and consequently fewer high-skilled migrants. Similarly, if low-skilled migrant workers cost as much as local workers in Scandinavian countries, there will be fewer admitted there than in Gulf oil exporters, where low-skilled migrants are generally paid less than local workers.

The migrant numbers–rights trade-off is straightforward but often misunderstood, prompting two points of emphasis. First, the relationships between migrant numbers and migrant rights are empirical descriptions of government policies, not normative statements of what labor migration policies should be. Second, the falling part of the X in Figure 6.1 for low-skilled workers refers to *temporary* workers, not settler immigrants. It would be poor public policy to admit low-skilled migrants as settlers and deny them access to services that could speed their integration, a point missed in some critiques of the numbers–rights trade-off (Cummins and Rodriguez, 2010).

Openness to low-skilled migrant workers and rights for them are rarely discussed together. Some migrant-sending governments, UN agencies, and non-governmental organizations (NGOs) that deal with migrant rights discuss the need for more governments to ratify and implement ILO and UN conventions that protect migrants, while other agencies of the same governments may send negotiators to the World Trade Organizations (WTOs) or World Bank and urge migrant-receiving governments to open doors wider to migrant service providers by exempting their citizens from minimum wage and

Number of migrants

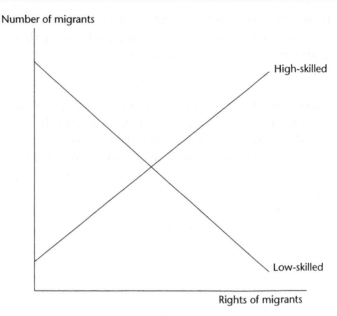

High-skilled

Low-skilled

Rights of migrants

Figure 6.1 Migrant numbers and migrant rights
Source: Author's own work.

work-related benefit programs to make them cheaper and to open up more opportunities for them.

The migrant numbers versus rights dilemma is apparent in General Agreement on Trade in Services (GATS) negotiations at the WTO. There are four major modes or ways to provide services across national borders: cross-border supply, consumption abroad, FDI or commercial presence, and Mode 4 migration, which the GATS refers to as the temporary movement of "natural persons." Unlike goods, services are often produced and consumed simultaneously, as with haircuts, and sometimes change consumers, as with medical services.

The major focus of GATS migration discussions is Mode 4 movements of service providers, who can be substitutes or complements to the other types of trade in services. For example, accountancy services can be provided online (Mode 1) rather than by sending an accountant abroad to audit financial statements (Mode 4); or the client could travel to the country where the service provider is located to receive services (Mode 2). Similarly, an IT service provider could visit a client abroad (Mode 4) or provide services to foreign clients via the internet (Mode 1).

Developing countries led by India want GATS negotiations to liberalize Mode 4 movements of service providers. They aim to persuade WTO member countries to reduce barriers to service providers from other WTO member countries by opening all sectors to foreign service providers with horizontal commitments, the norm in WTO Mode 4 commitments, so that migrant-sending countries do not have to determine which sectors are open to Mode 4 migrants. However, many Mode 4 commitments are unbound, meaning no opening, or they provide partial opening, as when they are unbound but accompanied by an "except for" list of occupations closed to migrants, for example when teachers are admitted but public school teachers must be citizens. The most extensive GATS free-movement commitments are for business visitors and intra-corporate transfers (Martin, 2006a).

Developing countries seek concessions or commitments from richer countries in four major areas in order to increase flows of migrant service providers. First, they want industrial countries to eliminate the economic needs tests often used to determine whether employers truly "need" foreign workers. Economic needs tests usually require employers to search for and fail to find local workers while offering at least government-set minimum wages in order to receive permission to recruit migrants. Failure to find local workers results in a certification of the need for migrant workers, usually from the Ministry of Labor, and this certification allows the Foreign Ministry to issue a visa to the foreigner specified by the employer.

Second, developing countries want migrant-receiving countries to expedite the issuance of visas and work permits, preferably by creating one-stop shops that bring together all relevant government agencies and establish timelines for action. Many migrant-sending countries want their GATS partners to process requests for foreigners quickly, and to develop appeals procedures for employers and foreigners whose requests for visas and work permits are denied.

Third, developing countries want the richer migrant-receiving countries to which most migrants move to facilitate the recognition of credentials earned at home, and to ensure that any necessary licenses needed to work in the host country are issued in a timely fashion. In this way, migrant-sending countries hope that their citizens can quickly obtain the recognition and licenses often required to work abroad.

Fourth, many migrant-sending countries want destination countries to exempt their citizens from participating in work-related benefit programs and the taxes that finance them. If destination countries exempt the wages paid to migrant service providers from the payroll taxes that finance pensions, unemployment, and other work-related programs, migrants and their employers would save the 20 to 40 percent that such taxes typically add to wages. Lower labor costs associated with migrants could, in turn, encourage employers to prefer to hire migrant service providers.

Each of these issues has a numbers versus rights component, as highlighted by the debate over whether migrant service providers should be required to receive at least the minimum wage in the destination country. Chaudhuri et al. (2004) emphasize that requiring migrant service providers to be paid minimum or wages equal to local workers in host countries may reduce the number who find jobs in them: "Wage-parity...is intended to provide a nondiscriminatory environment, [but] tends to erode the cost advantage of hiring foreigners and works like a de facto quota." Another Indian economist asserted that requiring equal wages for migrant and local workers "negates the very basis of cross-country labor flows, which stems from endowment-based cost differentials between countries" (Chanda, 2001: 635).

The tension between migrant numbers and migrant rights is difficult to resolve. UN agencies and governments that see migration as a shortcut to development want more doors opened to migrant workers, which is why they want to ease access and lower the costs of migrants to employers. To ensure that migrants depart at the end of their contracts, some World Bank economists have proposed that migrants post bonds before departure that would be forfeited if they fail to return. They reason that assuring migrant-receiving countries that migrants will not settle would persuade them to open doors wider to low-skilled migrants (Schiff, 2004).

Migrant rights groups, on the other hand, often highlight the low wages and poor working conditions of low-skilled migrant workers. They see migrant workers as victims of broader forces, from unequal development to climate change, and believe that people "forced" to cross national borders to work need protections from the many who would take advantage of them. Migrant advocates urge governments not to tie migrant workers to particular employers (Fudge, 2011), even though the rationale for admitting low-skilled migrants is to fill particular job vacancies, not to admit migrants to float around in the labor market.

The participants on the two sides of the numbers versus rights debates often perceive migrants very differently. Are most migrants rational economic actors who willingly trade fewer rights abroad for higher wages, as imagined by those who believe that larger numbers and more remittances should have higher priority, or are most migrants victims who deserve special protections after crossing borders, as the rights-oriented groups believe? The ILO wants to protect all workers, including migrants, and emphasizes that treating migrants equally helps to protect local workers from "unfair migrant competition." Some rights-oriented groups would go further, arguing for additional rights for migrants and their families because of the nature of the forces pushing and pulling them over national borders.

Closing Regulatory Gaps

Most meetings that discuss recruiters and migrant workers end with a call for more countries to ratify and implement ILO and UN conventions that protect migrant workers. Ratifications are a convenient scorecard, but their number may have little relationship to effective migrant worker protections because ratification by a country's government is simply the first step in a long process of implementation. After ratification, international conventions must be turned into national laws, and these national laws must be enforced effectively. In many countries, there is protective legislation covering migrant workers but little effective implementation.

The best protection from abusive recruiters and employers in all countries and at all times is giving workers the power to say no to high recruiter fees, false promises, and low wages. A worker's power to say no is greatest when there are decent wages and working conditions at home, so that economic development that gives workers decent jobs at home also gives them the power to protect themselves from abusive recruiters. Until then, what are the major regulatory gaps in government efforts to regulate recruiters, and how can they be reduced?

There are three major regulatory responses to recruiter violations of protective labor laws. First, governments establish penalties for violations and create new violations and penalties in response to specific cases of abuse. Second, governments may develop incentives for compliance, such as giving awards to "good" recruiters. Third, governments can change the framework of the recruiting industry by establishing government agencies that compete with private recruiters or have a monopoly on sending workers to particular destinations.

The first line of defense against abusive recruiters involves penalties for violations of recruitment regulations. Governments normally follow a three-step procedure to regulate recruiters, beginning with a requirement that they identify themselves by obtaining licenses and pass tests and post bonds to maintain licenses. Government agencies may inspect recruiters and solicit complaints to ensure that recruiters are in compliance with regulations, and mete out penalties for violations.

In practice, most applicants for recruiter licenses receive them; there are relatively few worker complaints filed with government agencies, and most complaints are settled privately between the complaining worker and the recruiter before a government agency makes a final determination that could result in loss of the recruitment license. Some governments issue recruitment licenses for only a year at a time under the theory that renewals provide an opportunity to check on the recruiter. However, frequent renewals may do more to discourage recruiters from developing partnerships with employers abroad that could lower costs over time rather than weed out bad recruiters.

For example, between 1992 and 2002, the Philippine Overseas Employment Administration (POEA) filed 650 cases against Filipino recruiters, but only sixty-six were recommended for criminal prosecution and resulted in a conviction, about 10 percent, a result attributed to the reluctance of many migrants to testify against recruiters and the inefficiency of the court system (Martin, 2006b: 17). The experience is similar in other countries. Workers may file complaints, but many are withdrawn or languish in administrative or court proceedings (Barauh, 2006).

The second option induces recruiters to comply with laws and regulations by providing incentives, such as rewarding compliance with benefits that range from lower fees and faster processing to symbolic awards. The third option is competition—as when foreign employers can recruit workers directly or utilize public agencies to move workers over borders—or creating monopolies that permit only public agencies to recruit, screen, and deploy migrant workers to employers abroad.

Regulating recruiters via penalties is problematic for several reasons. First, most recruiters are small, so that many inspectors are required to check effectively on diverse small businesses that may have many of their assets in the heads of owners and key employees rather than in an easy-to-understand bookkeeping system. When inspectors visit agencies from which there have been no complaints, exactly what do they look for? Do local laws require recruiters to keep records and allow inspectors to review them in the absence of complaints?

In some countries, there are enough complaints to keep inspectors busy so they do not have time to check on agencies without complaints. Worker complaints prompt inspectors to target particular recruiters, but the recruiter can often make the complaint disappear by giving the complaining worker what he/she wants, a foreign job. Experience in many countries with "good" regulatory and enforcement regimes demonstrates that many and often most complaints made against recruiters are withdrawn by workers. If recruiters learn that they can persuade workers to withdraw complaints, they may be tempted to violate regulations, hope that aggrieved workers do not complain, and deal privately with those who do, creating the exact opposite of the compliance regime desired.

Third, the penalty structure for recruiters can be problematic. For example, if one complaint prompts the government to stop processing all applications from a particular recruiter, workers may try to blackmail recruiters by filing complaints in order to get abroad quicker. On the other hand, if a complaint leads to an investigation and a hearing in which the government or a worker presents evidence and the recruiter responds, the recruiter can stay in business for months or years while fending off significant penalties. The complaining worker may be at a disadvantage in such areas if he or she is from a rural area and the recruiter and hearing are held in the capital city. If the hearing results in the worker being restored to the economic position he or she would have had before the recruiter violation, that is, if there are no fines or punitive damages, there is little deterrent effect from completed enforcement cases, since the penalty for the recruiter is to do what should have been done in the first place.

Regulatory gaps coupled with complexity allow recruiters to charge high fees to migrants. It can also be difficult for migrants to seek effective resolution of their complaints. Migrants must be able to file complaints with appropriate authorities. In many countries, NGOs help migrants to file complaints; without their assistance, it can be very difficult to set the complaint system in motion. Migrants often lack documentation of promises made by and fees paid to recruiters, making it hard to conduct investigations and impose penalties for violations.

7

Recruiter Incentives and Alternatives

This chapter begins with a review of options available to governments to induce recruiters to comply with protective laws and regulations, using the carrot of economic benefits such as codes of conduct and taxes and subsidies. It then turns to the evidence of the effectiveness of bottom-up enforcement, the normal process under which governments enact protective laws and regulations and rely on agency staff to enforce them, often in response to problems identified after workers file complaints.

Regulating recruiters is often a "wicked problem," one that is hard to define, ever changing, and defying easy solutions. Recruiters may act as gatekeepers to higher-wage jobs abroad, and use their control over foreign jobs to extract payments from workers. Governments try to keep maximum payments to recruiters below what workers are willing to pay, which means that overpayments are a form of "victimless crime" in the sense that workers who pay more than government-set maximums get what they want, a foreign job offering higher wages. This makes workers reluctant to complain, and when they do it is often because the recruiter did not send them abroad quickly. Recruiters can encourage workers to withdraw complaints by moving them to the front of the queue and sending them abroad.

The chapter next turns to the promises and pitfalls of bilateral labor agreements (BLAs), an alternative to private recruiters. The Korean Employment Permit System, the Canadian Seasonal Agricultural Worker Program, and Australian and New Zealand Pacific Island seasonal worker programs are often touted as best-practice models of programs to move workers over borders at minimal cost to migrants. They share the characteristic of having multiple goals, including filling vacant jobs in receiving countries, protecting workers during recruitment, and promoting development in migrant countries of origin. All these BLAs are subsidized from foreign aid and similar budgets, which may contribute to their effectiveness in comparison to BLAs that have proven more troublesome, including the Mexico–US Bracero agreements between

1942 and 1964 and the more recent Bangladesh–Malaysia and Burma, Cambodia, and Laos–Thai BLAs that focus primarily on filling vacant jobs.

Inducing Good Behavior

One way to strengthen migrant worker protections is to provide incentives for recruiters to comply with protective labor laws. These incentives can be symbolic, such as rewarding recruiters who agree to abide by a code of conduct and have no adjudicated complaints against them with a seal of approval that they can use to attract foreign employers or local workers. Alternatively, economically significant compliance incentives, such as lower fees for government services, preferred access to foreign job offers or local workers seeking jobs, and allowing A-rated recruiters to certify that they have followed government regulations, can persuade recruiters to abide by worker protection laws.

Most businesses have systems to ensure that employees strive to achieve the firm's goals, such as producing safe and useful products as efficiently as possible. Other systems promote compliance with government regulations on taxes, safety, and labor. Compliance depends on systems and audits. Systems acknowledge the importance of compliance to the firm, establish protocols to prevent problems or violations, and educate supervisors and workers on how to implement them consistently. Internal- and third-party audits, as well as internal complaint mechanisms, ensure that the protocols are being followed and help firms to avoid penalties for violations.

Codes of Conduct

Codes of conduct that include a requirement that participants abide by all relevant labor laws may induce compliance by recruiters. The International Confederation of Private Employment Agencies (CIETT) has a 10-point code of conduct that calls on recruiters to "comply with all relevant legislation, statutory and non-statutory requirements and official guidance covering Private Employment Agencies [PEAs]" (#2). PEAs or recruiters should "not charge, directly or indirectly ... any fees or costs to jobseekers and workers, for the services directly related to temporary assignment or permanent placement" (#4).[1]

CIETT is most active in industrial countries with significant temporary help industries, and includes as corporate members most of the major temp staffing

---

[1] CIETT spells out its agreement with the International Labour Organization (ILO), the International Organization for Migration (IOM), and other multinational efforts to improve recruitment and combat forced labor at www.ciett.org/index.php?id=45.

firms, from Adecco to Manpower. CIETT members in industrial countries and in major migrant-sending countries such as the Philippines are mostly temp staffing agencies that provide local workers to local businesses, as when Manpower sends employees to factories and offices for assignments that range in duration from weeks to months.

Temp staffing firms rarely charge fees to the workers they send to temporary jobs, but temp workers often earn lower wages than the permanent staff with whom they work, that is, temp workers pay for temp agency services in the form of lower wages rather than upfront fees (Luo et al., 2010). Temp employment is growing in most industrial and in many developing countries, as firms that face an uncertain demand for their goods and services prefer to hire easy-to-lay off temps rather than regular or permanent employees.

In the US, the average employment of temp firms rose from a million in 1990 or 1 percent of wage and salary employment to three million or over 2 percent of wage and salary employment by 2015.[2] The US temporary help services industry, the North American Industry Classification System (NAICS) (code 561320) employed almost three million workers in May 2015, including 600,000 laborers and material movers and 600,000 office and administrative support services workers.[3] Temp employees are paid lower wages than the "regular" employees with whom they work because of the fees charged by the temp agency to the business.

CIETT and the multinational temp agencies that dominate its ranks have worked closely with the ILO to implement a Fair Recruitment Initiative (FRI) based on Convention 181. The goals of the FRI are to prevent forced labor and human trafficking, protect migrant workers during the recruitment process, and reduce the cost of international labor migration and enhance migration's development outcomes.[4] CIETT members do not charge workers to avoid "situations of abuse, human trafficking and forced labor."[5] CIETT member recruiters may lawfully pay lower wages to the workers they place in jobs than regular employees, so long as they pay at least minimum wages, so that temp agency workers pay for recruitment services in the form of lower wages rather than upfront fees.

The ILO in 2016 published thirteen general principles and operational guidelines for fair recruitment for governments, employers, and recruiters. Their general principle is that "no recruitment fees or related costs should be charged to, or otherwise borne by, workers or job seekers," and is reinforced by

---

[2] Two-thirds of US temp firm employees are in three occupational groups: office and administrative support, transportation and material moving, and production occupations, often in manufacturing and especially in the southeastern US.

[3] Detailed data on temp employees is at http://www.bls.gov/oes/current/naics5_561320.htm.

[4] The FRI is described at www.ilo.org/global/topics/fair-recruitment/lang–en/index.htm.

[5] See: http://www.wecglobal.org/index.php?id=45.

operational guideline 6 (ILO, 2016a, #7). Another general principle says that "migrant workers should not require the employer's or recruiter's permission to change employers" (#12).

Some codes of conduct focus on recruiters who move workers over national borders. The IOM's International Recruitment Integrity System (IRIS) aims "to bring transformational change to part of the international [recruitment] industry" by encouraging recruiters to subscribe to twelve principles, from respect for laws (#2) to charging no recruitment fees for jobseekers (#4).

IRIS is voluntary, with participating recruiters allowed to have their businesses listed on an IOM-operated portal accessible to employers who post jobs and workers seeking jobs who post their qualifications (http://iris.iom.int/about-iris). Participating recruiters must agree to be "assessed" by a rating agency before they are allowed to post job openings. IRIS promises to help recruiters who want to post job offers but are not in compliance to achieve compliance and earn IRIS certification. IRIS has been in development for several years, but had not yet launched in 2016.

The Dhaka Principles for the Responsible Recruitment and Employment of Migrant Workers were developed by the Institute for Human Rights and Business (IHRB) and launched in June 2011 with the support of multinationals such as Nike who have goods assembled for them in factories in Asian countries, some of which hire migrant workers. The ten Dhaka principles call for no worker-paid recruitment fees, written contracts that workers understand, lawful wages paid on time, safe and decent work, and the right of workers to retain their passports and other documents (http://www.dhaka-principles.org).

The IHRB asks business leaders to require their suppliers to refrain from charging workers fees in order to get jobs. As with most codes that are imposed by buyers on their supply chains, the key to the effectiveness of the Dhaka Principles is monitoring to ensure compliance. The IHRB's Leadership Group for Responsible Recruitment has embraced the employer pays principle: "no worker should pay for a job—the costs of recruitment should be borne not by the worker but by the employer."[6] Note that this employer pays principle says nothing about workers paying for jobs in the form of lower wages after they are hired.

Many recruiter codes of conduct are industry and occupation specific, such as the World Health Organization's (WHO) 2010 Global Code of Practice on the International Recruitment of Health Personnel (www.who.int/hrh/migration/code/practice/en). The 15-page voluntary WHO code, mostly concerned with avoiding the exit of too many health-care workers from developing

---

[6] www.ihrb.org/focus-areas/migrant-workers/new-model-migrant-worker-recruitment.

countries, calls on Member States in Section 5.1 to "discourage active recruitment of health personnel from developing countries facing critical shortages of health workers." There are also codes of conduct for recruiters of domestic workers,[7] seafarers, and other occupations.

The International Labor Recruitment Transparency Project (http://www. recruitmenttransparency.org) takes a different approach, extracting data provided by employers and recruiters seeking certification to employ low-skilled migrant workers in the US and inviting workers, non-governmental organizations (NGOs), and others to rate employers and recruiters. The goal of this project is to allow users to flag abuses that range from employers withholding documents to failure to pay wages. The project faces a chicken and egg problem in the sense that there are few ratings of employers and recruiters, which gives potential workers little reason to turn to the website for information.

Codes of conduct generally work best where they are needed least. The recruiters most likely to abide by codes of conduct are those that already satisfy all or most of the principles and can adhere to the code of conduct at little additional cost. Proponents of codes of conduct hope that their seal of approval will help compliant recruiters to increase their business, so that market transactions will favor compliant recruiters over time.

An important presumption of codes of conduct is that foreign employers want to deal with good recruiters and have trouble identifying them, so that the code's seal or listing generates more job offers for good recruiters. Large-scale international labor migration is at least three decades old, and there are few examples of market forces "raising the bar" in recruitment by having employers favor recruiters with seals of approval from certifying organizations.

Many organizations want recruiters to do more than comply with labor laws in order to be certified. However, codes of conduct are often written in elastic ways that can be hard to interpret in concrete cases. The IRIS prohibitions on recruiting child labor and charging fees to jobseekers are straightforward, but what is IRIS's call for recruiters to have respect for decent work or to engage in transparent recruitment? How should such phrases be interpreted in particular cases?

Many developing countries have decent work plans to ensure that all workers have jobs that are safe and pay living wages. Many of these plans express an aspiration, since most workers in such countries lack decent jobs. For example, the ILO's Decent Work Country Programme for Nepal for 2013–17 calls for "promoting well-managed labor migration from Nepal...improving recruitment services by working with the government and private sector." The

---

[7] For details of the effort in Lebanon see: www.ilo.org/beirut/events/WCMS_241034/lang–en/index.htm. For seafarers in the Philippines, see: www.gmanetwork.com/news/story/269835/news/pinoyabroad/to-protect-pinoy-workers-recruitment-agencies-adopt-code-of-ethics.

performance indicators are new and modified laws and regulations and the adoption of gender-sensitive policies, not empirical measures of migrants obtaining decent jobs at home or abroad (ILO, 2014a: 15).

Translating codes of conduct into action items that can be audited is difficult. For example, if codes of conduct require complaint systems, who handles complaints and evaluates whether the remedies are fair and are implemented? Collective bargaining agreements (CBAs) are codes of conduct negotiated between employers and unions, and they often contain very detailed language spelling out rights and responsibilities and grievance and arbitration mechanisms to resolve complaints. The number of complaints about particular provisions in a CBA may serve as a guide to items that are renegotiated in subsequent CBAs. If CBAs are a model, recruiter codes of conduct must become far more detailed, have robust complaint and implementation mechanisms, and be adjusted to deal with recurring problems.

Codes of conduct can be defensive or offensive efforts to preserve or gain market share. Many are *defensive*. For example, food safety codes of conduct were largely a defensive reaction to illnesses and deaths linked to tainted produce that reduced the demand and prices for all producers of a commodity, that is, mistakes by one grower create the externality of lower prices for all growers (Martin, 2016). Similarly, codes of conduct in the Bangladeshi garment industry were defensive, aimed at preserving sewing orders and jobs despite unsafe sewing factories that led to many worker deaths.[8] Bangladeshi codes helped manufacturers to stay in business, preserving jobs for the women who dominate the workforces of the sewing factories. When non-compliant producers impose negative externalities on an entire sector, the defensive response is collective action to produce safe food or make factories safer.

Most codes of conduct in international labor recruitment are *offensive* efforts to increase demand for the services of good recruiters. The theory behind offensive codes is that many foreign employers want to use good recruiters, but have difficulty finding them, an information gap overcome by the certifying organization. However, it is not clear how much unmet employer demand there is for "good recruiters," and how hard it would be for foreign employers who want to deal with good recruiters to find them. The emergence of IRIS and other voluntary codes of conduct will help to determine whether

---

[8] The eight-story Rana Plaza building in Savar that housed five sewing factories collapsed April 24, 2013, killing over a third of the 3,000 workers who made clothes for export, the deadliest accident in the history of the garment industry. Structural flaws in the building were discovered on April 23, 2013, prompting the closing of some ground-floor businesses but not the sewing factories on the upper floors, which had heavy generators to provide electricity during regular brownouts. Bangladesh exported clothing worth $18 billion in 2012 from 5,000 factories that employed four million workers. With garments 80 percent of Bangladeshi manufacturing exports, the government worked with the garment-sewing industry to develop a code of conduct to preserve jobs. See: https://migration.ucdavis.edu/mn/more.php?id=3851.

there is an unmet demand from employers for recruiters who abide by codes that call for obeying the laws needed to obtain and retain government licenses, and perhaps going beyond them to protect the migrant workers they deploy.

Systems to ensure compliance with laws and codes are often more important than audits, which are snapshots of compliance at a particular time and place. The goal of compliance systems is motion picture compliance at all times. An audit snapshot that results in certification for two or three years does not mean that the recruiter or employer is always in compliance, especially if audits are announced beforehand or workers are coached on what to say to auditors.

Compliance sometimes has a pass–fail quality, but it can be just as important to know if a firm or recruiter scored 54 or 74 points on a scale on which 75 points means compliance. Both are failing scores, but the 74 points indicates almost in compliance, while the 54 suggests many violations. In labor law compliance, inspectors may cite recruiters for violations of laws that are easy to police, such as whether the recruiter has required insurance and bonds, rather than more complex violations that may be difficult to prove because of incomplete records that would require additional investigator time to resolve. In other words, the violations cited by inspectors under time pressure may not reflect all violations.[9]

Agunias (2013) proposes a hybrid code of conduct and a ranking system for recruiters. Government regulators could rank recruiters by criteria that include efficiency and compliance, such as number of workers sent abroad the previous year and the number of complaints against recruiters that were upheld by authorities. Agunias also urged formalization of the often informal means by which recruiters find workers, such as regulating the subagents who travel between rural villages to find workers willing to go abroad.

Requiring subagents and others in the networks between licensed recruiters and workers to register with the government could be problematic because of their diversity. Some subagents are returned migrants, while others are professionals such as teachers and doctors; most in both groups refer workers to

---

[9] These observations are based on work with the US Department of Labor's (DOL) Wage and Hour Division (WHD), which enforces federal labor laws. WHD has 1,000 investigators who recovered $247 million in back wages for 240,000 workers in FY15 (October 1, 2014 through Sepember 30, 2015). Most investigations are triggered by worker complaints, but WHD is trying to increase compliance in industries where violations are common, including agriculture, construction, and restaurants, with agency-initiated or targeted inspections.

Investigators face real trade-offs. When DOL found what appeared to be very high worker earnings at Oregon blueberry farms, it accused the farms of having ghost employees, workers who helped the very fast pickers. DOL threatened to place a "hot goods" hold on harvested blueberries unless the growers admitted to having ghost employees. They did, and then sued to recover the money. A federal judge agreed with the growers that DOL "unfairly stacked the deck" against them, and voided their DOL fines, highlighting the difficulty of enforcing labor laws that protect low-skilled workers. See: https://migration.ucdavis.edu/rmn/more.php?id=1837.

licensed recruiters on a part-time basis. It may be possible to register and monitor full-time subagents who recruit for a particular recruiter, but they may be a small minority of on-the-ground recruiters. Just as governments may want to distinguish professional "scalpers" who regularly buy tickets to popular events and seek to sell them for more than face value from those who occasionally scalp extra tickets, so it is likely to be difficult to distinguish regular from occasional subagents.

During the 1990s, when the unemployment rate in Midwestern states was below 3 percent and meatpackers were searching for workers for their "disassembly lines," Iowa enacted a Non-English-Speaking Employees Law that required workers recruited from more than 500 miles away to sign a document in their language that spelled out the job and wages. If the employee quit the job within four weeks of arriving in Iowa, the employer was responsible for paying return transportation. The law was often called the IBP law after the state's then largest meatpacker, which was constantly searching for new workers to replace those who quit (Grey, 1996).

The 1991 bill failed for several reasons. First, IBP did not recruit out-of-state workers directly. Instead, IBP offered $250 to *anyone* who referred a worker who was hired and stayed in the job at least 2 months, whether the recruiter was a current employee or a full- or part-time recruiter. Workers showed up at IBP and were hired, and their referring agent received the payment from IBP after the new employee worked the minimum required time. Second, employers were exempt from paying return transportation if they fired the worker rather than waiting until the worker quit, giving employers an incentive to terminate poor performers.

Economic Incentives

Codes of conduct may provide economic incentives for recruiters to obey labor laws if they generate more business, but economic benefits in the form of lower costs may do more to encourage recruiter compliance with protective laws. There are two types of economic incentives that could improve recruiter behavior, micro and macro, although the lines between them can be blurred. Micro-incentives affect individual recruiters, while macro-incentives affect the recruitment industry.

Micro-incentives to influence recruiter behavior fall into three major categories—costs, taxes, and publicity. Good or A-rated recruiters could pay lower fees and or receive faster government processing of the paperwork required to send workers abroad; A-rated recruiters can be granted tax exemptions and tax credits; and A-rated recruiters can receive awards that generate more business. If such incentives raise revenues more than any increased costs, recruiters have incentives to achieve and maintain compliant or A-ratings.

The first cost savings could come from the government agencies that regulate recruiters and handle approvals to deploy workers abroad. The staff in these agencies often know the recruiters who are submitting worker contracts for approval. Analysts often have informal systems to distinguish recruiters who are likely to be in full compliance from those who are not. Making this informal rating system explicit would offer an incentive for recruiters to earn and maintain an A-rating that provided economic benefits, since A-rated recruiters could be charged lower fees to reflect the savings in agency staff time.

There are two issues with ABC rating systems: what criteria must be satisfied to earn an A-rating, and what benefits accrue to recruiters with an A-rating. For example, one way to determine which recruiters deserve an A-rating is to require them to be in business at least 2 years and to have no valid complaints filed against them. Over time, A-rated recruiters could be allowed to skip some steps in the deployment process. For example, if they use a standard contract that was approved by the government, the workers they deploy could skip in-person checks of contracts, saving workers the cost of traveling to the capital city for pre-departure contract checks. Most recruiters would have a B-rating, and would be treated as they currently are, accompanying migrants to government agencies for contract checks. C-rated recruiters would be subject to close scrutiny, and could be charged extra fees to cover the cost of processing their contracts and workers.

The second micro-incentive could function via the tax system. A-rated recruiters could be exempted from value-added taxes (VAT) on their revenues and taxes on their profits. Recruiters who send workers to foreign jobs that pay more than destination country minimum wages, or who satisfy similar criteria, could receive subsidies from the government, just as foreign investors sometimes receive subsidies and tax holidays in exchange for investments that create jobs and bring new technologies into a country. Since labor migration provides jobs, generates remittances, and can result in the return of workers with new skills and ambitions, the same rationale that justifies government assistance to foreign investors can also justify subsidies and tax breaks for recruiters.

The third incentive channel through which governments can recognize individual recruiters is with awards and recognition. Awards can raise the profile of good recruiters, helping them to obtain more business as they are recognized at public events. A-rated recruiters can accompany the country's leaders abroad, just as business people often accompany government delegations to sell their goods. Receiving the implicit endorsement of government leaders abroad can help recruiters to gain business, especially with public-sector foreign employers. Recruiters can also gain credibility with workers at home as desirable intermediaries. Table 7.1 summarizes these micro-incentives.

Macro-incentives and policies can reshape the recruitment industry and its relationships with employers and workers by favoring larger over smaller

Table 7.1 Micro- and macro-incentives for recruiters

Micro	Action	Justification	Impact
Cost savings	Charge A-rated recruiters lower fees & allow them to skip some procedures	A-rated recruiters abide by laws and regs and impose lower costs on gov. staff	Provides an incentive for recruiters to earn and maintain A-rating
Taxes	Exempt A-rated recruiters from some taxes	Migration promotes development, so A-rated recruiters should receive the same benefits as others that speed development	Could provide significant economic incentives to earn and maintain A-rating
Awards	Awards for A-rated recruiters that can be used to attract more business	Awards are similar to codes of conduct that aim to help A-recruiters earn more business	Accompanying gov. leaders abroad can introduce A-recruiters to "good" employers, including gov.-linked employers
Macro			
Consolidation	Favor fewer & larger recruiters to achieve economies of scale & increase efficiency of regulation	Comprehensive recruiters can be one-stop shops that offer training and skills certification, and on return certify skills earned abroad	Comprehensive recruiters can develop operating procedures to ensure compliance; violations hurt their reputation
Direct recruitment	Allow foreign employers to recruit workers directly rather than via recruiting agencies that must be owned by citizens	Can remove a layer in the migration process that adds to worker-paid costs	Foreign employers would likely send hiring managers familiar with local workers' skills and the requirements of the job abroad
Favor recruiter–employer partnerships	Favor stable partnerships between foreign employers and particular recruiters by *not* posting all job offers so that all recruiters compete to fill them	Stable partnerships allow both parties to invest and recoup their investments with more placements over time	An example is seafarers, with shipping companies and recruiters investing in schools and training to desired standards

Source: Author's assessment (see chapter text, pp. 142–4).

recruiters, permitting foreign employers to recruit workers directly, and encouraging long-term partner relationships between employers and recruiters rather than short-term agent transactions. Larger recruiters can achieve economies of scale that lower their costs per worker deployed, can develop market power and avoid destructive competition that allows foreign employers to charge recruiters for jobs, and can become comprehensive one-stop shops for employers and migrants, offering everything from training for foreign jobs and skills certification to placement in foreign jobs and handling travel arrangements.

Comprehensive recruiters can develop standard procedures for preparing workers for departure and maintain contact with them while they are employed abroad. As workers abroad near the end of their contracts, recruiters can remind them of end-of-contract and other benefits they have earned and certify any skills acquired abroad for future local or foreign employers. Fewer and larger recruiters are easier for regulatory agencies to monitor.

Many migrant-sending governments require foreign employers to use local-citizen recruiters to find workers, that is, they prohibit foreign employers from recruiting their citizens directly. Foreign employers of highly skilled workers usually travel to the country and interview candidates that a local recruiter has assembled before selecting workers. Employers usually pay for the services of a local recruiter to assemble skilled workers for selection because of the value of having good worker–job matches.

Foreign employers rarely travel to interview low-skilled migrants, meeting them in most cases when they arrive at the workplace. This allows recruiters to send workers who are willing to pay for jobs rather than those who are most qualified. If foreign employers could recruit workers directly, they would likely send hiring managers familiar with workers in the sending country to interview and select workers at job fairs and other venues. Direct hiring could improve job placement outcomes if hiring managers in the destination know more than local recruiters about the work to be performed abroad and the capabilities of the workers being interviewed.

Finally, migrant-sending governments can favor stable employer–recruiter relationships that allow both employers and recruiters to invest in training and deployment. This is what occurs in seafaring, where shipping companies contribute to training schools operated by the manning companies from whom they recruit workers. Both parties benefit, as shipping companies approve the curriculum and know that graduates are trained seafarers, while recruiters recoup their investment in training by making many placements over time. The result can be win–win–win, as workers pay low fees for training and placement, recruiters earn modest but steady returns, and shipping companies get trained workers.

Several recruiters have developed, often with the support of foundations, no-fee agencies to deploy low-skill workers. FSI Worldwide (www.fsi-worldwide.com) began as a specialist recruiter of Nepalese security guards and broadened into a provider of workers to fill jobs in maritime and service occupations as a no-fee recruiter, which won FSI a Business Leaders Award to Fight Human Trafficking at the World Economic Forum in 2013, a year during which FSI placed about 2,000 workers from Nepal, Kenya, and India in Afghanistan and Iraq as well as United Arab Emirates (UAE) and the UK. FSI does not collect money from the workers it places in foreign jobs, even if migrant-sending country laws allow fees from workers. FSI uses its own staff rather than agents on commission throughout the recruitment and deployment process and audits its offices and staff regularly to detect cases of staff accepting payments from workers. CEO Tristan Forster, who spent 12 years with Nepali Gurkhas, argues that the three I's of *insist* on no fees, *invest* in staff, and *inspect* to avoid corruption, increases the productivity of the migrants that FSI places in foreign jobs (IOM, 2013).

The Fair Hiring Initiative (FHI) (www.fairhiringinitiative.com) aims to send domestic Filipino workers abroad at no cost to the worker. FHI believes that ethical recruitment systems in which employers pay all recruitment fees will improve worker productivity abroad, but has struggled to obtain large numbers of job offers. Gordon (2015: 52) notes that "good recruiters" such as FSI and FHI "struggle to stay in business because they must compete with other recruiters who do not adhere to the same high standards," and recommends pressure on employers to use only ethical recruiters as a strategy to improve the recruitment industry.

Bottom-up Enforcement via Complaints

Codes of conduct and economic incentives such as A-ratings, tax advantages, and awards are top-down approaches to improving recruiter compliance with laws and regulations that protect migrant workers. An alternative to top-down incentives is the current bottom-up approach of enforcement to maintain compliance with protective laws and regulations, as when worker complaints lead to penalties that induce lawful recruiter behavior.

Numerous studies have documented the difficulties facing migrants who complain about recruiters in migrant-sending countries, and most conclude there is little justice for aggrieved migrants (Paoletti et al., 2014; Farbenblum et al., 2013; IOM, 2016). These studies call on governments to redouble their efforts to enact and enforce protective laws (Jones, 2015). The IOM (2016) study is typical, ending with eleven recommendations that include rating recruiters based on a code of conduct, requiring recruiters to undergo training, regulating subagents, reducing litigation costs for workers who file complaints against recruiters, and making foreign employers jointly liable with recruiters for recruiter violations of regulations.

Laws and regulations to protect migrant workers from abusive recruiters that are developed with the help of international organizations may satisfy international norms, but their enforcement can be ineffective for reasons that range from workers not knowing about their rights to slow adjudicative procedures that favor recruiters over migrants. In some cases, international organizations urge governments to remove side doors that save workers money but evade government checks of contracts and pre-departure orientations aimed at informing and protecting workers, making the judgment that these protective steps justify their cost to workers.

There are three major reasons why worker complaints do not lead to enforcement that induces changes in recruiter behavior. First, low-skilled migrants often lack documents to prove recruiter violations, since they are not accustomed to operating in a world of contracts and receipts. Many find it hard to navigate complaint procedures, which often require paperwork to document violations and evidence. Second, migrants who have borrowed money to go abroad may be reluctant to borrow more to hire a lawyer in the hope of getting back some of their money, especially if they lack receipts and other evidence. Third, recruiters can encourage migrants to withdraw their complaints by settling privately with them, often paying only some of what the migrant demanded. If migrants file complaints, and the recruiter prepares a defense, the migrant may accept half of what he or she feels is owed rather than waiting for several years for first decisions and appeals.

Migrants would make more complaints, and recruiters would be more inclined to obey laws and regulations, if there were effective enforcement. However, it is hard to overemphasize the social differences between low-skilled migrants and the recruiters, government agency staff, and adjudicators from whom they seek redress. Low-skilled migrants from rural areas are "different" from the city-based people they must deal with to go abroad, including recruiters and those who regulate them. Many migrants begin the complaint process believing that the deck is stacked against them, a major factor that encourages settlement or abandonment of complaints.

Most reports on the recruitment industry in migrant-sending countries end with a list of recommendations (Gordon, 2015; Farbenblum et al., 2013; Jones, 2015; Paoletti et al., 2014), including decentralization of government agencies, so that rural migrants do not have to travel to the capital city or regional centers to press their complaints. Other recommendations would allow government agencies to impose administrative sanctions quickly on errant recruiters, allowing agencies to issue fines that must be paid or put into escrow if the recruiter appeals to the courts, an effort to shift some of the pain from alleged violations onto the shoulders of recruiters. Finally, all reports call for more education of migrants and support for NGOs to help migrants to file complaints and seek justice from recruiters who violated their rights.

Education of migrants, speedier justice, and more resources to monitor recruiters and deal with migrant complaints about them are desirable, and are often listed as goals by migrant-sending governments. The practical issue facing many governments is how to balance the need for resources to improve regulation of the recruitment industry with other government priorities, including sending more workers abroad to generate more remittances. Competing priorities should not obscure the fact that governments could at low cost implement policies to improve education and compliance, including developing standard contracts and educating workers about them. Many migrant-sending governments say they want standard contracts, but give up when destination governments say that contracts between foreign employers and migrant workers are "market determined." When low-skilled workers seek foreign jobs, foreign employers who can recruit in many countries have more bargaining power, which is why standard contracts would help to protect workers.

Even with a more efficient system to deal with migrant complaints about recruiters in migrant-sending countries, there may not be justice for migrants because of the social gaps between recruiters, officials, and adjudicators on the one hand, and migrants on the other. Conversations with government officials reveal that many believe migrants who obtain contracts to work abroad at higher wages have "won the lottery," giving them little excuse to complain. Many government staff frequently interact with recruiters, and are more likely to see recruiters rather than migrants as their clients, an example of regulatory capture. The common practice of government agencies contacting recruiters after complaints are filed to get their side of the story often makes it clear to migrants that they should settle rather than fight. These social gaps are reinforced if migrants are disproportionately from minority groups.

Enforcement can have a top-down quality if inspectors randomly check recruiters to ensure that they are in compliance with laws and regulations. However, in most countries, there are more than enough complaints to keep enforcement staff busy, so few enforcement agencies conduct random audits of recruiters.

There are also difficult human aspects of foreign employment that defy easy solutions. Many migrants going abroad for the first time have never performed the job they are expected to fill abroad. It is very hard for a migrant who may have never held a wage job before to understand the need to be punctual in reporting for work, to stand or sit for long periods and take breaks only when other workers do, or to work outdoors in unfamiliar weather. Migrants from rural areas of poorer countries may be accustomed to hard work, but work in agriculture is often seasonal, and non-farm work is often interrupted by intermittent supplies or electricity. Migrants who complain of "hard work" abroad often say that there were no unplanned breaks due to lack of supplies or electricity.

One way to educate migrants would be for governments or recruiters to film workers abroad as they perform their jobs and explain what they are doing in the local language. Such films could be far more effective at educating migrants than pre-departure seminars led by college-educated teachers who have never done the work that the migrants will be performing abroad. Films of migrants working abroad could be shown on regular TV or made available via the internet for phones, so that workers have a more realistic idea of what work abroad entails and are in a better position to ask questions of agents and subagents who offer foreign jobs.

More information will not end the problems of workers who arrive abroad in debt and work very hard in hot temperatures fueled by caffeine for fear that they will be fired as unsatisfactory workers. Debt, anxiety, and caffeine may have contributed to heart attacks and deaths among Nepalis in Qatar.[10] The *Associated Press* (AP) in December 2016 reported that an average 1,500 Nepali men leave every day for work abroad, and six Nepalis who have died abroad are returned daily. Many died in their sleep, from so-called Sudden Unexplained Nocturnal Death Syndrome.[11] AP emphasized that both the Nepali and Qatari governments ban recruiters from charging fees to migrants, but noted that almost all low-skilled Nepalis pay for foreign jobs. Some 10 percent of the 28 million Nepalis are abroad, and remittances to Nepal are over $6 billion a year.

Solutions for workers new to the job include education at home as well as break-in and training periods abroad, regulations that limit outdoor work during periods of high heat, and advice on the health consequences of caffeine-fueled drinks. Media reports focus on the evils of sponsorship systems that tie migrant workers to a particular employer and the high fees charged by recruiters that put migrants in debt. However, even if these problems ended, there will still be a need to help workers who have to adapt to a new country and a new type of work.

Visual materials can help to educate migrants, but only if they know what job they will do abroad. Many workers in pre-departure training do not know whether they will be caring for the elderly or children abroad, highlighting the need to link workers in training at home with the jobs they will fill abroad. Migrants going abroad as laborers may not know whether they will work during the day or at night or whether they will work in the presence of machinery. Visual materials that help migrants to see themselves doing the job should be accompanied by accurate information on exactly what job a migrant will fill abroad. The fact that many migrants in training before departure do not know exactly what job they will perform abroad speaks volumes about how low-skilled migrants are viewed as interchangeable.

---

[10] Owen Gibson, 2014. The hundreds of migrant workers dying as a brand new Qatar is built. *The Guardian*, May 14. There were an estimated 1.4 million migrant workers in Qatar in 2014, including 22 percent each from India and Pakistan, 16 percent from Nepal, 13 percent from Iran, 11 percent from the Philippines, and 8 percent each from Egypt and Sri Lanka.

[11] Martha Mendoza, 2016. At Escalating Rate, Nepalis Working Abroad Return Home Dead. *Associated Press*, December 21, www.foxbusiness.com/markets/2016/12/21/at-escalating-rate-nepalis-working-abroad-return-home-dead.html.

Wicked Problems: Trafficking

When the supply of labor exceeds the demand for it, low-skilled workers are willing to pay recruiters to get higher-wage jobs abroad. Governments can set maximum worker-paid fees at zero or one month's foreign earnings, but they cannot easily enforce such caps if workers are willing to pay more (Agunias, 2013: 7–8).[12]

Regulating the fees that low-skilled workers pay to get foreign jobs when the supply of workers exceeds the demand for them is an example of a "wicked problem," defined by Conklin (2005) as a problem not fully understood, ever changing, and defying durable solutions. Wicked problems are symptoms of other problems, such as developing an alternative to the worker-willingness-to-pay model used to allocate limited foreign jobs among many low-skilled workers. Wicked problems often involve complex interdependencies, so that solving one aspect of the problem creates another problem, as when prohibiting young women from going abroad to be domestic workers, or preventing migrants from going to work in countries at war, pushes them to leave illegally or via third countries and reducing protections that may be scant in the first place.

In the case of migrant workers and recruitment fees, the fundamental issue is that governments do not want worker-paid fees to be the mechanism to allocate limited foreign jobs among citizens eager to work abroad. However, they do not offer another allocation tool, seeking instead to defy the laws of supply and demand by limiting what recruiters can charge workers. The effect of maximum fee regulations is to drive worker payments underground, where they take the form of non-documented payments, loans and deductions from wages, or payments for required training at the foreign workplace.

The durable solution to protecting migrant workers is development that offers decent work at home, an empowerment that allows migrants to reject high fees for foreign jobs. The ILO's decent work agenda is aspirational, urging governments to offer

> opportunities for work that is productive and delivers a fair income, security in the workplace and social protection for families, better prospects for personal development and social integration, freedom for people to express their concerns, organize and participate in the decisions that affect their lives and equality of opportunity and treatment for all women and men.[13]

---

[12] See the discussion of zero-cost migration for Nepalis headed to Qatar. Governments in both countries agreed that employers were to pay all visa and travel costs in 2005, and re-signed the agreement in 2015, but Nepalis nonetheless pay for jobs in Qatar. See: www.nepalitimes.com/blogs/thebrief/2015/06/28/zero-cost-migration/.

[13] The ILO's Decent Work Agenda was incorporated into Goal 8 of the UN's 2030 Agenda for Sustainable Development; see: www.ilo.org/global/topics/decent-work/lang–en/index.htm.

However, until decent work is universal, what can be done to improve protections for migrant workers?

The easy solution is to enact laws and regulations. The bedrock principle of the current system is the assumption that, if it is unlawful to charge workers anything or more than one month's foreign earnings, recruiters will comply to avoid penalties. Workers who pay too much are expected to complain to governments, who penalize and put out of business offending recruiters. The result should be an industry of compliant recruiters and a narrowing of gaps between the goals spelled out in regulations, such as low or no worker-paid migration costs, and the realities of large worker payments. However, even the Philippines has been unable to prevent low-skilled migrants from paying more than government-set maximum fees.

The ILO and many governments pay special attention to recruiters and others who may overcharge migrant workers and place them into positions of forced labor, defined in ILO Convention 29 (1930) as "work or service which is exacted from any person under the menace of a penalty," with exceptions for compulsory military service, work required after a conviction in court, and "minor communal services performed by the members of a community in the direct interest of the community." The ILO estimated in 2015 that some 21 million workers were subject to forced labor, including a quarter who were victims of forced sexual exploitation and two-thirds who were victims of forced labor, almost always in the private sector.[14]

One victim of forced labor is one too many, but the multiple campaigns against trafficking or "modern slavery" sometimes suggest that most migrant workers are victims. Many organizations funded by governments and foundations train border and regular police to detect victims of slavery and trafficking, in part because of reports such as the Global Slavery Index, which estimated there were almost 46 million people "subject to some form of modern slavery" in 2016 based on "surveys conducted by Gallup," up from 30 million in 2013.[15] The ILO raised its estimate of forced laborers from 12 million in 2005 to 21 million in 2012, including 9 million who moved within their own countries or over national borders.

The Palermo Protocol to Prevent, Suppress and Punish Trafficking in Persons, especially Women and Children, approved in 2000, defined trafficking to include three elements: an act (such as migration), a means (coercion), and a purpose (exploitation).

---

[14] For details see: www.ilo.org/global/standards/subjects-covered-by-international-labour-standards/forced-labour/lang–en/index.htm.

[15] http://www.globalslaveryindex.org/findings/. The data for twenty-seven countries were extrapolated to cover 167 countries.

Specifically, trafficking is

> the recruitment, transportation, transfer, harboring or receipt of persons, by means of the threat or use of force or other forms of coercion, of abduction, of fraud, of deception, of the abuse of power or of a position of vulnerability or of the giving or receiving of payments or benefits to achieve the consent of a person having control over another person, for the purpose of exploitation...sexual exploitation, forced labor or services, slavery or practices similar to slavery, servitude or the removal of organs...The consent of a victim of trafficking in persons to the intended exploitation...shall be irrelevant where any of the means [such as coercion] have been used.

The UN Office on Drugs and Crime (UNODC) monitors trafficking under the Palermo Protocol, and issues periodic reports on the extent of trafficking. Its most recent report (UNODC, 2014) noted that most trafficking victims were subjected to sexual exploitation, and 40 percent of the 40,000 victims of trafficking detected between 2010 and 2012 were subject to forced labor. Some 34,000 offenders were prosecuted between 2010 and 2012, and 13,000 convicted. UNODC's report on recruiters is vague on details of workers abused by recruiters, citing reports prepared by others to suggest that many low-skilled workers are exploited by recruiters (UNODC, 2015). UNODC called on more countries to ratify and implement international conventions and protocols, more policing to detect trafficking victims, and more prosecution of traffickers.

The stories of individuals who are victims of trafficking are often heartbreaking, and the good news is that there are relatively few such victims.[16] Andrees (2006: 179) acknowledged that "there is little research into the extent" of labor trafficking, and that "there is a wide spectrum [among traffickers]...ranging from sophisticated criminal networks at one end to semi-legal private agencies at the other." Andrees emphasized that it is often difficult to persuade the victims of trafficking to testify, either for fear about what may happen to their families at home or because they would have to acknowledge their illegal status in the country.

The fact that some migrants are trafficked and enslaved should not obscure the fact that almost all of the international migrants who cross borders voluntarily for higher wages are not subject to forced labor abroad. The willingness of governments to fund anti-trafficking projects, and the publicity earned by the NGOs who carry out government-funded programs, sometimes leave the impression that most migrants are trafficked, putting the emphasis on finding and prosecuting offending recruiters. It is more realistic to think of recruiters as merchants of labor engaged in the legitimate business of moving workers over borders, but often operating in ways that raise costs to workers.

---

[16] For a review of the issues with estimates of modern-day slaves, see Glenn Kessler, 2015. Why you should be wary of statistics on 'modern slavery' and 'trafficking.' *Washington Post*, April 24, www.washingtonpost.com/news/fact-checker/wp/2015/04/24/why-you-should-be-wary-of-statistics-on-modern-slavery-and-trafficking/.

Recruiters and Contractors

Experience shows that it is difficult to enforce recruitment regulations governing items such as worker-paid fees when the economic incentives of migrants encourage them to pay more. If decent work at home and penalties on recruiters cannot reduce worker overpayments, could government incentives to recruiters substitute for payments from migrants? Micro-incentives combined with policies that favor fewer and larger recruiters, allow foreign employers to recruit workers directly, and encourage stable foreign employer–local recruiter partnerships may do more to protect migrant workers than incremental improvements to the current penalty-based system.

Experience regulating labor contractors or gangmasters who recruit and often employ low-skilled workers within countries highlights the challenges. International recruiters move workers over national borders, and generally do not act as the employer of migrant workers abroad. Labor contractors or gangmasters usually hire local and foreign-born workers who have few other job options, and often act as their employer as they move from one farm or business to another.

Table 7.2 summarizes the essential differences between recruiters who move low-skilled workers over national borders and contractors who hire low-skilled workers within a country. The types of jobs and workers involved are similar whether the recruiter operates internationally or the contractor operates nationally, so that jobs tend to be low wage and in difficult-to-regulate sectors, and workers tend to be low skilled and with few other job options. In both cases, there are often violations of sometimes detailed laws and regulations that can be hard to enforce because they fall into gray areas, as when recruiters do not charge any fees to domestic workers they place abroad, but require them to undergo paid training as soon as they arrive abroad, the cost of which is deducted from their wages. Similarly, contractors can pay workers required wages and benefits, but charge them for ancillary services that range from rides to work to cashing paychecks. Even detailed laws and aggressive enforcement cannot easily repeal supply and demand conditions that encourage workers to accept contractor-provided services. Table 7.2 summarizes these similarities.

Many factors, including the often competitive and low-profit nature of industries that use recruiters and the fact that workers are often desperate for jobs and wages, allow intermediary contractors to take advantage of workers. Governments have difficulty enforcing protective labor laws in such situations, prompting an acclaimed labor economist in the 1950s, after studying US government efforts to regulate farm labor contractors and protect seasonal farm workers, to conclude that "the brightest hope for the welfare of seasonal agricultural workers lies with the elimination of the jobs on which they now

Table 7.2 Recruiters and contractors

	Recruiters	Contractors	Notes
Jobs	Fill jobs in competitive industries that offer low wages and are hard to regulate, e.g. ag, domestic work, construction	Fill jobs that offer low wages and are often seasonal; workers in crews are often seen as interchangeable	Farmers make investments that assume contractors will find enough workers to fill harvesting jobs
Workers	Low-skilled and often from rural areas. Need to get foreign job offer, navigate bureaucracy, and perform satisfactorily abroad	Usually hire workers without other job options ("getting a seasonal farm work force requires poverty at home and misery abroad" Fisher (1953))	Workers' social networks should lower recruiter costs over time, but exit procedures aimed at protecting migrants can limit cost savings
Environment	Widespread violation of often detailed protective laws, e.g. maximum fees evaded through charges for training or other services	Widespread violation of often detailed protective labor laws via charges for services, e.g. rides to work, housing, check cashing	Migrants often withdraw complaints if recruiters send them abroad. Contractor relatives may provide ancillary services
Laws	Detailed in response to abuses, making it hard to be in full compliance	Detailed in response to abuses. California contractors say that hiring farm workers is second only to hiring child actors in its complexity	Fisher (1953) concluded that the best way to protect workers from contractors is to eliminate their jobs

Source: Author's assessment (see chapter text, pp. 152–3).

depend" (Fisher, 1953: 148). Fisher thought that the US government would not be able to improve protections for seasonal farm workers employed by contractors, and advocated freer trade, subsidized mechanization, and other policies to eliminate seasonal farm jobs.

Governments have made often heroic efforts to regulate the contractors who employ low-skilled workers. The US Migrant and Seasonal Agricultural Workers Protection Act (MSPA)[17] follows the same three procedures to regulate farm labor contractors that are used to regulate recruiters who move workers over borders, that is, require them to identify themselves and obtain licenses and post bonds, educate workers about their rights and explain how they can file complaints of violations, and strictly regulate the ancillary services that contractors can provide to the workers they employ, from transportation to housing to check cashing. Despite laws and enforcement, most US farm labor contractors whose operations are inspected are found to be in violation of at least some laws and regulations.

---

[17] MSPA is explained at https://www.dol.gov/whd/mspa/index.htm.

Even if governments could regulate labor contractors effectively, the contracting system includes perverse incentives. For example, a farmer facing weather and other risks has an incentive to request too many workers too soon to harvest crops, since the farmer does not pay as workers wait to go to work. Labor contractors, on the other hand, have incentives to promise more workers than they have and sooner than they may be available in order to win the farmer's business. The results of these perverse incentives are frequent complaints of "farm labor shortages" from farmers when contractors do not deliver promised workers. These shortage complaints receive far more publicity than the unemployment common among farm workers even during the peak of the harvest system as they wait for work to begin.[18]

A centralized system that included an honest demand for and supply of labor would be far more efficient at assembling the minimum number of workers necessary to complete the work. Hiring halls rationalized the hiring of longshoremen who load and unload ships, gave the unions operating the halls the power to allocate workers, and made dockworkers blue-collar elites in many countries. Unions often operate hiring halls to allocate jobs in the construction trades, so that employers with union contracts must use the union hiring hall to find carpenters, electricians, and plumbers. Union-run hiring halls were tried in California agriculture in the 1970s, but were abandoned in the face of both employer and worker opposition, as employers complained that the union did not send them workers whom they had hired in previous seasons and workers complained when family groups were broken up by being sent to different farms (Martin, 2003; Pawel, 2009).

Contractors, called gangmasters or labor providers in the UK, are regulated in similar ways. The UK Gangmasters (Licensing) Act of July 2004 requires farm and fishery labor contractors as well as those who supply workers to food processing industries to register with a Gangmasters Licensing Authority (GLA), which issues licenses, inspects gangmasters, and follows up on worker complaints.[19] The act makes it a criminal offense to operate as a gangmaster without a license, and empowers agents enforcing the act to inspect gangmasters and their records.

The GLA was created in response to the drowning in February 2004 of twenty-three Chinese migrants in Morecambe Bay, who were picking cockles, a seafood delicacy similar to clams that are exported to Holland for processing and then shipped to Spain and the Far East (Balch, 2010). When

---

[18] For examples of farm labor shortage complaints, see: https://migration.ucdavis.edu/rmn/more.php?id=1692. In many cases, farmers see workers as interchangeable workers rather than individuals, as when they talk of a shrinking "labor pool" from which to draw seasonal workers when they are needed.

[19] The GLA's mission is "Protecting vulnerable workers in UK food and drink processing and packaging, agriculture and shellfish gathering." http://www.gla.gov.uk

the Gangmasters (Licensing) Act was enacted, there were an estimated 10,000 gangmasters in the UK, including 3,000 active in agriculture; by 2015, the GLA reported only 1,000 active licenses.

Media reports suggest that British supermarkets encourage produce firms and farmers to compete with each other on price, which tends to drive down wages and leads to labor exploitation.[20] Many gangmasters did not pay all required taxes on the wages of the workers they employed, and some were complicit in benefit fraud, as when they hired workers who were also collecting unemployment or welfare benefits. While some gangmasters are large businesses that have established record keeping and control systems, others are operated by persons with no business experience and few records (Rees, 2006).

The GLA is generally praised as necessary but not sufficient to reduce the exploitation of migrant workers. Oxfam (2009) praised the GLA for "improving labor rights, standards for workers and creating a more level playing field for employers," but a 2012 report commissioned by the government recommended that the GLA be abolished, concluding that its enforcement activities could be handled more efficiently by existing enforcement units (Beecroft, 2012). The GLA was moved from the Department of Food, Environment and Rural Affairs to the Home Office in April 2014, when it reported "more and more cases of vulnerable people being exploited" in the UK.

Contractors or labor providers are active in most countries with sectors that have seasonal sectors such as agriculture and food processing, which hire large numbers of low-skilled workers. The workers available to fill seasonal jobs often have few alternatives, making them vulnerable to contractors who themselves may have little bargaining power with the farmers and produce firms who turn to them for workers. In this competition, reducing costs is a top priority, and the effects are often felt by low-wage workers in the form of low wages and insecure work.

Bilateral Agreements

One alternative to recruiters are BLAs or memoranda of understanding (MOU) between governments that eliminate or restrict the roles of private recruiters. The ILO welcomes BLAs and MOU that lay out the rights and responsibilities of governments in migrant-sending and -receiving countries, including Germany's seasonal worker program and NZ's Recognized Seasonal Scheme, in its good practices database.[21]

---

[20] Felicity Lawrence, 2005. Migrant workers: The official solution: license gangmasters and let more migrants work. *The Guardian*, January 10.

[21] The good practices database is at www.ilo.org/dyn/migpractice/migmain.listPractices? p_theme=O2.

The term "bilateral" suggests that agreements are negotiated by governments in migrant-sending and -receiving countries. In reality, most BLAs are written by governments in receiving countries and offered to sending countries, which may be able to extract limited modifications. In this sense, unilateral guest worker programs such as the US H-2 programs for low-skilled guest workers may be more effective than many BLAs in protecting migrants. For example, the US H-2 programs prohibit US employers from charging any fees to the guest workers they recruit (GAO, 2015).

Korean Employment Permit System

One BLA introduced in response to problems regulating recruiters is the Korean Employment Permit System (EPS). The EPS was introduced in 2003 and since 2007 has been the only way for most Korean small and medium-size enterprises (SMEs) to hire non-ethnic Koreans from outside the country.

Under the previous industrial trainee system, the Korean Federation of Small Businesses beginning in 1994 arranged for the entry of foreigners from China and Southeast Asian countries to work in manufacturing firms with fewer than fifty employees. Trainees were paid less than the Korean minimum wage because their employers were supposed to provide them with training. The training was minimal, and the industrial trainee system soon became a cheap-labor program with high costs to workers.

Most trainees paid recruiters and others in their home countries for Korean trainee slots, which means they arrived in debt. Many Korean employers deducted some of these recruitment costs from worker wages, prompting some trainees to "run away" from the employer to whom they were assigned because they could earn more as illegal workers than as legal trainees. By 2000, it was reported that 85 percent of trainees had run away from their assigned employers, prompting some employers to take actions that became human rights abuses to prevent runaways.[22]

The ILO worked closely with the Korean government to develop the EPS guest worker program. The government sets an annual quota on how many slots will be available for new or first-time workers; 32,890 in 2015, and for migrants who were previously employed in Korea, 9,510 in 2015. These quotas are allocated by sector in Korea, so that 85 percent go to small Korean manufacturers, and by country of origin, so that several thousand workers can arrive from fifteen Asian countries. Between 2004 and 2011, when more than 300,000 migrants were admitted under the EPS, Vietnam accounted for 77,000 admissions or 26 percent, followed by Thailand and the Philippines with 14 percent each (Kim, 2015: 8).

---

[22] For details see: https://migration.ucdavis.edu/mn/more.php?id=2267.

The admissions process begins with eligible Korean employers requesting permission from a government agency to employ EPS guest workers by showing that local workers are not available. The BLA specifies that foreigners aged 18 to 40 who want to be EPS workers in Korea pass a test of the Korean language in their countries of origin, and health and security checks to be placed on lists maintained by government agencies from which Korean employers select workers, sometimes after Skype interviews conducted with the help of translators.

Government agencies are not allowed to charge workers to be placed on the list, but potential EPS workers must pay for the Korean language training, whose cost ranges from $10 to $10,000; some trainers suggest that learning Korean with them will lead to faster selection by Korean employers. A 2013 survey of agencies in migrant-sending countries reported that the workers selected to work in Korea paid an average $925 to learn Korean and buy tickets to Korea, much less than the $3,500 to $5,000 in migration costs paid by trainees in the pre-EPS era (Park, 2013).

Employers and selected migrant workers sign Standard Labor Contracts that detail wages and working conditions, including hours of work, accommodations, and other work-related items. Migrant workers receive 20 hours of orientation and training after arriving in Korea, and must enroll in four insurance programs—Departure Guarantee Insurance, Return Cost Insurance, Casualty Insurance, and Wage Guarantee Insurance.[23]

Migrant workers receive 3-year E-9 visas that can be renewed for another 22 months. After 4 years and 10 months, they must leave Korea for at least 3 months, but may return to their previous Korean employer without retaking the Korean language test. The EPS is subsidized by Korea's foreign aid budget, and the Happy Return program offers training and support at home to departing E-9 foreign workers who want to open a business in their country of origin. Happy Return also helps returning migrants to apply for jobs at Korean companies in their country of origin.[24]

Some migrant workers stay in Korea when their contracts end and work illegally. Kim (2015: 18) reported that overstay rates for EPS migrants were about 8 percent, and noted that some employers encouraged migrants to overstay because of the time and uncertainty involved in getting a replacement

---

[23] Employers deduct 8.3 percent from worker wages to deposit into the Departure Guarantee Insurance, which migrants receive if they depart as required. The processes for receiving permission to hire migrant workers under the EPS, being selected, and enrolling in the four insurance programs is at https://www.eps.go.kr/en/view/view_02.jsp.

[24] Human resource development (HRD) communicates with migrants at 6 and 3 months prior to their departure dates to advise them of Happy Return and related services. Migrants can learn skills on Sundays at vocational training institutions in Korea, and can receive certificates while employed in Korea attesting to their skills, which can be presented to Korean-owned firms in their country of origin.

migrant worker.[25] Governments in Nepal, Vietnam, and other countries from which some migrants overstay require their citizens to post bonds of $5,000 to $10,000 that are forfeited if migrants do not return when required, reasoning that too many overstays can lead to a reduction in the quota for the country, that is, reducing overstay rates is necessary for opening up job slots for more workers.[26]

The EPS is considered a model BLA, and the conversion from migrant trainees to migrant workers is generally praised by worker advocates. However, a 2010 HRD survey found that a quarter of migrants thought employers had violated their contracts (Kim, 2015: 28), usually because employers did not pay overtime wages or failed to record all hours worked. Some advocates say that, despite the fact that most migrants are relatively well-educated and have passed tests of Korean, they are afraid to complain for fear of being fired and forced to leave Korea. A related criticism deals with health and safety. Korea's Labor Standards Act applies only to workplaces with five or more workers and excludes agriculture and fisheries, sectors that also employ migrants (Kim, 2015: 32).

The Korean EPS is a clear improvement over the previous trainee system and a model in a continent with some of the highest-cost migration corridors for workers. Many of the complaints about the EPS reflect the realities of small workplaces around the world, where enforcement of labor laws is difficult because of often close relationships between employers and workers, especially if the employer also provides housing for employees. The EPS, whose administration in migrant-sending countries is subsidized by the foreign aid budget, may be a model for governments that want to make labor migration processes fairer and less costly.

Canada–Mexico Seasonal Agricultural Workers Program

Canada's Commonwealth Caribbean and Mexican Seasonal Agricultural Workers Program (SAWP), which has been admitting Caribbean workers since 1966 and Mexican workers since 1974 to fill seasonal farm jobs, is another best-practice model program. Procedures to recruit workers and to protect them while employed abroad are spelled out in government-to-government MOU[27] and employer–worker contracts.

---

[25] Under Korean law, foreigners in the country for 5 continuous years could apply for permanent residence status.

[26] Governments justify these bonds under an externality argument, so that if too many of their citizens run away from an assigned employer or overstay, the country's quota of visas may be reduced. Lawful behavior by migrants abroad opens more opportunities for citizens to work in the destination country.

[27] The MOU between Canada and Mexico, Jamaica, and other Caribbean countries are intergovernmental administrative arrangements, not binding international treaties.

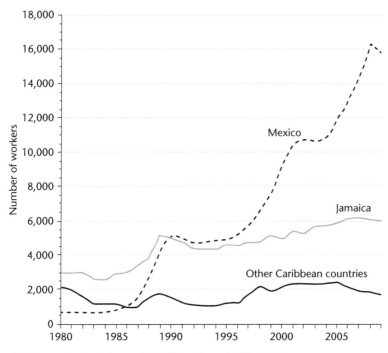

Figure 7.1 Annual admissions of SAWP workers, 1980–2009

Source: Calculations by author based on data from Citizenship and Immigration Canada (CIC), Facts and Figures, 2009. See: http://www.cic.gc.ca/english/resources/statistics/.

The SAWP "matches workers from Mexico and the Caribbean countries with Canadian farmers who need temporary support during planting and harvesting seasons, when qualified Canadians or permanent residents are not available." There are about three Mexican workers admitted for each Jamaican, the second-largest origin country (Figure 7.1). In 2012, some 29,000 farm jobs were certified to be filled with SAWP workers, about the same as in previous years. Two-thirds of SAWP workers were in Ontario in 2012, almost 20 percent in British Columbia (BC), and 10 percent in Quebec.

The admissions process begins with Canadian farmers who try and fail to recruit Canadian workers[28] by offering the higher of the minimum or prevailing wage.[29] Canadian minimum wages vary by province, from C\$10.70 in Atlantic Canada in 2016 to C\$11.25 in Ontario, the province with a third of Canadians and over half of SAWP workers. If efforts to recruit Canadian workers fail, and the government determines that the presence of SAWP

---

[28] Most discussions refer to insufficient "reliable" local workers, that is, there are unemployed Canadians, but they do not want to fill seasonal farm jobs.

[29] The prevailing wage is determined by the Canadian government or is the wage paid by the farmer to Canadians doing similar work.

159

workers will not depress wages of similar Canadian farm workers, farmers are certified by Service Canada to recruit SAWP workers by promising them at least 240 hours of farm work for at least 6 weeks of work.[30]

After Service Canada approves farmers to hire SAWP workers, most farmers turn to non-profit organizations created by farmers to recruit and transport SAWP workers to their farms: Foreign Agricultural Resource Management Service (FARMS) in Ontario and FERME in Quebec. In most cases, there is little recruitment of new workers, since Canadian farmers specify or "name" over three-fourths of the SAWP workers they want to hire, usually workers who were employed the previous season or the relatives of current or past-season workers. If new workers are required, labor ministries in Jamaica and Mexico maintain lists of workers who would like to be selected to work in Canada.

SAWP workers are not supposed to pay recruitment fees before departure, but some do. On June 23, 2008 Canadian Border Services Agency (CBSA) inspectors asked eighty Mexicans with valid SAWP permits whether they had paid recruitment fees and, when they said yes, they were not admitted to BC. CBSA says that workers who pay recruitment fees can be denied entry into Canada because they might not leave at the end of their work contracts.[31]

Most farmers advance the cost of airfare and visas (C$155), but deduct some travel and other costs from workers' wages.[32] SAWP workers are covered by Canada's national health insurance upon arrival, and employers deduct health insurance premiums from worker wages to help cover costs. SAWP workers and their employers also pay premiums for the (un)employment insurance (UI) program, even though SAWP workers are generally not eligible for UI benefits because they cannot remain unemployed in Canada looking for jobs. Employers offer free housing to SAWP workers on their farms; this is inspected by Canadian authorities before workers arrive and by government liaison agents from Jamaica and Mexico after workers arrive.

SAWP workers may stay in Canada up to 8 months, and on average they stay 22 weeks or 5.5 months, often working 60 to 70 hours a week. About 2,000 Canadian farms hire SAWP workers. Hydroponic or greenhouse tomatoes are an especially important employer of SAWP workers. Canada is the largest producer of greenhouse tomatoes in North America, and two-thirds of Canada's greenhouse tomatoes are grown around Leamington, Ontario, the self-described tomato capital of the world. Production peaks between April and November,

---

[30] Most discussions of available Canadian workers refer to insufficient "reliable" local workers, that is, there are unemployed Canadians, but they do not want to fill seasonal farm jobs.

[31] For details see: http://migration.ucdavis.edu/rmn/more.php?id=1328.

[32] BC does not allow farmers to recoup transportation costs from SAWP workers, but does allow farmers to deduct 6 percent of gross wages or a maximum C$450 to cover housing costs from SAWP workers' wages. The Mexican consulate in BC handles employer requests for SAWP workers and arranges for workers to travel to BC.

when long hours of daylight contribute to average yields of over 500 metric tons per hectare.

Farmers evaluate each SAWP worker at the end of the season. SAWP workers are required to present their employer's evaluation to a government agency at home to be selected for the next season. Farmers and farm organizations can "blacklist" particular workers and not hire them in the future, and government agencies in sending countries can blacklist particular Canadian farmers and not approve sending workers to them. However, Canadian farmers blacklisted by the Mexican government can turn to the Caribbean for workers.

FARMS, FERME, and other farmers' organizations that arrange travel to bring SAWP workers to Canada and deploy them to member farms are involved in reviewing the operation of the program in periodic meetings with the Canadian, Mexican, and Caribbean governments. There is no formal role for worker organizations in these review-of-SAWP operations meetings, and the sending country governments are assumed to represent the interests of their workers. Mexican and Caribbean government liaison officers interact with workers from their countries while they are in Canada, to sometimes mixed reviews when SAWP workers complain that their government's officials are more interested in maximizing the number of Canadian jobs available rather than dealing with the grievances of particular workers.[33]

The SAWP program for Caribbean workers, mostly from Jamaica, is slightly different, since Jamaica and most other Caribbean governments require SAWP workers to agree to have 25 percent of their Canadian wages deducted and sent to a liaison office in Canada. This office keeps 5 percent of each worker's wages and forwards 20 percent to the worker's account at home, prompting some workers to complain of delays in receiving these forced savings and the low exchange rate at which they are converted. In Jamaica, members of parliament nominate new workers to participate in SAWP, and the Jamaican government in 2004 promised to do more to ensure that the workers who were nominated had experience doing farm work.[34]

Farmers can also hire foreign workers under the agricultural stream of the Temporary Foreign Worker Program (TFWP), which began in 2002 as the Pilot Project for Occupations Requiring Lower Levels of Formal Training, a unilateral program that offers fewer protections for guest workers.[35] There are three

---

[33] Some workers and NGOs say that government liaison officers in Canada generally favor Canadian employers rather than their citizen workers because they value high-wage jobs and remittances more than worker complaints. If workers make complaints, government liaison officers discuss them with employers, but the remedy may be removing the worker from the farm and returning him or her to their country of origin.

[34] Most Caribbean countries allow returning workers to bring $500 worth of electronics and other goods home duty free at the end of their contracts; many pack these goods in barrels to send home. See: http://migration.ucdavis.edu/rmn/more.php?id=824.

[35] See: https://www.tbs-sct.gc.ca/hidb-bdih/initiative-eng.aspx?Hi=39&YrAn=2016.

sub-programs or streams: for live-in caregivers, for agricultural workers, and for other low-skill workers filling jobs in construction, restaurants, meatpacking, and other sectors.

Workers admitted under the TFWP must be offered at least 30 hours of work a week at a wage below the median hourly wage for the province in which the job is located. In 2016, employers offering accommodation and food service jobs (NAICS 72) or retail trade jobs (NAICS 44–45) in provinces with an unemployment rate of 6 percent or higher were not allowed to request additional migrants under the TFWP. Employers are allowed to have up to 20 percent TFWP migrants, although farmers and private homes and health-care facilities hiring caregivers are exempt from this cap.[36]

The number of low-skilled migrants admitted more than doubled from 101,300 in 2002 to 251,200 in 2008, and rose further to 338,200 in 2013. Most low-skill migrant workers are filling year-round non-farm jobs for up to 2-year visas that can be renewed, giving TFWP workers a maximum 4 years in Canada.

An agricultural stream under the TFWP admitted almost 8,000 foreign workers in 2012, mostly Guatemalans employed in Quebec. The Guatemalan–Quebec program was developed in 2003 with the help of the International Organization for Migration to ensure clean recruitment. The farmer-created Quebec-based FERME used both IOM and recruiter Amigo Laboral to obtain Guatemalan workers. IOM exited the recruitment business in 2013, and FERME could obtain workers from seven recruiters by 2016, including five operated by ex-IOM staff. Muir (2016) recounted stories of recruiters charging potential migrants $2,000 and more for passports, visas, health checks, and training, and emphasized that many of the Guatemalans who take out loans to be trained to work in Canada are never selected by Canadian farmers.

Foreigners admitted under the SAWP can return to Canada indefinitely, while foreigners admitted under the TFWP can stay in Canada a maximum 4 years. The SAWP is governed by bilateral MOU and the recruitment of new workers is overseen by a government agency in the sending country, while the TFWP is a unilateral program that allows Canadian employers to recruit guest workers anywhere and in any manner they choose.

The SAWP is limited to producers of fruits, vegetables, horticultural crops, and tobacco and sod, while the TFWP is open to all farm employers, including livestock producers. SAWP allows farm employers who pay for worker transportation to Canada to deduct from worker wages half of the airfare to get to Canada (typically C$630) and requires employers to offer housing to workers at no charge. SAWP employers must provide housing on the farm where the

---

[36] See: www.esdc.gc.ca/en/foreign_workers/hire/median_wage/low/requirements.page.

migrant works at no charge, while TFWP farm employers can provide housing off the farm and charge guest workers for their housing.

Most farmers and workers are satisfied with the SAWP, but the United Food and Commercial Workers (UFCW) union calls SAWP "Canada's dirty little secret." The UFCW operates Agriculture Workers Alliance support centers for SAWP workers and has tried to organize some of them. Mayfair Farms in Portage La Prairie, Manitoba, signed the first contract covering SAWP workers with a UFCW in June 2008; it linked future wage increases to increases in the provincial minimum wage and provided a C$1 an hour overtime premium for work done after 70 hours a week.

The UFCW–Mayfair contract was troublesome. Some of Mayfair's SAWP workers complained that the UFCW negotiated a C$0.15 an hour raise, but charged them $4 a week in union dues. Others said that they wanted to work 12 to 14 hour days and 100 hours a week, but Mayfair limited them to 70 hours a week to avoid the overtime pay required by the contract. In June 2009, Mayfair's SAWP workers voted 26:0 to decertify UFCW. Migrant advocates charged that the Mexican consul warned Mayfair's SAWP workers they could be blacklisted if they did not vote for decertification.[37]

The UFCW has also had mixed experiences representing SAWP workers in BC. The British Columbia Labor Relations Board certified the UFCW to represent forty SAWP workers at Greenway Farms in Surrey, BC, in August 2008, and the UFCW won an election to represent seventy SAWP workers at Sidhu & Sons Nursery in BC in March 2010. In these cases, the UFCW represented only the SAWP workers on the farm, not the Canadian workers.

In the Sidhu case, after a vote to decertify the UFCW, some Sidhu SAWP workers petitioned the BC Labor Relations Board to overturn the decertification vote, alleging that Mexican labor attachés encouraged the decertification effort. The Mexican government tried to have its conduct before the decertification vote in the Sidhu case declared immune from Canadian law, a position rejected by Canadian courts in February 2015. The Mayfair and Sidhu cases highlight what the UFCW says is the Mexican government acting on behalf of Canadian employers rather than Mexican SAWP workers.[38]

The North–South Institute supported several studies of the SAWP program that concluded it helped Canadian farmers to recruit and employ reliable low-skilled workers. Verma (2002) emphasized the inherent difficulty meeting SAWP objectives—administer the SAWP in ways that avoid depressing wages and working conditions—is very hard if most workers are SAWP migrants who are vulnerable to losing their jobs and the right to be in Canada. Workers

---

[37] For details on the Mayfair Farms case, see: http://migration.ucdavis.edu/rmn/more.php?id=1488.

[38] https://migration.ucdavis.edu/rmn/more.php?id=1893.

who want to be named by their employer to return next season are unlikely to complain.

The Institute for Research on Public Policy (IRPP) interviewed 600 Mexican and Jamaican farm workers in 2012 and found that most returned to Canada for an average eight seasons. Many SAWP workers complained of isolation on the farms where they worked, but two-thirds said they would like to become Canadian immigrants (Hennebry, 2012).

The SAWP is an example of a circular migration program that fills seasonal jobs with workers from lower-wage countries, most of whom return year after year. The Mexican government in a January 2015 press release called the SAWP

> a model of bilateral cooperation between the two countries, guaranteeing employ-
> ment to farm workers and making it possible to maintain a temporary migration
> flow that is orderly, circular and secure, and above all, one that fully respects the
> workers' labor, social and human rights.[39]

Researchers point out gaps in the SAWP between goals and outcomes. Since at least 85 percent of SAWP workers have been employed in Canada before, farmers get the services of experienced workers without paying them higher wages. Hennebry and Preibisch (2012) praise the cooperation between governments to administer the SAWP, transparency in selection of workers, and health insurance for SAWP workers upon their arrival in Canada, but note that there is no formal program to recognize worker qualifications in Canada or after they return to Mexico, and there is no path for SAWP workers to become Canadian immigrants. If the alternative to SAWP is illegal migration and contractors assembling crews of workers to fill seasonal farm jobs, as in California and other areas of the US, the SAWP can be considered a best practice, a "model despite flaws" (Basok, 2007).

There is less evidence that the SAWP has promoted stay-at-home development in worker areas of origin. Most returned SAWP workers improved their housing and spent more on their children's health and education than similar families without migrants and remittances, but many continue to migrate year after year to fill seasonal farm jobs in Canada. The upward mobility in the SAWP case may be intergenerational, as the children of SAWP workers who obtained more health care and education elect to stay in Jamaica or Mexico.

The SAWP is part of a larger debate in Canada over guest workers versus immigrants, and whether guest workers should be considered intending immigrants. Canada admitted 260,000 immigrants in 2014, equivalent to 0.7 percent of its population, and plans to accept 300,000 in 2016, including refugees. Canada has traditionally admitted immigrants rather than guest

---

[39] https://embamex2.sre.gob.mx/canada/index.php/en/press/press-releases/1292-jan15.

workers, but during the economic boom beginning in 2000, the government allowed employers to have easy access to guest workers. The number of guest workers rose rapidly, so that by the end of 2014 there were 353,000 foreigners in Canada under the TFWP and International Mobility program. Stories of employers favoring guest workers over Canadians prompted the government to tighten regulations and remind employers of their obligations to give priority to Canadians to fill vacant jobs.

The SAWP is sometimes touted as a model for the US, which has far more Mexican-born farmworkers. The National Agricultural Worker Survey found that at least 70 percent of the workers on US crop farms in 2014 were born abroad, usually in Mexico, and that most of these foreign-born farmworkers were not authorized to work in the US (www.doleta.gov/agworker/naws.cfm). US farmers who anticipate labor shortages may hire legal guest workers under the H-2A program by following procedures similar to those of the SAWP, that is, try and fail to find US workers, provide free housing to the H-2A guest workers, and pay the special H-2A minimum wage.

For most of the past three decades, US farmers found it easier to hire unauthorized rather than H-2A guest workers, in part because H-2A regulations require US farmers to pay all recruitment costs rather than share them as with the SAWP. However, the slowdown in unauthorized Mexico–US migration since the 2008–09 recession has encouraged more farmers to use the H-2A program to obtain seasonal workers, mostly from Mexico but also from fifty other countries. The number of jobs that the US Department of Labor certified to be filled with H-2A guest workers rose from 59,100 in FY06 to 165,700 in FY16, emphasizing that the US, with a much larger labor-intensive agriculture than Canada, employs far more guest workers in agriculture.

Australia and New Zealand Pacific Island Schemes

Australia has a Seasonal Worker Program (SWP) and New Zealand a Recognized Seasonal Employers (RSE) scheme to allow workers from eleven Pacific Island Countries (PICs) to fill seasonal farm jobs. The labor and foreign affairs ministries in each receiving country, and those in sending countries charged with labor and development, are involved in the design and administration of programs that aim for win-win-win outcomes—filling jobs in destination countries, enabling workers to earn higher wages and send home remittances, and promoting development in PICs that often offer few opportunities for low-skilled workers to increase their earnings.

The New Zealand (NZ) RSE is older and larger than the Australian SWP. The RSE involved 6,500 Pacific Island workers in 2013–14, versus 2,000 in the SWP, and the RSE ceiling for 2015–16 is 9,500, twice the 4,500 for the SWP

(Curtain, 2015).[40] Wages are lower in NZ, from which many fruits and vegetables that meet exacting quality standards are exported to Europe. Wages are higher in Australia, where many producers aim to keep labor costs low to sell fruits and vegetables in domestic markets and to Asian countries. NZ producers who receive higher prices for their exported produce can afford higher labor costs than Australian producers who deliver fruits and vegetables to the country's two dominant supermarket chains on time and at low cost.

The NZ RSE began April 30, 2007 after farmers complained of too few workers to harvest wine grapes, kiwifruit and apples. NZ exports half of the commodities produced on 5,500 commercial horticultural farms with the help of a peak 40,000 seasonal workers in March–April, including 60 percent who are hired in the Hawke's Bay and Bay of Plenty regions. With fewer un- and under-employed NZ workers and working holidaymakers (foreign youth earning money while touring NZ) available to harvest their crops, gangmasters or contractors filled the gap with crews of foreign students and other migrants, some of whom were not authorized to work.

Uncertainty about the supply of harvest labor and illegal work prompted farmers and the government to look for a new source of legal workers to fill seasonal jobs. The World Bank, noting that half of the populations of the PICs are under 24 and that 60 percent of youth are NEETs, that is, not in education, employment, or training, was seeking more wage work for Pacific Island workers, including in Australia and NZ (Luthria et al 2006; Haque and Packard, 2014).

The final factor effectuating the RSE was the UN's High-Level Dialogue on migration and development in fall 2006, which urged governments to open more channels for migrants from lower-wage countries to increase remittances and speed development. This development benefit was highlighted in a NZ government submission to an Australian Parliamentary Inquiry in 2015, which emphasized the triple wins from the RSE: filling vacant jobs in NZ, generating more jobs for NZ workers, and promoting development in the Pacific Islands (New Zealand Government Submission, 2015).

As with other seasonal farm labor programs, the Australia and NZ programs give local workers the first chance to fill farm jobs. This means that farmers must try and fail to recruit local workers by offering at least the minimum wage or the prevailing wage for the work to be done. There have been few complaints of NZ farmers refusing to hire available local workers, and the government has been relatively effective in reducing the use of labor contractors who in the past provided unauthorized farm workers.

Once certified to employ PIC workers, NZ farm employers must offer contracts that guarantee PIC migrants at least 240 hours and 30 hours a week at the

---

[40] Admissions of PIC workers to NZ in 2015–16 were about 8,500.

minimum wage of NZ$14.75 ($9.65) an hour after April 1, 2015. Farm employers must provide the migrants they employ with housing, health insurance, and pastoral care, such as transportation for banking and religious services. Farmers must also pay half of the cost of a return ticket for PIC migrants.

NZ employers can recruit PIC workers directly or select workers from lists prepared by local governments. For example, the Tongan government used village committees to rank the "work-ready" men and women who wanted to work in NZ by criteria such as honesty, being a hard worker, and knowing some English; about 5,000 or 20 percent of Tongan men between 20 and 60 registered to work in NZ in 2008. Before departing, migrant workers must obtain passports and undergo health checks and police clearances as well as complete a pre-departure orientation. Most PIC migrants remain in NZ for up to 7 months, but migrants from Kiribati and Tuvalu can stay in NZ up to 9 months because of their higher travel costs.

The number of RSE migrants was capped at 5,000 until 2008, when the ceiling was raised to 8,000 and to 9,000 in 2014. There have been about 7,000 RSE migrants in NZ in recent years, making them almost 20 percent of peak employment. PIC workers earn an average NZ$2,400 ($2,000) a month for an average 5 months in NZ, and remit half of what they earned to their families; an NZ Government Submission in 2015 reported that RSE migrants had average net earnings of NZ$5,500 a year ($3,667). The major skills acquired in NZ include better English, improved abilities to manage time and money, and perhaps an improved work ethic. However, the fruit and wine grapes produced in NZ are not produced in the Pacific Islands, making experience with these crops of limited use at home.

Employers say that, because most RSE migrants do not have experience picking fruit, newly arrived workers require training and a break-in period to become proficient workers. However, since most RSE migrants return year after year, employers recoup their training expenses via the higher prod-uctivity of returning workers. The workers have few complaints, although some note that they incur living costs when there is no work and that some employers set piece rates so low that workers earn only the minimum wage. Piece-rate workers normally earn more than the minimum wage, giving them an incentive to work fast without close supervision.[41]

Evaluations suggest the RSE has been successful in filling jobs with rural and less educated Pacific Islanders who earn more in NZ than they would earn at home. The third hoped-for win is faster development. If migration speeds development, its effects should soon be visible in migrant-sending villages. Gibson et al. (2008) found that RSE migrants averaged 17 weeks of work in NZ

---

[41] Some New Zealand employers had to raise piece rates so that RSE workers earned at least the minimum wage at the rate at which they were able to work.

and had average net earnings of NZ$5,700 ($3,400) after paying for half of their airfare and living expenses. They concluded that per capita incomes in Pacific Island households with at least one member in the RSE were 40 percent higher than similar households without migrants, suggesting that migration to NZ raised incomes far more than microfinance and conditional cash transfers in other developing countries. Households with participants in the RSE were also more likely to improve their homes, buy durable goods, and keep 15–18-year-olds in secondary school.

Vanuatu provided over a third of RSE migrants in recent years, followed by 20 percent from Tonga, 15 percent from Samoa, and almost 10 percent from Thailand; over 80 percent of RSE migrants were from seven Pacific Island countries. Most are men: 85 percent of those admitted in 2012–13 from Vanuatu under the RSE were men, as were 88 percent of those from Tonga admitted to Australia under the SWP (ILO, 2015c).

There are several looming tensions. First, farm employers prefer experienced workers to benefit from their higher productivity, but rehiring experienced workers can mean fewer opportunities for new Pacific Islands' workers to participate, which may slow the development impacts of working abroad. Second, more workers want to be employed in NZ than there are jobs. If the pool of workers from which NZ employers can select increases faster than NZ job opportunities, the result may be slower development if workers who anticipate being selected shun local opportunities in anticipation of going to NZ.

The third issue is the future of the RSE. The high value of the NZ dollar and welfare reforms that may add to the supply of farm workers in NZ has kept the number of guest workers below the 9,000 quota. On the other hand, if NZ fruit and wine exporters can achieve some kind of a fair trade label for commodities produced with the help of PIC workers, they may continue to hire them in order to receive premium prices. GlobalGap, a European organization that certifies farm compliance with Good Agricultural Practice in food safety, sustainable production methods, worker and animal welfare, responsible use of water, and compound feed and plant propagation materials, has accredited ten times more producers in NZ than in Australia.

The Horticulture and Viticulture Seasonal Working Group, which includes representatives of government, employers, and unions, is charged with developing medium- and long-term strategies for the NZ horticultural industry. NZ industry groups say that the availability of reliable PIC migrants has encouraged them to expand production and exports of horticultural commodities.

Australia's Pacific Seasonal Worker Pilot Scheme (PSWPS) was launched in 2008 with up to 2,500 seasonal work visas available to PIC migrants. Even though Australia has a far larger agricultural sector, relatively few Pacific Islanders were admitted under the PSWPS, largely because local Australian workers and working holidaymakers have been available to fill seasonal farm jobs. Some Australian farmers complain that the fees charged by the three officially approved labor-hire firms are too high, and that some of the PIC migrants selected to work on their farms "know how to read a pay slip but don't know what an orange is," suggesting a weak work ethic.[42] Connect Group, one of the approved labor providers, in turn complained that some farmers prefer to use local contractors and unauthorized workers rather than PIC migrants.[43]

The reason for relatively few PIC migrants in Australia is because local Australian workers and working holidaymakers have been available to fill seasonal farm jobs.[44] As in NZ, local contractors assembling crews of some-times unauthorized immigrants and others compete to provide workers to farmers at costs that can be lower than hiring PIC migrants.[45] Working holidaymakers or backpackers are foreign youth from many countries who are in Australia to work and holiday on visas that are valid for up to a year.

Since 2006, backpackers can stay in Australia 2 years if they work at least 88 days in agriculture, forestry, fishing, construction, and mining during their first year. About 90 percent of backpackers who stayed 2 years worked in agriculture during year 1, and about 90 percent of farmers said they were satisfied with backpackers (Curtain, 2015). Farmers do not have to advertise for Australian workers before hiring backpackers, although they must try to recruit local workers before hiring PIC migrants.[46]

Australia renamed the PSWPS the Seasonal Worker Program (SWP) and made it permanent on July 1, 2012. The annual quota was raised to 12,500 (and eliminated June 18, 2015), and SWP workers were allowed to work in

[42] Australia, New Zealand, 2010. *Migration News* 17(2). https://migration.ucdavis.edu/mn/more.php?id=3603.

[43] Approved SWP employers are listed at http://employment.gov.au/seasonal-worker-programme.

[44] Australian farmers in 2008 said they needed 22,000 more seasonal workers; up to A$700 million in fruit rotted for lack of labor to pick it. See: http://migration.ucdavis.edu/rmn/more.php?id=1349.

[45] For example, in 2008, the minimum wage in the Swan Hill area for farmworkers was supposed to be A$17, when some contractors reportedly paid A$12 and charged workers for housing and rides to work. Contractors officially received a 5 percent commission from the farms to which they supply workers, but many augment this commission with other charges levied on workers. Local reports are that larger farms run by investment partnerships are most likely to use reputable contractors. See: http://migration.ucdavis.edu/rmn/more.php?id=1349.

[46] There are two backpacker visas: 417 for developed countries, with 183,000 visas granted in 2013–14, and 462 for developing countries, with 10,000 visas granted in 2013–14. Until 2015, only those with 417 visas could stay a second year after working in selected sectors their first year, but now all backpacker visa holders can stay two years with qualifying work in their first year. Howes expects more backpackers to switch from horticulture to tourism in Northern Australia to earn a second-year visa. With backpackers since 2015 able to work for one employer for 24 months, backpackers essentially have 2-year temporary work visas with employers who do not have to test the labor market for Australian workers (see: http://devpolicy.org/a-big-week-for-pacific-labour-mobility-backpacker-reforms-20150625/.)

both crop agriculture and hotels in some areas. SWP workers must be offered enough work in Australia to gain a "net financial benefit" of at least A$1,000 (about 1 month's work). SWP workers can stay in Australia up to 6 months without their family members, or 9 months for workers from Kiribati, Nauru, and Tuvalu. Three-fourths of the first waves of SWP workers admitted have been from Tonga.

The SWP operates similarly to the RSE. Australian employers must first try to recruit local workers and, if this recruitment fails, they can be certified to employ PIC migrants. Employers must pay transportation to the work site, but can deduct from worker pay up to $500 for international travel and $500 for domestic travel from the worker's arrival place in Australia to the workplace. PIC migrants must be guaranteed at least 30 hours of work a week, and employers must show that employment in Australia is in the migrant's best interest, although the previous requirement that employers offer a minimum 14 weeks of Australian employment was dropped. Contractors are allowed to employ PIC migrants if they have been in business at least 5 years and "have a record of compliance with immigration and workplace relations requirements."

Most of the Approved Employer farmers using the SWP are satisfied, saying that PIC migrants are "more dependable, enthusiastic and productive than local workers or working holidaymakers" (Doyle and Howes, 2015). Many of the farms using the SWP to obtain PIC migrants are larger and grow crops that have relatively long growing seasons. In surveys, farmers want the government to shift the cost of transportation to workers (in 2005 the government allowed SWP employers to pay and then deduct the cost of domestic travel from worker wages) to eliminate requirements to provide housing for SWP workers, and to end required advertising to find local workers.[47]

Doyle and Howes concluded that the SWP must be made cheaper for employers if the Australian government wants to increase the number of PIC migrants. Farm employers may also have to reorient from shorter- to longer-term thinking. Backpackers are cheaper than PIC migrants because there is no need for farmers to try to find local workers before hiring them and no requirement to provide backpackers with accommodation and other services. However, if backpackers are employed only 4–6 weeks, the employer may have to train replacements. A PIC migrant employed for 6 months, and returning year after year, may prove cheaper over time if productivity increases with experience.

---

[47] One recruiter asserted that: "The farmer's request should be sufficient evidence that a genuine need exists and that there are an insufficient amount of reliable workers to fill the need," see: http://devpolicy.org/reforming-the-swp-a-recruiters-perspective-20150227/.

Other Bilateral Labor Agreements

There are more than 200 BLAs, MOU, and similar arrangements[48] between governments to manage the movement of workers over national borders; two-thirds were signed after 2005 (Wickramasekara, 2015a). BLAs vary greatly in length, detail, and roles for private recruiters. Even when BLAs ban licensed recruiters from moving workers over borders, they often allow consultants and others to help employers and workers to navigate migration processes and procedures.

An evaluation of the provisions of 144 BLAs found that few complied with all twenty-seven provisions of the model BLA developed by the ILO in 1949 to manage international labor migration (Wickramasekara, 2015a). The Canada–Mexico SAWP had the most provisions of the ILO model contract, eighteen of twenty-seven, including provisions governing recruitment and social security and specifying a minimum wage. Of course, having an ILO-recommended provision in a BLA does not mean that it is implemented.

Some BLAs specify particular private recruiters to screen workers for foreign employers. For example, MOU agreements between the Philippines and several Canadian provinces signed in 2008 require Canadian provincial authorities to send approved job offers to the Philippines Department of Labor and Employment (DOLE), which in turn distributes them to licensed Filipino recruiters. In this case, both the Canadian government and DOLE verify that the job offer satisfies their standards, DOLE ensures that only licensed recruiters are involved in finding Filipino workers, and both countries cooperate to ensure that employers pay all recruitment costs.

Do BLAs rather than private recruiters result in lower costs for workers? In the case of Korea, the answer appears to be yes, as studies agree that worker-paid costs have fallen by half or more since government agencies replaced private recruiters. However, there are two caveats about the EPS. First, the EPS is subsidized from Korea's foreign aid budget, so that some of the costs of making workers aware of the EPS and encouraging them to return and reintegrate in their countries of origin are covered by foreign aid funds. Second, there is significant opportunity cost to workers, since many learn Korean and pass the Korean language test but are not selected to work in Korea.

The Bangladesh–Malaysia BLA is more problematic. After policy changes in both countries left 15,000 Bangladeshis stranded at Malaysian airports in September–October 2007, the Malaysian government banned the recruitment

---

[48] BLAs are normally legally binding instruments between nation states, as with investor protection agreements, while MOU are not legal but are used frequently to manage labor migration.

of new Bangladeshi workers.[49] In 2013 a BLA was signed that forbade private recruiters from sending Bangladeshis to work on Malaysian plantations and set the maximum worker-paid fee at 40,000 taka ($515). Bangladeshi recruiters protested that they had invested to "open the market" in Malaysia for Bangladeshis, and now could not place workers there.

When the Bangladesh–Malaysia BLA was signed in 2013, there was talk of sending 100,000 Bangladeshis a year to Malaysian plantations. However, after 2 years, fewer than 10,000 Bangladeshis went to Malaysia under the BLA. Instead, a "travel now, pay later" system evolved under which recruiters and smugglers arrange transportation to Malaysia in exchange for up to $2,000 which is deducted from the Malaysian wages of Bangladeshi migrants, equivalent to more than 8 months' pay.

A profile of workers employed by Malaysia's Felda Global, one of the world's largest producers of crude palm oil, highlighted the challenges of protecting migrant workers.[50] Felda Global acknowledged that 34,000 or 85 percent of its plantation workers are foreigners, and most are provided by contractors who do not pay migrants the promised wages and sometimes do not pay them at all as they are shuffled from one contractor to another. Workers employed directly by Felda Global, a member of the Roundtable on Sustainable Palm Oil, said they were paid promised wages and treated well, a sharp contrast with the experiences of the employees of contractors.[51]

All workers in peninsular Malaysia should be paid at least RM900 ($240), the monthly minimum wage after January 1, 2013, but employers may deduct the cost of the levy, RM 590 a year in plantations, as well as the cost of housing for workers, often RM50 a month.[52] Many employers pay the annual levy upfront and deduct it from worker wages each month, and by withholding migrants' passports give them incentives to ensure that they do not "run away." The contractors may pay the minimum wage, but recoup some of the wages paid workers via monopoly stores that sell food and supplies to workers who often live on the plantations far from stores. Felda Global says that it is reducing the

---

[49] Some 200 Malay recruiters were allowed to bring 300,000 Bangladeshis to Malaysia in 2007, and some 200,000 arrived before the Malaysian government suspended further recruitment in October 2007. One reason was high costs. Officially, Bangladeshis were to pay no more than 84,000 taka ($1,080), but many reported paying 200,000 taka. In 1999, Malaysia suspended the recruitment of Bangladeshis, and lifted the ban in 2006.

[50] Syed Zain Al-Mahmood, 2015. Palm-Oil Migrant Workers Tell of Abuses on Malaysian Plantations. *Wall Street Journal*, July 27. http://www.wsj.com/articles/palm-oil-migrant-workers-tell-of-abuses-on-malaysian-plantations-1437933321.

[51] The Roundtable on Sustainable Palm Oil certifies that plantations comply with environmental and social standards.

[52] Felda Global says that workers must work at least 26 days a month to earn the full minimum wage. Some workers say that they do not receive enough work to earn the minimum wage despite Malaysian laws requiring employers to offer sufficient work to earn the minimum wage each month.

use of contractors, monitors the wages and working conditions of workers brought to farms by contractors, and suggested that the abuses highlighted in the profile are an exception.

Many plantations prefer to hire irregular Indonesians provided by contractors rather than Bangladeshis sent via the Bangladeshi–Malaysia BLA. The Indonesians are more familiar with palm oil production, which involves cutting 50 to 60 pound bunches of the fruit of oil palms that grow near the top of 40 to 50 foot-high trees using a sickle attached to a long pole. Indonesia is the world's largest producer of palm oil, and Indonesian workers who paid less for jobs are more willing to accept deductions from their wages for the levy and housing.

Malaysia produces about 40 percent of the world's palm oil, and was upgraded in 2015 from a Tier 3 to a Tier 2 country in the annual US Department of State (DOS) Trafficking in Persons Report; Tier 3 countries are not making significant efforts to reduce human trafficking. Malaysia was one of twelve countries negotiating the Trans-Pacific Partnership (TPP) free-trade agreement, and US law prohibits the signing of free-trade agreements with countries on the Tier 3 list, prompting suggestions that DOS upgraded Malaysia in order to allow it to sign the TPP. President Trump withdrew the US from TPP negotiations.

Labor migration in Bangladesh and Malaysia is marked by corruption in both countries. The shortcomings of the Bangladesh–Malaysia BLA prompted the Malaysian government in September 2015 to give Synerflux Sdn Bhd, co-owned by former Malaysian home minister Azmi Khalid, a monopoly on bringing Bangladeshis to Malaysia. Khalid previously co-owned Bestinet, which allegedly charged high fees to Indonesian and Nepalese migrants.[53] If the Bangladeshi Workers Management System is implemented, Synerflux would collect job orders from Malaysian employers and use selected Bangladeshi recruiters to find workers to fill them.

From an Organization of the Petroleum Exporting Countries to an Organization of Labor Exporting Countries?

In 1960, four oil exporters met in Baghdad to form the Organization of Petroleum Exporting Countries (OPEC), which expanded and shocked the world in the 1970s with oil price hikes. The price of oil rose from $3 a barrel in 1973 to $37 a barrel in 1980, most industrial countries experienced recessions, and manufacturing shed thousands of jobs as the era of cheap energy ended.

---

[53] Details at http://www.thedailystar.net/frontpage/firm-dubious-records-charge-154780.

Cartels aim to restrict the supply of a commodity in order to increase its price. Most eventually fail because individual cartel members have incentives to cheat, to provide a slight discount from the cartel price in order to sell more, with the discount often concealed in a rebate for lower quality or in some other fashion. OPEC's power over the price of oil has shrunk, but OPEC remains a symbol of one of the most effective commodity cartels ever established by governments.[54]

Could countries that send workers abroad develop an Organization of Labor Exporting Countries (OLEC), a union of migrant-sending countries that sets minimum wages and working conditions for workers employed outside their country of citizenship? There have been many proposals for OLEC-type organizations, with proponents laying out the benefits that could flow to migrant-sending countries if they rather than foreign employers could dictate the terms for the employment of their citizens.

The argument runs as follows. Governments in migrant-sending countries invest in the health and education of citizens who spend some of their most productive years abroad. By setting minimum wages and standards for their citizens employed abroad, OLEC governments could withhold labor from employers in countries that do not have minimum wages and offer few work-related benefits. If OLEC controlled enough of the supply of migrant workers, migrant-receiving countries would have to agree to OLEC terms in order to obtain foreign workers.[55]

The anticipated virtuous circle would have OLEC governments doing a better job of screening and training workers so that they are more productive abroad and governments in migrant-receiving countries collecting work-related taxes on the higher earnings of migrant workers. In some variations, governments in migrant-receiving countries would remit some of these taxes to governments in migrant-sending countries to pay for the workers' education.

Could an OLEC be formed and achieve the success of OPEC? If an OLEC raised the cost of migrant workers, would recruiters send more workers abroad illegally, so that workers wind up paying more for foreign jobs and having fewer protections abroad? More importantly, with the number of workers growing much faster than the number of jobs in many developing countries, would migrant-sending countries cheat by turning a blind eye to non-regulated departures?

There are many other questions. Could an OLEC prevent a country such as Nepal from sending workers abroad at a temporarily lower wage in order to

---

[54] Governments of OPEC countries own the oil in the ground, and charge royalties on oil as it is extracted.

[55] Sami Mahroum, 2016. An OPEC for Migrant Labor? *Project Syndicate* August 19, at: https://www.project-syndicate.org/commentary/an-opec-for-migrant-labor-by-sami-mahroum-2016-08.

increase remittances to rebuild after an earthquake? Allowing such exceptions could very quickly undermine any OLEC, as member countries act in their sovereign interest rather than in the interest of the cartel; this is perhaps the major reason why an OLEC has been more discussion than reality ever since Jordan's Crown Prince Hassan at the ILO's annual conference in June 1977 called for countries that receive migrant workers to compensate migrant-sending countries. He warned that if they did not, migrant-sending countries could form a labor-sending cartel.

8

Employers, Recruiters, and Workers

Merchants of labor are the glue of international labor market recruiters, the intermediaries between workers in one country and jobs in another. They have long been considered necessary evils to fill less-desirable jobs. Private recruiters today are involved in the movement of most of the 10 million workers who cross national borders each year, generating annual revenues of $10–$20 billion.

Worker-paid migration costs are a concern for three reasons. First, they are high, absorbing from low-skilled workers 1–10 months foreign earnings and diverting money that could go to migrants and their families into the pockets of better-off recruiters and others in the migration infrastructure. Survey data show that recruiters often add little value to worker–job matches, that is, they neither ensure that workers have the skills employers need, nor put workers in the jobs best suited to their skills.

Second is the regressive nature of recruitment costs, with lower-skill and lower-wage workers paying more in migration costs than high-skilled migrants because the supply of low-skilled workers is larger than the demand for them. Highly skilled workers invest in earning degrees and obtaining certification of their skills. The fact that there are fewer high-skilled workers relative to the demand for them, and that the costs of poor worker–job matches rise with the level of skills, means that employers are willing to invest more to recruit high-skilled workers and to pay their migration costs.

Third is the lack of transparency about recruitment costs. No one knows exactly how much low-skilled workers pay for foreign jobs. Media reports suggest that many workers pay far more than one month's foreign earnings to get contracts for jobs abroad, and exposés of workers who arrive abroad in debt can leave the impression that most workers pay a significant fraction of their foreign earnings to recruiters and others. The survey data do not agree with this conventional wisdom, finding instead that most low-skilled workers returning from Gulf oil-exporting countries had relatively low migration costs.

Matching workers with jobs is a core function of labor markets and subject to extensive government regulation. Governments enact laws that lay out minimum standards, from wages and benefits to safe working conditions, and rely on workers to complain in order to enforce these regulations. This same approach is used to regulate recruiters, who are generally required to identify themselves by obtaining licenses. Recruiter activities are regulated, often quite closely, by mandates to pass tests of their knowledge of regulations, post bonds, and abide by maximum fee and other constraints on their businesses. Workers are educated about recruiter regulations, and their complaints prompt investigations of suspect recruiters.

This three-pronged approach of licensing, regulation, and acting on complaints has not prevented some workers from paying very high recruitment fees. As a result, there is a quest for new regulations, more worker education and enforcement, and bilateral agreements (BLAs) to reduce worker-paid costs (Jones, 2015). However, doing more of what had not protected migrant workers during recruitment may not be the most effective approach.

There are several truths about the recruitment of low-skill migrant workers. First, matching workers with jobs has costs that must be paid by someone—employers, recruiters, or workers. Second, passing laws that require employers to pay all worker recruitment costs is not realistic if there are more workers than jobs. Worker willingness to pay is one means of allocating scarce foreign jobs, and declaring high payments illegal and not offering an alternative allocation mechanism simply drives worker payments underground. Third, even in the world's highest cost migration corridors that move workers to and from jobs in Gulf Coooperation Council (GCC) countries, most workers pay less than 10 percent of their foreign earnings in recruitment costs.

Could economic incentives *induce* recruiters to comply with protective labor laws? Recruiting is an economic business in which profits are the difference between revenues and costs. Relying on complaints and penalties has not prevented recruiters from overcharging workers, largely because recruiters can encourage most workers to withdraw complaints by giving them what they want—a foreign job that offers higher wages. If government incentives could raise the revenue of good recruiters more than fines raise the costs of bad recruiters, market forces may provide an incentive for more recruiters to comply with protective labor laws.

Incentive systems that reward compliant recruiters can also help to transform the recruitment industry, changing it from many small and family-owned agents who engage in frequent one-time transactions into fewer and larger partners of foreign employers who standardize worker contracts, achieve economies of scale that reduce costs, and have reputations worth protecting as they place more workers abroad over time. A migration system based on long-term partner recruiters is likely to be more efficient and protective of workers than the current system based on agents competing for one-time business.

Reducing Worker-Paid Costs

International labor migration is a normal market transaction that is often expensive for worker participants. They make payments to recruiters and others for foreign jobs, pay for documents and health and similar checks, and pay for pre-departure training. Migrants also incur opportunity costs as they travel to recruiters, government agencies, and training centers. Once abroad, workers may pay for recruitment indirectly in the form of lower-than-average wages and benefits.

Interviews with workers in Korea, Kuwait, and Spain found that most earned at least five times more abroad than they could earn at home while paying less than a month's foreign earnings in migration costs. Migration costs were a lower share of earnings in Korea, where migrants may stay up to 5 years, than in Spain, where migrants were employed less than a year in agriculture. Migrants in Kuwait paid the highest migration costs and had the lowest earnings, paying an average 4 months of Kuwaiti earnings in migration costs. There were differences between corridors: Bangladeshis and Egyptians paid more than Indians and Sri Lankans.

Workers returning from Qatar, Saudi Arabia (SA), and the United Arab Emirates (UAE) paid the equivalent of 1–9 months' earnings for their jobs. Filipinos returning from Qatar paid a month's Qatari earnings for their jobs, while Ethiopians returning from SA paid 4 months' Saudi earnings. Indians returning from Qatar paid 2 months' Qatari earnings for their jobs, while Nepalese paid more than 3 months of their Qatari earnings. Pakistanis paid the most, 9 months' earnings for jobs in SA and the UAE.

Recruiting is an economic business, and licensed recruiters are trying to maximize profits. The current regulatory model aims to protect workers by penalizing recruiters who violate protective laws. However, recruiter–worker interactions are often victimless crimes in the sense that some workers willingly pay recruiters more than legal maximums in order to ensure that they are selected to fill foreign jobs. Relying on worker complaints to ensure compliance in such situations is unlikely to be effective.

An alternative to the stick of enforcement is the carrot of government incentives that increase the revenue of good recruiters. Governments can offer three major economic incentives to induce better recruiter behavior: lower processing costs, tax breaks, and awards and introductions. Good or A-rated recruiters can be exempted from some or all fees, providing recruiters with some of the revenue that would otherwise come from migrant workers.

The justification for lower fees is that governments need to spend less to check on good recruiters and the workers they send abroad.

Similarly, good recruiters can be exempted from VAT and other taxes that consume 15 percent to 25 percent of revenues. The justification for giving good recruiters tax breaks is the same as that for offering incentives to foreign investors. Just as foreign investment can bring new technologies and create jobs, so sending workers abroad can speed development at home, justifying tax exemptions and subsidies for good recruiters. Awards and the opportunity to accompany political leaders abroad can help good recruiters to expand their business, giving them a leg up in the competition with other recruiters.

There are alternatives to recruiter incentives, including more enforcement, codes of good recruiter conduct, and BLAs. Each is problematic. For example, more enforcement is unlikely to eliminate violations of regulations that are in conflict with market realities. If governments ban worker-paid fees or set maximum fees too low, worker payments will be made in ways that are hard to track as a means of allocating scarce foreign jobs. Data and experience suggest that *if* governments nonetheless want to keep recruiter fees below market rates, the best strategy is to ban all worker-paid fees, since allowing some worker-paid fees opens the door to hard-to-trace additional payments.

If governments succeed in keeping worker-paid recruitment fees below what workers are willing to pay, workers are likely to pay for their recruitment in other ways. For example, requiring employers to pay all recruitment costs for domestic workers can prompt recruiters to require new arrivals abroad to undergo training whose costs are deducted from wages, opening another door for recruiters to collect payments from workers. There are many examples of recruiters or recruiter-affiliates providing training to low-skilled workers who would like to work abroad and, so long as this "training" is not required to obtain a particular job, it is lawful to have workers pay for training.

Codes of good conduct are premised on the assumption that employers want to use good recruiters and cannot find them. Over the past decade, there have been several efforts to form associations that certify recruiter compliance with a code of conduct, but there is not yet convincing evidence that codes of conduct have raised recruiter standards. More important may be supply-chain compliance programs, as when brand names insist that their contract manufacturers who hire migrant workers do not charge migrants for jobs. Apple in 2015 barred its contract manufacturers from charging workers for jobs, and reported that it required them to reimburse 4,500 workers about $4 million in 2014, an average $900.[1] The effectiveness of supply-chain compliance systems

---

[1] http://www.apple.com/supplier-responsibility/labor-and-human-rights/.

depends on how they operate day to day rather than on the few days when audits are conducted (Martin, 2016).

The International Labour Organization (ILO) has consistently called for BLAs that substitute government agencies for private recruiters, taking private profits out of recruitment. Giving government agencies a monopoly on recruitment could eliminate recruiter fees, but runs the risk of sparking corruption if there are more workers than jobs and inefficiency in sending workers abroad. The bilateral programs that are often touted as best practices, from the Korean Employment Permit System (EPS) to the New Zealand Recognized Seasonal Employers (RSE) system, are relatively small, involving fewer than 50,000 workers a year and often subsidized from the aid budgets of the richer country.

Moving Forward

Worker-paid migration costs are the new frontier to make the international labor migration system more efficient and protective of migrant workers, with world leaders acknowledging the "enormous gains to be made by lowering costs... especially [those paid] by low-skilled migrants." The shared global goal in the wake of the 9/11 terrorist attacks of reducing remittance costs to shrink the informal money transfer channels used by migrants which could also be used by terrorists is not exactly analogous for migrants, since reducing recruitment costs transfers money from employers and recruiters to migrants.

There are other differences between remittances and recruitment. Lowering the cost of sending small sums over borders can increase the flow of remittances via regulated financial institutions, an example of demand elasticity, that is, when prices go down, the quantity or volume goes up, bolstering revenues for money transfer firms. International labor migration is different because the demand for foreign workers is determined in migrant-receiving countries, and they may not increase migrant worker admissions in response to lower recruitment costs. Indeed, if employers pay recruitment costs, the demand for migrant workers is likely to fall.

What should governments do? Migrant advocates urge adoption and implementation of laws that require employers to pay all migration costs for the migrant workers they employ, and call on governments to enact and enforce regulations that lead to employer-pays-all costs outcomes, that is, they seek a definitive solution to a wicked problem. This book argues that a better way of conceptualizing the worker-paid migration cost problem is to consider incremental economic interventions rather than aiming for solutions.

The current system, which rations jobs in a non-transparent way that results in workers paying high and variable costs, is hard to defend. However, it is also hard to imagine a world in which low-skilled migrants move under the aegis of government agencies that charge little or nothing for worker–job matching services. This book assumes that private recruiters are here to stay, and recommends ways to change the behavior of recruiters to benefit them and the low-skilled workers they place in foreign jobs.

Moving low-skilled workers over national borders is a complex process fraught with challenges. Most of those involved in regulating the movement of low-skilled workers over borders earn far more than the migrants they place and help to protect. The fact that the migrants are low skilled means there can be misunderstandings that complicate the regulation of recruiters, as it can be frustrating to obtain credible evidence of oral promises and payments for which there are no receipts. Neither the regulatory apparatus nor the recruitment industry employs large numbers of returned migrants, making it hard to inject migrant experiences into the industry and its regulation.

Migration is a journey of hope and fear, hope for economic betterment due to higher foreign wages and fear of complex and costly migration processes at home and unknown jobs abroad. Protecting low-wage migrant workers as they move from poorer to richer countries defies easy solutions. The best protection is obvious: empowering workers to say no to high fees and low wages by providing good jobs at home; but this leaves the question of how to regulate international labor migration effectively until decent work in all countries is achieved. Making the migration process more transparent and efficient with incentives for good recruiter behavior can reap dividends for employers, migrants, and both sending and receiving societies.

Sustainable Development Goals and Migration Costs

World leaders at the UN's Millennium Summit in 2000 agreed on eight Millennium Development Goals (MDGs) to be achieved by 2015, including eliminating extreme poverty and hunger, increasing education and improving child and maternal health, and promoting global partnerships for development (www.un.org/millenniumgoals). The MDGs, the most broadly supported poverty reduction goals ever set by world leaders, were based on three pillars: raising basic standards of living, increasing social, economic and political rights, and improving infrastructure.

The MDGs called attention to the potential of faster development to improve the lives of the world's poorest people. The first MDG, to halve the proportion of the world population living in dire poverty by 2015, was achieved in 2010, when the World Bank estimated that 21 percent of the world's people lived on less than $1.25 a day, down from 43 percent in 1990, with China accounting for half of the decline in extreme poverty (World Bank, 2010). Countries including Brazil and Mexico reduced extreme poverty by transferring cash to the poorest families.

The MDGs were replaced in 2015 by seventeen Sustainable Development Goals (SDGs) to be met by 2030 (www.un.org/sustainabledevelopment/sustainable-development-goals). They include ending poverty and hunger, ensuring healthy lives and education, achieving gender equality and inclusive economic growth, providing safe water and fostering viable cities, and making the global economy and biosphere sustainable. To counter criticism that progress toward achieving many of the MDGs could not be measured easily, the SDGs include 169 target indicators to allow citizens to measure their country's progress toward just, peaceful, and inclusive societies.

Goal 10 is to reduce inequality within and among countries. Target 10.7 calls on governments to "facilitate orderly, safe, regular and responsible migration and mobility of people, including through the implementation of planned and well-managed migration policies." Indicator 10.7.1 measures the recruitment costs borne by employees as a proportion of yearly income earned in country of destination.[1]

---

[1] A related target is to reduce "to less than three percent the transaction costs of migrant remittances and eliminate remittance corridors with costs higher than five percent" by 2030. Indicator 10.c.1 is "remittance costs as a proportion of the amount remitted."

Definitions

How should the worker-paid recruitment costs be defined and measured to track progress under SDG Indicator 10.7.1? There are four major worker-paid costs to consider:

1. general and specific training (including language) costs to prepare for jobs overseas;
2. the financial costs of obtaining contracts for jobs abroad, completing exit procedures, and traveling to the foreign job;
3. the opportunity costs of wages not earned at home while training and preparing to go abroad;
4. the social costs associated with separation from family and friends, and restrictions on rights while employed abroad.

Most studies focus on the second type of costs, the financial costs of workers who obtain foreign jobs.

Measuring worker-paid financial costs raises several issues. First, since highly trained workers generally pay low or no migration costs, should the cost of training undertaken by doctors and nurses that prompts foreign employers to pay their recruitment costs be included? Some doctors and nurses pay for their training, while others attend public institutions at little or no cost, raising the question of whether only private costs should be considered or whether public costs to train highly skilled workers who go abroad should also be considered?

Other training-related cost questions include whether the opportunity costs that arise in the form of wages not earned while studying should be included or ignored? Most surveys that ask workers what they paid to obtain foreign jobs do not include the cost of K-12 education and advanced schooling that could lead to a job at home or abroad, and they ignore tuition and other out of pocket costs as well as the opportunity cost of studying rather than working.

Some types of training are aimed specifically at work abroad, such as seafarer or cruise ship worker training, raising the question of whether the costs of training-that-will-pay-off-only-abroad should be included as a recruitment cost? Does it matter if governments require workers to undergo training before they can depart, as when domestic workers must undergo training before departure in some countries?

Second, which financial costs incurred to obtain the current foreign job should be included? Almost all surveys include the costs incurred to learn about the job, obtain a contract to fill the job, complete pre-departure procedures and obtain passports and visas as well as health and police clearances, and the cost of internal and international travel.

What about the costs of past failed efforts to work abroad? From the worker's point of view, past efforts that did not result in a foreign job should be included in the cost of the current successful effort. However, if past failed efforts to go to one country are attributed to the current job in another country, migration costs in a particular corridor could be raised artificially, biasing costs in a bilateral migration-cost matrix.

Third, should opportunity and social costs be included? Most worker surveys ignore opportunity and social costs because they are hard to measure accurately and are likely to vary widely from worker to worker; it is also hard to determine exactly how policy changes could affect opportunity and social costs. Similarly, it is difficult to measure the effects of the emigration of particular types of workers, such as the effects of the out-migration of health-care workers on those left behind. Difficulty in measuring what may be subjective costs means that opportunity and social costs are not included in cost of migration studies.

Interviewing Workers

SDG indicator 10.7.1 calls for measuring worker-paid financial costs as a share of annual foreign earnings. Unlike remittances, where remitter firms can be surveyed to determine what they charge to send $200 or $300 via various corridors, it is widely believed that recruitment cost data must be obtained from workers because recruiters will not report accurately the amounts they receive from workers.

Interviewing workers is expensive, and it would be useful to conduct surveys of recruiters in corridors where there is also worker-reported cost data to compare what recruiters and workers report, and whether any discrepancies can be explained. If the cost data provided by recruiters prove reliable, it is far cheaper to survey recruiters than workers.

Most migration-cost data are obtained from workers, who can be asked about the financial costs they incurred to get foreign jobs in three places: as they depart, during their employment abroad, or as they return. There are advantages and disadvantages of interviewing in each place. Asking departing workers what they paid provides a sampling frame if, for example, each one hundredth worker is interviewed, but departing workers may not know their net foreign earnings and may be reluctant to report that they paid excessive recruitment fees for fear that they may not be allowed to leave.

Interviewing workers while they are employed abroad has the advantage of providing accurate foreign earnings data, but there may be recall bias in reporting financial costs before departure. There are two major sampling issues: where to interview workers, and who should conduct the interviews.

There are three major options to collect worker-paid cost data in the country of employment. First, countries such as Canada, Korea, and Singapore conduct orientation sessions for some or all newly arrived workers, and a sample of new arrivals could be asked what they paid to get their jobs. The cost data are likely to be accurate, but newly arrived workers may not yet know their earnings.

Second, labor attaches posted in countries of employment could ask a sample of workers employed abroad about their migration costs.[2] Using labor attaches should reduce language issues and may have the added benefit of educating migrant-sending

---

[2] Baruh (2016: 24) reports that the Philippines had fifty labor attaches abroad, followed by nineteen for India, eighteen each for Pakistan and Sri Lanka, seventeen for Bangladesh, and thirteen each for Indonesia and Thailand. Except for Thailand, most were in Gulf Coooperation Council (GCC) countries.

governments about the migration costs and foreign earnings of their citizens, but additional resources would likely be required, since labor attaches are often already overstretched. A reliable sampling frame would have to be developed, since interviewing only workers who come to consulates with problems may generate a biased sample.

Third, receiving-government statistical agencies could interview migrant workers at home or work. Many labor force surveys are household based, meaning that workers are interviewed where they live rather than where they work. Household surveys can obtain data on more than employment and earnings, including income, reasons for not-working, and other socio-demographic data. However, it may be hard to obtain an accurate sampling frame for a household survey that includes migrant workers, especially those who live in nonstandard housing such as barracks and domestic workers who live with their employers.

Interviewing workers at work raises other issues. Employer or establishment surveys often rely on reports from employers of how many workers they employ and the wages they pay, and these data are often reported separately for production workers and supervisors and for men and women. Employer surveys could distinguish foreign-born and local workers, and within the foreign-born separate workers by visa status, but the result is likely to provide only employment and earnings data, not cost of migration data.

One workplace-centered survey, the US National Agricultural Workers Survey (www. doleta.gov/agworker/naws.cfm), interviews largely immigrant workers employed in agriculture. The National Agricultural Worker Survey (NAWS) was begun in 1989 because the household-based Current Population Survey was believed to miss many immigrant farm workers. The NAWS stratifies farm employers by size, samples workers within these strata by asking employers for permission to interview workers at work or at home, and pays workers $20 to participate in a survey that takes 45 minutes to complete. The NAWS costs the federal government about $5 million a year, with a private contractor interviewing 3,000 farm workers around the US at a cost of about $1,600 per interview. The NAWS may serve as a model for other governments wanting to survey hard-to-reach migrant workforces.

Fourth, workers could be interviewed as they returned from jobs abroad, especially to countries that have special desks for returning migrants, including Indonesia, Mexico, and the Philippines. Interviewing returning workers has the advantage of providing a sampling frame at relatively low cost, but could miss workers who return via means other than airports and seaports with migrant reception centers. Every hundredth worker could be asked to complete the survey, although an incentive may be needed to obtain cooperation from workers who have been away from waiting families for several years.

The most promising way to collect data on worker-paid migration costs as a share of foreign earnings is to collect data from workers while they are employed abroad. The lowest cost method in countries with orientation programs for newly arrived workers is to conduct interviews with a sample of new arrivals during their orientation. The second-lowest cost option is to use consular officials to interview their fellow citizens, but the cost of training and ensuring uniform survey methods may be high. There is potential to use migration-cost modules in labor force surveys to collect data from a larger sample of migrant workers at low cost, but only if more countries believe that such data are important (Clemens, 2009).[3]

Interviewing migrant workers via household or workplace surveys is likely to provide the most reliable data, but would take time and resources to implement. In a household survey, being foreign-born could be the first screen, followed by type of visa, but statistical agencies would have to be sensitive to groups that may not be well-represented in extant household surveys such as domestic workers. Country of destination (CoD)-government or contractor staff who conduct household surveys could interview a sample of migrant workers, with appropriate help to deal with various languages and cultural sensitivities, including assuring those being interviewed that their answers are confidential.

Costs, Loans, and Earnings

What cost data should be collected from migrant workers? Usual questions include what workers paid for the current job and the various components of the total charge, beginning with payments made to get the contract such as visa and agent fees, the costs of required documents and checks, including passports, visas, health, criminal, language, skills and other tests, internal and international travel costs, and any required payments to government migrant worker welfare funds or insurance funds.

In a labor force survey, there is likely space only for major migration-cost categories, and some workers may report only the lump sum payment to an agent or recruiter. Workers can be asked if employers or anyone else reimbursed them any of the migration costs they incurred.

Many workers borrow money to go abroad. Workers could be asked if they borrowed money to obtain the contract, from whom and at what interest rate, and the current status of the loan. These questions deal with worker-paid costs in the sense that borrowing money to work abroad can increase migration costs.

The third set of questions deals with jobs and earnings at home and abroad. Workers can be asked about employment and earnings in their current job, usual hours of work and work-related benefits, and employment and earnings before departure to estimate the wage wedge between migrant-sending and -receiving countries. Answers to these questions determine whether migration is economically worthwhile for workers, and the data can help to determine relationships between worker-paid costs and higher wages abroad.

Finally, workers could be asked about their rights abroad, and their perceptions of how they are treated while employed abroad. Usual questions include whether workplaces have unions and whether the migrant joined, whether migrants had deductions from their wages for work-related benefit programs, including workers compensation for injuries, unemployment insurance, pension programs, general health insurance, and bonuses, and whether migrants received benefits from such programs. Workers can

---

[3] Clemens (2009: 15–16) urges more migration modules on labor force and household surveys, and reporting the data from individuals in a single database to expedite answering questions such as the earnings payoff from working abroad.

also be asked about their perceptions of discrimination, religious freedom, and other aspects of life abroad.

Many cost, loan, and job- and life-related questions can be answered only by workers. Some of the questions may be sensitive, especially those dealing with worker perceptions of their rights while employed abroad.

Next Steps

The worker cost survey data summarized in Part 2 did not include data from the recruiters who collect most worker payments. An alternative approach would be to interview recruiters about worker-paid migration costs and to compare the results with worker surveys.

If recruiter- and worker-reported costs vary, there may be reasons, including the unwillingness of recruiters to acknowledge (over)charging workers and not knowing of worker payments to subagents and others in the migration chain. However, surveying labor intermediaries would have the advantage of being far less costly than surveying workers, analogous to calling money transfer firms and asking what they charge to send $200 between two countries in a particular corridor, and would provide an immediate basis to ask why costs for a particular type of worker vary within a corridor.

The best way forward would be to collect data from workers on what they paid to get jobs abroad, interview recruiters in some of the corridors for which worker-reported cost data are available to compare worker-reported and recruiter-reported cost data, and hold focus groups with workers, recruiters, employers, and others to reconcile worker- and recruiter-reported data on migration costs. There could also be meetings with government agencies that conduct household and labor force surveys to determine their capacity and willingness to add migration-cost modules to ongoing surveys, and meetings with labor attaches to determine the feasibility of them undertaking migration-cost surveys.

Bibliography

Abella, Manolo. 2004. The Recruiter's Share in Labour Migration, in Douglas Massey and Edward Taylor, eds., *International Migration. Prospects and Policies in a Global Market.* Oxford: Oxford University Press, 201–11. www.oxfordscholarship.com/view/10.1093/0199269009.001.0001/acprof-9780199269006.

Acosta, Pablo, Emmanuel Lartey, and Federico Mandelman. 2009. Remittances and the Dutch Disease. *Journal of International Economics* 79(1): 102–16. http://econpapers.repec.org/article/eeeinecon/v_3a79_3ay_3a2009_3ai_3a1_3ap_3a102-116.htm.

Adams, Richard and John Page. 2003. International Migration, Remittances, and Poverty in Developing Countries. World Bank Policy Research Working Paper Series 3179. https://ideas.repec.org/p/wbk/wbrwps/3179.html.

Agunias, Dovelyn. 2010. *Migration's Middlemen: Regulating Recruitment Agencies in the Philippines–United Arab Emirates Corridor.* Washington, DC: Migration Policy Institute. www.migrationpolicy.org/news/costs-private-recruitment-agencies-migrant-labor-sometimes-outweigh-benefits-mpi-study.

Agunias, Dovelyn. 2013. *What We Know: Regulating the Recruitment of Migrant Workers.* Washington, DC: Migration Policy Institute. www.migrationpolicy.org/research/what-we-know-regulating-recruitment-migrant-workers.

Akerlof, George. 1970. The Market for Lemons: Quality Uncertainty and the Market Mechanism. *Quarterly Journal of Economics* 84(3): 488–500. http://qje.oxfordjournals.org/content/84/3/488.short.

Amnesty International. 2009. Disposable Labour: Rights of Migrant Workers in South Korea. www.amnesty.org/en/documents/ASA25/001/2009/en/.

Andrees, Beate. 2006. Combating Criminal Activities in the Recruitment of Migrant Workers, in Christiane Kuptsch, ed., *Merchants of Labor.* Geneva: ILO, 175–84. www.ilo.org/public/english/bureau/inst/publ/books.htm.

Arango, Joaquin. 2013. *Exceptional in Europe? Spain's Experience with Immigration and Integration.* Washington, DC: Migration Policy Institute. www.migrationpolicy.org/research/exceptional-europe-spains-experience-immigration-and-integration.

Atoyan, Ruben, Lone Engbo Christiansen, Allan Dizioli, Christian Ebeke, Nadeem Ilahi, Anna Ilyina, Gil Mehrez, Haonan Qu, Faezeh Raei, Alaina Rhee, and Daria Zakharova. 2016. Emigration and Its Economic Impact on Eastern Europe. IMF Staff Discussion Notes No. 16/7. www.imf.org/external/pubs/cat/longres.aspx?sk=42896.0.

Autor, David (ed.). 2009. *Studies of Labor Market Intermediation.* Chicago, IL: University of Chicago Press. http://press.uchicago.edu/ucp/books/book/chicago/S/bo6407656.html.

Baffes, John, Ayhan Kose, Franziska Ohnsorge, and Marc Stocker. 2015. The Great Plunge in Oil Prices. World Bank. PRN 15/01/. http://documents.worldbank.org/ curated/en/726831468180852545/The-great-plunge-in-oil-prices-causes-consequences- and-policy-responses.

Balch, Alex. 2010. *Managing Labour Migration in Europe: Ideas, Knowledge and Policy Change*. Manchester: Manchester University Press. www.manchesteruniversitypress. co.uk/9780719080722/.

Barajas, Adolfo, Ralph Chami, Connel Fullenkamp, Michael Gapen, and Peter Montiel. 2009. Do Workers Remittances Promote Economic Growth? July. WP/09/153. https://www.imf.org/external/pubs/cat/longres.aspx?sk=23108.0.

Barauh, Nilim. 2006. The Regulation of Recruitment Agencies, in Christiane Kuptsch, ed., *Merchants of Labor*. Geneva: ILO, 37–46. www.ilo.org/public/english/bureau/ inst/publ/books.htm.

Barkat, Abul, Md. Ismail Hossain, and Ehsanul Hoque. 2014. The Cost, Causes of and Potential Redress for High Recruitment and Migration Costs in Bangladesh. Inter- national Labour Organization, ILO Country Office for Bangladesh, Dhaka. www.ilo. org/dhaka/Whatwedo/Publications/WCMS_303633/lang–en/index.htm.

Baruh, Nilim. 2016. Labor Migration Infrastructure and Services in Countries of Origin in Asia, in Asian Development Bank Institute, *Labor Migration in Asia: Building Effective Institutions*, Ch. 2, 18–29. https://www.adb.org/publications/labor-migration-asia- building-effective-institutions.

Basok, Tanya. 2007. *Canada's Temporary Migration Program: A Model Despite Flaws*. Washington, DC: Migration Policy Institute. www.justicia4migrantworkers.org/bc/ pdf/SAWP-A_Model_Despite_Flaws.pdf.

Beecroft, Adrian. 2012. *Report on Employment Law*. www.gov.uk/government/publica tions/employment-law-review-report-beecroft.

Bhagwati, Jagdish. 2003. Borders beyond Control. *Foreign Affairs* 82(1, January-February): 98–104. https://www.foreignaffairs.com/articles/2003-01-01/borders-beyond-control.

Booth, Philip. 2013. Qatar World Cup Construction Will Leave 4,000 Migrant Workers Dead. *The Guardian*, September 26. www.theguardian.com/global-development/ 2013/sep/26/qatar-world-cup-migrant-workers-dead.

Borjas, George. 2016. *We Wanted Workers. Unraveling the Immigration Narrative*. New York: Norton. http://books.wwnorton.com/books/We-Wanted-Workers/.

Callen, T., Cherif, R., Hasanov, F., Hegazy, A., and Khandelwal, P. 2014. Economic Diversification in the GCC: Past, Present, and Future. IMF Staff Note 14/12. https:// www.imf.org/external/pubs/cat/longres.aspx?sk=42531.0.

Chanda, Rupa. 2001. Movement of Natural Persons and the GATS. *World Economy* 24(5, May): 631–54. http://onlinelibrary.wiley.com/doi/10.1111/1467-9701.00373/abstract.

Chanda, Rupa. 2004. Movement and Presence of Natural Persons and Developing Coun- tries: Issues and Proposals for the GATS Negotiations. South Centre Working Paper 19. May. http://www.southcentre.int/ https://books.google.co.uk/books/about/Movement_ and_Presence_of_Natural_Persons.html?id=P3u9HAAACAAJ&redir_esc=y.

Chaudhuri, Sumanta, Aaditya Mattoo, and Richard Self. 2004. Moving People to Deliver Services: How Can the WTO Help? *Journal of World Trade* 38(3): 363–94. http://elibrary.worldbank.org/doi/abs/10.1596/1813-9450-3238.

Clemens, Michael. 2009. Migrants Count. Five Steps toward Better Migration Data. www.cgdev.org/publication/migrants-count-five-steps-toward-better-migration-data.

Clemens, Michael. 2011. Economics and Emigration: Trillion-Dollar Bills on the Sidewalk? *Journal of Economic Perspectives* 25(3): 83–106. https://www.aeaweb.org/issues/204.

Clemens, Michael, Claudio Montenegro, and Lant Pritchett. 2009. The Place Premium: Wage Differences for Identical Workers across the US Border. HKS Faculty Research Working Paper Series RWP09-004. https://dash.harvard.edu/bitstream/handle/1/4412631/Clemens%20Place%20Premium.pdf?sequence=1&sa=U&ei=5XFQU8nFAcq zyATciYHgCw&ved=0CFAQFjAJ&usg=AFQjCNEt7UC3z08FQcyAA6PyGZy44q0AaQ.

Collier, Paul. 2013. *Exodus: How Migration is Changing our World.* Oxford: Oxford University Press. https://global.oup.com/academic/product/exodus-9780190231484?q=collier&lang=en&cc=us.

Conklin, Jeff. 2005. Wicked Problems & Social Complexity, Ch. 1 of Dialogue Mapping: Building Shared Understanding of Wicked Problems. Wiley. www.wiley.com/WileyCDA/WileyTitle/productCd-EHEP000878.html.

Cummins, Matthew and Francisco Rodriguez. 2010. Is There a Numbers versus Rights Trade-off in Immigration Policy? What the Data Say. *Journal of Human Development and Capabilities* 11: 281–303. http://www.tandfonline.com/doi/full/10.1080/194528 21003696855.

Curtain, Richard. 2015. New Zealand's RSE and Australia's SWP: Why Do Different Outcomes? Mimeo. April 29. https://www.imi.ox.ac.uk/events/seasonal-worker-programs.

de-Bel Air, Francoise. 2015. Demography, Migration, and the Labour Market in the UAE. GLMM Explanatory Note No. 7/2015. http://cadmus.eui.eu/bitstream/handle/1814/36375/GLMM_ExpNote_07_2015.pdf?sequence=1.

de Guchteneire, Paul, Antoine Pécoud, and Ryszard Cholewinski (eds.). 2009. Migration and Human Rights: The United Nations Convention on Migrant Workers' Rights. www.unesco.org/new/en/social-and-human-sciences/themes/international-migration/publications/migration-and-human-rights/.

de Haas, Hein. 2010. Migration and Development: A Theoretical Perspective. *International Migration Review* 44(1): 227–64. http://onlinelibrary.wiley.com/doi/10.1111/j.1747-7379.2009.00804.x/abstract.

Del Carpio, Ximena, Caglar Ozden, and Mauro Testaverde. 2013. Immigration in Malaysia: Assessment of its Economic Effects. World Bank. http://www.knomad.org/events/immigration-in-Malaysia.

Demaret, Luc. 2006. Private Employment Agencies. The Challenges Ahead from the Workers' Perspective, in Christiane Kuptsch, ed., *Merchants of Labor.* Geneva: ILO, 159–68. www.ilo.org/public/english/bureau/inst/publ/books.htm.

Doyle, Jesse and Stephen Howes. 2015. Seasonal Worker Program: Demand-side Constraints and Suggested Reforms. World Bank. https://openknowledge.worldbank.org/handle/10986/21491.

Dustman, Christian, María Casanova, Michael Fertig, Ian Preston, and Christoph M. Schmidt. 2003. The Impact of EU Enlargement on Migration Flows. Home Office Report 25/03. http://discovery.ucl.ac.uk/14332/1/14332.pdf.

The Economist (Asia edn). 2015. Going to Debt Mountain. Working Abroad is no Bargain. February 12. www.economist.com/news/asia/21643235-working-abroad-no-bargain-going-debt-mountain.

EIU (Economist Intelligence Unit). 2016. Measuring Well-Governed Migration. https://publications.iom.int/books/measuring-well-governed-migration-2016-migra tion-governance-index.

Farbenblum, Bassina, Eleanor Taylor-Nicholson, and Sarah Paoletti. 2013. *Migrant Workers' Access to Justice at Home: Indonesia*. New York, NY: Open Society Foundations. http://www.law.unsw.edu.au/profile/bassina-farbenblum/publications.

Fisher, Lloyd. 1953. *The Harvest Labor Market in California*. Cambridge, MA: Harvard University Press. https://books.google.com/books/about/The_Harvest_Labor_Mar ket_in_California.html?id=hgc0AAAAIAAJ&hl=en.

Fix, Michael and Neeraj Kaushal. 2006. *The Contributions of High-Skilled Immigrants*. Washington, DC: Migration Policy Institute. www.migrationpolicy.org/research/con tributions-high-skilled-immigrants.

Forstenlechner, I. and E. J. Rutledge. 2011. The GCC's "Demographic Imbalance": Perceptions, Realities and Policy Options. *Middle East Policy Council* 18(4). http:// www.mepc.org/journal/middle-east-policy-archives/gccs-demographic-imbalance-perceptions-realities-and-policy-options?print.

Fox, Louise. 2016. Why Are Worker Benefits and Protections So Limited in Developing Economies? Brookings Blum Roundtable. www.brookings.edu/multi-chapter-re port/the-future-of-work-in-the-developing-world/?hs_u=plmartin@ucdavis.edu&utm_ campaign=Global+Economy+and+Development&utm_source=hs_email&utm_medium= email&utm_content=32637885.

Fudge, Judy. 2011. The Precarious Migrant Status and Precarious Employment: The Paradox of International Rights for Migrant Worker. October. https://papers.ssrn. com/sol3/papers.cfm?abstract_id=1958360.

Gabriel, Christina and Helene Pellerin (eds.). 2008. *Governing International Labour Migration*. London and New York, NY: Routledge. https://books.google.com/books? id=Q8I-tFA7aukC&pg=PR8&lpg=PR8&dq=Gabriel,+Christina+and+Helene+Pellerin. +2008.+Governing+International+Labour+Migration.&source=bl&ots=4aBaHZXyNa& sig=-4OZ7uogajHHmNPD9pYE4eIkytU&hl=en&sa=X&ved=0ahUKEwipwtOtoqTSAh VQxWMKHQhbDfQQ6AEIJjAG#v=onepage&q=Gabriel%2C%20Christina%20and% 20Helene%20Pellerin.%202008.%20Governing%20International%20Labour%20Migr ation.&f=false.

Gallagher, Anne T. 2015. Exploitation in Migration: Unacceptable but Inevitable. *Journal of International Affairs* 68: 55–74. http://works.bepress.com/anne_gallagher/33.

GAO (General Accountability Office). 2015. H-2A and H-2B Visa Programs. March 6. http://www.gao.gov/products/GAO-15-154.

GCIM (Global Commission on International Migration). 2005. Migration in an Intercon-nected World. New Directions for Action. Geneva. https://www.unitar.org/ny/sites/ unitar.org.ny/files/GCIM%20Report%20%20PDF%20of%20complete%20report.pdf.

Gibson, John, David McKenzie, and Halahingano Rohorua. 2008. How Pro-poor is the Selection of Seasonal Migrant Workers from Tonga under New Zealand's Recognized

Seasonal Employer (RSE) program? *Pacific Economic Bulletin* 23(3): 187–204. https://ideas.repec.org/p/crm/wpaper/0807.html.

Giloth, Robert (ed.). 2004. *Workforce Intermediaries for the 21st Century*. Philadelphia, PA: Temple University Press. http://muse.jhu.edu/books/9781439903865?auth=0.

GLMM (Gulf Labour Markets and Migration). 2017. Gulf Labour and Migration News. http://gulfmigration.eu.

Gordon, Jennifer. 2015. Global Labour Recruitment in a Supply Chain Context. June 24. www.ilo.org/global/publications/working-papers/WCMS_377805/lang–en/index.htm.

Gravel, Eric. 2006. ILO Standards Concerning Employment Services, in Christiane Kuptsch, ed., *Merchants of Labor*. Geneva: ILO, 145–54. www.ilo.org/public/english/bureau/inst/publ/books.htm.

Grey, Mark. 1996. Meatpacking and the Migration of Refugee and Immigrant Labor to Storm Lake, Iowa. Mimeo. https://migration.ucdavis.edu/cf/more.php?id=154.

Haque, Tobias and Truman Packard. 2014. Well-being from Work in the Pacific Island Countries. World Bank. http://documents.worldbank.org/curated/en/2014/01/19485962/well-being-work-pacific-island-countries.

Held, David, Anthony McGrew, David Goldblatt, and Jonathan Perraton. 1999. *Global Transformations: Politics, Economics, and Culture*. Stanford, CA and Cambridge: Polity Press. http://www.sup.org/books/title/?id=1565.

Hennebry, Jenna. 2012. Permanently Temporary? Agricultural Migrant Workers and Their Integration in Canada. IRPP No. 26. http://irpp.org/research-studies/study-no26/.

Hennebry, Jenna and Kerry Preibisch. 2012. A Model for Managed Migration? Re-examining Best Practices in Canada's Seasonal Agricultural Worker Program. *International Migration* 50(February): S319–S340. http://onlinelibrary.wiley.com/doi/10.1111/j.1468-2435.2009.00598.x/abstract;jsessionid=EAC124BEAB8CFC5F2E4CEF6DC8E76CE1.f02t04?userIsAuthenticated=false&deniedAccessCustomisedMessage=.

Hertog, Steffen. 2013. The Private Sector and Reform in the Gulf Cooperation Council. Kuwait Programme on Development, Governance, and Globalization in the Gulf States. http://www.lse.ac.uk/middleEastCentre/kuwait/documents/the-private-sector-and-reform-in-the-gcc.pdf.

Hertog, Steffen. 2012. A Comparative Assessment of Labor Market Nationalization Policies in the GCC, in *National Employment, Migration and Education in the GCC. The Gulf Region: Economic Development and Diversification*. Berlin: Gerlach Press. http://eprints.lse.ac.uk/46746/1/A%20comparative%20assessment%20of%20labor%20market%20nationalization%20policies%20in%20the%20GCC(lsero).pdf.

Houseman, Susan, Arne Kalleberg, and George Erickcek. 2003. The Role of Temporary Agency Employment in Tight Labor Markets. *Industrial and Labor Relations Review* 57 (1, October): 105–27. http://research.upjohn.org/jrnlarticles/49/.

Hvidt, M. 2013. Economic Diversification in GCC Countries: Past Record and Future Trends. Research Paper, Kuwait Programme on Development, Governance, and Globalization in the Gulf States. http://www.lse.ac.uk/middleEastCentre/kuwait/documents/economic-diversification-in-the-gcc-countries.pdf.

IDMC (Internal Displacement Monitoring Centre). 2016. Global Report. http://internal-displacement.org/.

ILO (International Labor Organization). 2004. Resolution Concerning a Fair Deal for Migrant Workers in a Global Economy. http://www.ilo.org/global/topics/labour-migration/WCMS_178658/lang–en/index.htm.

ILO (International Labor Organization). 2006. Multilateral Framework on Labor Migration. Non-Binding Principles and Guidelines for a Rights-Based Approach to Labor Migration. Geneva. www.ilo.org/public/english/protection/migrant/areas/multilateral.htm.

ILO (International Labor Organization). 2007. Guide to Private Employment Agencies—Regulation, Monitoring and Enforcement. Geneva. www.ilo.org/sapfl/Informationresources/ILOPublications/lang–en/docName–WCMS_083275/index.htm.

ILO (International Labor Organization. 2014a. Decent Work Country Programme, Nepal 2013-2017. www.ilo.org/kathmandu/country/WCMS_235929/lang–en/index.htm.

ILO (International Labor Organization. 2014b. Fair Migration: Setting an ILO agenda, Report of the Director General, International Labour Conference, 103rd Session, 2014, Report I (B) www.ilo.org/ilc/ILCSessions/103/reports/reports-to-the-conference/WCMS_242879/lang–en/index.htm.

ILO (International Labor Organization). 2015a. ILO Global Estimates of Migrant Workers. December 15. www.ilo.org/global/topics/labour-migration/publications/WCMS_436343/lang–en/index.htm.

ILO (International Labor Organization). 2015b. World Social Protection Report 2014-15: Building Economic Recovery, Inclusive Development and Social Justice. http://www.ilo.org/global/research/global-reports/world-social-security-report/2014/WCMS_245201/lang–en/index.htm.

ILO (International Labor Organization). 2015c. Submission 31 to the Australian Federal Parliament Joint Standing Committee on Migration. www.aph.gov.au/Parliamentary_Business/Committees/Joint/Migration/Seasonal_Worker_Programme/Submissions.

ILO (International Labor Organization). 2016a. General Principles and Operational Guidelines for Fair Recruitment. www.ilo.org/global/topics/fair-recruitment/WCMS_536755/lang–en/index.htm.

ILO (International Labour Organization). 2016b. Key Indicators of Labour Market. www.ilo.org/global/statistics-and-databases/research-and-databases/kilm/WCMS_498929/lang–en/index.htm.

IOM (International Organization for Migration). 2013. Global Eye on Human Trafficking. September. http://publications.iom.int/books/global-eye-human-trafficking-issue-13-september-2013.

IOM (International Organization for Migration). 2016. Research on Labour Recruitment Industry between United Arab Emirates, Kerala (India) and Nepal. http://www.wam.ae/en/news/emirates/1395278548097.html.

Ishizuka, Futaba. 2013. International Labor Migration in Vietnam and the Impact of Receiving Countries' Policies. IDE-JETRO DP 414. http://www.ide.go.jp/English/Publish/Download/Dp/414.html.

Jones, Katherine. 2015. Recruitment Monitoring and Migrant Welfare Assistance. What Works? IOM. www.iom.int/sites/default/files/migrated_files/What-We-Do/docs/Recruitment-Monitoring-Book.pdf.

Juridini, Ray. 2016. Ways Forward in Recruitment of Low-skilled Migrant Workers in Asia–Arab States Corridor. ILO. http://www.ilo.org/beirut/publications/WCMS_519913/lang–en/index.htm.

Kenny, Charles. 2012. Getting Better: Why Global Development Is Succeeding—And How We Can Improve the World Even More. Basic Books. http://charleskenny.blogs.com/weblog/2009/06/the-success-of-development.html.

Kim, Min Ji. 2015. The Republic of Korea's Employment Permit System (EPS): Background and Rapid Assessment. International Migration Paper No. 119. www.ilo.org/global/topics/labour-migration/publications/WCMS_344235/lang–en/index.htm.

Kuptsch, Christiane (ed.). 2006. *Merchants of Labor*. Geneva: ILO. www.ilo.org/public/english/bureau/inst/publ/books.htm.

Kwong, Peter. 1998. Forbidden Workers Illegal Chinese Immigrants and American Labor. New Press. http://thenewpress.com/books/forbidden-workers.

Lindquist, Johan. 2010. Labour Recruitment, Circuits of Capital and Gendered Mobility: Reconceptualizing the Indonesian Migration Industry. *Public Affairs* 83(1): 115–32. http://scholar.google.com/citations?view_op=view_citation&hl=en&user=NaxXGHQAAAAJ&citation_for_view=NaxXGHQAAAAJ:qjMakFHDy7sC.

Lowell, Lindsay and Philip Martin. 2012. Managing the Dynamic Science and Engineering Labor Market in the United States. International Migration Review. Vol 46. No 4. Pp 1005–12. http://onlinelibrary.wiley.com/doi/10.1111/imre.12008/abstract

Luo, Tian, Amar Mann, and Richard Holden. 2010. The Expanding Role of Temporary Help Services from 1990 to 2008. *Monthly Labor Review* August. www.bls.gov/opub/mlr/2010/08/art1full.pdf.

Luthria, Manjula, Ron Duncan, Richard Brown, Peter Mares, and Nic Maclella. 2006. At Home and Away: Expanding Job Opportunities for Pacific Islanders through Labor Mobility. World Bank. http://documents.worldbank.org/curated/en/2006/09/7202441/pacific-islands-home-away-expanding-job-opportunities-pacific-islanders-through-labor-mobility.

McKenzie, David. 2005. Paper Walls are Easier to Tear Down: Passport Costs and Legal Barriers to Emigration. World Bank Policy Research Working Paper No. 3783. http://elibrary.worldbank.org/doi/book/10.1596/1813-9450-3783.

Marshall, Ray. 2011. Value-Added Immigration: Lessons for the United States from Canada, Australia, and the United Kingdom. http://www.epi.org/publication/value-added-immigration/.

Martin, Philip. 1993. Trade and Migration: NAFTA and Agriculture. IIE. *Policy Analyses in International Economics* 38. http://bookstore.piie.com/book-store/73.html.

Martin, Philip. 1998–99. Economic Integration and Migration: The Case of NAFTA. *UCLA Journal of International Law and Foreign Affairs* 3(2, Fall/Winter): 419–41. http://heinonline.org/HOL/LandingPage?handle=hein.journals/jilfa3&div=22&id=&page=.

Martin, Philip. 2003. *Promise Unfulfilled: Unions, Immigration, and Farm Workers*. Ithaca, NY. Cornell University Press. www.cornellpress.cornell.edu/book/?GCOI=80140100792940.

Martin, Philip. 2005. Mexico–US Migration, in Gary Hufbauer and Jeffrey Schott, eds., *NAFTA Revisited: Achievements and Challenges*. Washington, DC: Institute for International Economics, Ch. 8, 438–65. http://bookstore.piie.com/book-store/332.html.

Martin, Philip. 2006a. GATS, Migration, and Labor Standards. IILS Discussion Paper 165/ 2006. www.ilo.org/public/english/bureau/inst/publications/discussion/dp16506.pdf.

Martin, Philip. 2006b. Regulating Private Recruiters. The Core Issues, in Christiane Kuptsch, ed., *Merchants of Labor*. Geneva: ILO, 13–26. www.ilo.org/public/english/ bureau/inst/publ/books.htm.

Martin, Philip. 2009. *Importing Poverty? Immigration and the Changing Face of Rural America*. London: Yale University Press. http://yalepress.yale.edu/yupbooks/book. asp?isbn=9780300139174.

Martin, Philip. 2011. International Labor Migration: The Numbers–Rights Dilemma, in Rey Koslowski, ed., *Global Mobility Regimes*. New York, NY: Palgrave Macmillan, Ch. 11, 201–18. http://www.palgrave.com/us/book/9780230116924.

Martin, Philip. 2012. Climate Change, NAPAs, Agriculture, and Migration in LDCs. ISIM. http://isim.georgetown.edu/work/past/climatemigration.

Martin, Philip. 2014a. The United States: The Continuing Immigration Debate, in James Hollifield, Philip Martin, and Pia Orrenius, eds., *Controlling Immigration. A Global Perspective*. Stanford, CA: Stanford University Press. www.sup.org/book. cgi?id=22520.

Martin, Philip. 2014b. Germany: Managing Migration in the 21st Century, in James Hollifield, Philip Martin, and Pia Orrenius, eds., *Controlling Immigration. A Global Perspective*. Stanford, CA: Stanford University Press. www.sup.org/book.cgi?id= 22520.

Martin, Philip. 2014c. The H-2A Program; Evolution, Impacts, and Outlook, in David Griffith ed., *(Mis)managing Migration. Guestworkers' Experiences with North American Labor Market*. Santa Fe, NM: SAR Press, Ch. 2, 33–62. http://sarweb.org/index.php? sar_press_mismanaging_migration.

Martin, Philip. 2016. Labor Compliance in Fresh Produce: Lessons from Food Safety. Choices. http://www.choicesmagazine.org/choices-magazine/submitted-articles/labor- compliance-in-fresh-produce–lessons-from-food-safety.

Martin, Philip and Elizabeth Midgley. 2010. Immigration in America. Population Refer- ence Bureau. June. www.prb.org/Publications/PopulationBulletins/2010/immigration update1.aspx.

Martin, Philip, Manolo Abella, and Christiane Kuptsch. 2006. *Managing Labor Migration in the Twenty-First Century*. London: Yale University Press. http://yalepress.yale.edu/ yupbooks/book.asp?isbn=0300109040.

Martin, Susan. 2014. *International Migration Evolving Trends from the Early Twentieth Century to the Present*. Cambridge: Cambridge University Press. www.cambridge. org/us/academic/subjects/politics-international-relations/international-relations-and- international-organisations/international-migration-evolving-trends-early-twentieth- century-present.

Maxwell, Nan. 2006. The Working Life: The Labor Market for Workers in Low-Skilled Jobs. Upjohn. www.upjohn.org/publications/upjohn-institute-press/working-life-labor- market-workers-low-skilled-jobs.

Maybud, Susan and Christiane Wiskow. 2006. Care Trade. The International Brokering of Health Care Professionals, in Christiane Kuptsch, ed., *Merchants of Labor*. Geneva: ILO, 223–38. www.ilo.org/public/english/bureau/inst/publ/books.htm.

Migrant Forum. 2014. Joint and Several Liability of Recruitment/Placement Agencies with the Principal/Employer under Philippine Laws. http://www.mfasia.org/.

Miller, David. 2016. Strangers in Our Midst. The Political Philosophy of Immigration. Harvard. www.hup.harvard.edu/catalog.php?isbn=9780674088900.

Miller, Mark and Philip Martin. 1982. *Administering Foreign-Worker Programs: Lessons from Europe.* Lexington, MA: Lexington Books. https://books.google.com/books/about/Administering_Foreign_Worker_Programs.html?id=AUuyAAAAIAAJ.

Monthly Labor Review. 2013. Industry Employment and Output Projections to 2022. December. www.bls.gov/opub/mlr/2013/article/industry-employment-and-output-projections-to-2022.htm.

Muir, Gwendolyn. 2016. The Cost of Managed Migration. Briarpatch Magazine. http://briarpatchmagazine.com/articles/view/the-cost-of-managed-migration.

Naidu, Suresh, Yaw Nyarko, and Shing-Yi Wang. 2014. Worker Mobility in a Global Labor Market: Evidence from the United Arab Emirates. NBER Working Paper No. 20388. http://www.nber.org/papers/w20388.

NASA. 2009. Global Climate Change: NASA's Eyes on the Earth. http://climate.nasa.gov/keyIndicators/.

New Zealand Government Submission. 2015. Submission 10 to the Australian Federal Parliament Joint Standing Committee on Migration. July. www.aph.gov.au/Parliamentary_Business/Committees/Joint/Migration/Seasonal_Worker_Programme/Submissions.

Omar Mahmoud, Toman and Christoph Trebsech. The Economics of Human Trafficking and Labour Migration: Micro-evidence from Eastern Europe. https://ideas.repec.org/p/lmu/muenar/19321.html.

Omelaniuk, Irena (ed.). 2012. Global Perspectives on Migration and Development. Springer. www.springer.com/us/book/9789400741096.

Oxfam. 2009. An Evaluation of the Gangmasters Licensing Authority. http://policy-practice.oxfam.org.uk/publications/an-evaluation-of-the-gangmasters-licensing-authority-126001.

Paoletti, Sarah, Eleanor Taylor-Nicholson, Bandita Sijapati, and Bassina Farbenblum. 2014. Migrant Workers' Access to Justice at Home: Nepal. Open Society Foundations. http://www.law.unsw.edu.au/profile/bassina-farbenblum/publications.

Park, Young-bum. 2013. Temporary Low-skilled Migrant Worker Program in Korea: Employment Permit Scheme. Arbor. http://arbor.revistas.csic.es/index.php/arbor.

Parreñas, Rhacel. 2015. *Servants of Globalization: Migration and Domestic Work.* Stanford, CA: Stanford University Press. http://www.sup.org/books/title/?id=21323.

Passel, Jeffrey and D'Vera Cohn. 2016. Overall Number of U.S. Unauthorized Immigrants Holds Steady Since 2009. Pew Hispanic. www.pewhispanic.org/2016/09/20/overall-number-of-u-s-unauthorized-immigrants-holds-steady-since-2009/.

Pattisson, Pete. 2013. Nepalese Workers in Qatar: Exploitation of Migrants Starts at Home. *The Guardian.* October 2. www.theguardian.com/world/2013/oct/02/nepalese-migrants-qatar-exploitation-home.

Pawel, Miriam. 2009. *The Union of Their Dreams: Power, Hope, and Struggle in Cesar Chavez's Farm Worker Movement.* New York, NY: Bloomsbury Press. http://unionoftheirdreams.com/home.php.

PRB (Population Reference Bureau). 2016. *World Population Data Sheet*. www.prb.org.

Pritchett, Lant. 2006. *Let Their People Come: Breaking the Gridlock on Global Labor Mobility*. Washington, DC: Center for Global Development. www.cgdev.org/content/publications/detail/10174/.

Rahman, Mizanur. 2011. Recruitment of Labor Migrants for the Gulf States. The Bangladeshi Case. ISAS WP 132. https://www.files.ethz.ch/isn/133099/ISAS_Working_Paper_132_-email_-__Recruitment_of_Labour_06092011180556.pdf.

Rapoport, Hillel. 2016. Migration and globalization: what's in it for developing countries? *International Journal of Manpower* 37(7): 1209–26. http://www.emeraldinsight.com/doi/abs/10.1108/IJM-08-2015-0116.

Ratha, Dilip. 2005. Remittances. A Lifeline for Development. *Finance and Development* 42 (4, December). www.imf.org/external/pubs/ft/fandd/2005/12/basics.htm.

Rees, Dan. 2006. New Measures to Tackle Exploitation in the UK Agricultural Industry, in Christiane Kuptsch, ed., *Merchants of Labor*. Geneva: ILO, 217–22. www.ilo.org/public/english/bureau/inst/publ/books.htm.

Riley, John. 2001. Silver Signals. Twenty-Five Years of Screening and Signaling. *Journal of Economic Literature* 34(June): 432–78. www.aeaweb.org/articles.php?doi=10.1257/jel.39.2.432.

Ruhs, Martin. 2013. *The Price of Rights: Regulating International Labor Migration*. Princeton, NJ: Princeton University Press. http://press.princeton.edu/titles/10140.html.

Ruhs, Martin and Bridget Anderson (eds.). 2010. *Who Needs Immigrant Workers? Labour Shortages, Immigration, and Public Policy*. Oxford: Oxford University Press. https://global.oup.com/academic/product/who-needs-migrant-workers-9780199580590?cc=us&lang=en&.

Schiff, Maurice. 2004. When Migrants Overstay Their Legal Welcome: A Proposed Solution to the Guest-Worker Program. IZA Discussion Papers 1401, Institute for the Study of Labor (IZA). https://ideas.repec.org/p/iza/izadps/dp1401.html.

Schuster, Liza. 2003. *The Use and Abuse of Political Asylum in Britain and Germany*. Abingdon: Routledge. www.routledge.com/The-Use-and-Abuse-of-Political-Asylum-in-Britain-and-Germany/Schuster/p/book/9780714683201.

Shah, Nasra and Philippe Fargues. 2012. *The Socio-Economic Impacts of GCC Migration*. Cambridge: Gulf Research Centre. http://grm.grc.net/index.php?pgid=Njk=&wid=Mjc.

Sirkeci, Ibrahim, Jeffrey Cohen, and Dilip Ratha (eds.). 2012. *Migration and Remittances during the Global Financial Crisis and Beyond*. Washington, DC: World Bank. https://openknowledge.worldbank.org/handle/10986/13092.

Skeels, Jack. 1969. Perspectives on Private Employment Relations. *Industrial Relations* 8(2): 151–61. http://onlinelibrary.wiley.com/doi/10.1111/j.1468-232X.1969.tb00474.x/abstract.

Spence, Michael. 1973. Job Market Signaling. *Quarterly Journal of Economics* 87(August): 355–74. http://qje.oxfordjournals.org/content/87/3/355.short?rss=1&ssource=mfc.

Sullivan, Daniel. 1989. Monopsony Power in the Market for Nurses. *Journal of Law and Economics* 32(2, part 2, October): s135–s178. www.nber.org/papers/w3031.

Talani, Leila. 2014. *The Arab Spring in the Global Political Economy*. Basingstoke: Palgrave Macmillan. www.palgrave.com/page/detail/the-arab-spring-in-the-global-political-economy-leila-simona-talani/?K=9781137272188.

Teitelbaum, Michael. 1992–93. The Population Threat. *Foreign Affairs* Winter. www. foreignaffairs.com/articles/1992-12-01/population-threat.

Teitelbaum, Michael. 2015. The Truth about the Migrant Crisis: Tragic Choices, Moral Hazards, and Potential. *Foreign Affairs* September. www.foreignaffairs.com/articles/western-europe/2015-09-14/truth-about-migrant-crisis.

UN DESA (Department of Economic and Social Affairs). 2015. International Migration Report 2015. http://www.un.org/en/development/desa/population/migration/index.shtml.

UN Secretary General. 2013. International Migration and Development. www.un.org/en/development/desa/population/theme/international-migration/.

UNDP (United Nations Development Program). 2009. Overcoming Barriers: Human Mobility and Development. Human Development Report. http://hdr.undp.org/en/content/human-development-report-2009.

UNHCR (United Nations High Commissioner for Refugees). 2015. *UNHCR Statistical Yearbook 2014*, 14th edn. http://www.unhcr.org/en-us/statistics/country/566584fc9/unhcr-statistical-yearbook-2014-14th-edition.html.

UNODC (United Nations Office of Drugs and Crime). 2014. Global Report on Trafficking in Persons. www.unodc.org/unodc/en/human-trafficking/publications.html#Reports.

UNODC (United Nations Office of Drugs and Crime). 2015. The Role of Recruitment Fees and Abusive and Fraudulent Recruitment Practices of Recruitment Agencies in TiP. www.unodc.org/unodc/en/human-trafficking/publications.html#Reports.

US Department of State. Annual. Trafficking in Persons Report. http://www.state.gov/j/tip/rls/tiprpt/.

Verma, Veena. 2002. The Mexican and Caribbean Seasonal Agricultural Workers Program: Regulatory and Policy Framework, Farm Industry Level Employment Practices, and the Future of the Program Under Unionization. www.nsi-ins.ca/publications/the-mexican-and-caribbean-seasonal-agricultural-workers-program-regulatory-and-policy-framework-farm-industry-level-employment-practices-and-the-future-of-the-program-under-unionization/.

Wickramasekara, Piyasiri. 2013. Regulation of the Recruitment Process and Reduction of Migration Costs: Comparative Analysis of South Asia. October. http://papers.ssrn.com/sol3/papers.cfm?abstract_id=2478461.

Wickramasekara, Piyasiri. 2015a. Bilateral Agreements and Memoranda of Understanding on Migration of Low Skilled Workers: A Review. March. ILO. www.ilo.org/global/topics/labour-migration/publications/WCMS_385582/lang–en/index.htm.

Wickramasekara, Piyasiri. 2015b. South Asian Gulf migration to the Gulf: A Safety Valve or a Development Strategy? *Migration and Development* 51): 99–129. www.tandfonline.com/doi/full/10.1080/21632324.2015.1039770.

World Bank. 2005. Global Economic Prospects. The Economic Implications of Remittances and Migration. http://go.worldbank.org/5VKCMARHP0.

World Bank. 2009. Reshaping Economic Geography. https://openknowledge.worldbank.org/handle/10986/5991.

World Bank. 2010. Global Monitoring Report 2010: The MDGs after the Crisis. https://openknowledge.worldbank.org/handle/10986/2444.

World Bank. 2015. Migration and Development Brief 24. Remittances Growth to Slow Sharply in 2015, as Europe and Russia Stay Weak; Pick Up Expected Next Year. April 13. http://go.worldbank.org/R88ONI2MQ0.

World Bank. 2016. World Development Indicators. https://openknowledge. worldbank.org/bitstream/handle/10986/23969/9781464806834.pdf.

Xiang, Biao and Wei Shen. 2009. International Student Migration and Social Stratification in China. *Education and Development in Contemporary China* 29(5): 513–22. www. sciencedirect.com/science/article/pii/S073805930900042X.

Yellen, Janet. 1984. Efficiency Wage Models of Unemployment. *American Economic Review*. May: 200–5. https://ideas.repec.org/a/aea/aecrev/v74y1984i2p200-205.html.

Index

Tables and figures are indicated by an italic *t* and *f* following the page number.